I0105116

Charles Franklin Dunbar

Laws of the United States

Relating to Currency, Finance and Banking from 1789 to 1891

Charles Franklin Dunbar

Laws of the United States
Relating to Currency, Finance and Banking from 1789 to 1891

ISBN/EAN: 9783743408319

Manufactured in Europe, USA, Canada, Australia, Japa

Cover: Foto ©Suzi / pixelio.de

Manufactured and distributed by brebook publishing software (www.brebook.com)

Charles Franklin Dunbar

Laws of the United States

LAWS

OF

THE UNITED STATES

RELATING TO

CURRENCY, FINANCE, AND BANKING

FROM 1789 TO 1891.

COMPILED BY

CHARLES F. DUNBAR,

PROFESSOR OF POLITICAL ECONOMY IN HARVARD UNIVERSITY.

BOSTON:

GINN AND COMPANY.

1891.

Copyright, 1891,
By Charles F. Dunbar.

PREFACE.

In making this collection, my object has been to bring within the easy reach of students and teachers of Political Economy and History the important parts of our national legislation respecting Currency, Coinage, Loans, and Banking. For this purpose the Acts of Congress have been carefully examined, and the leading provisions upon these subjects are now presented in their chronological order, following with precision the text given in the Statutes at Large. Acts and provisions of less consequence in financial history, but still likely to require occasional attention, have been abridged or described in their natural connection. Finally, acts and provisions seldom referred to in ordinary use, as, for example, those relating to small loans, to banks in the District of Columbia, and to minor coinage, together with most provisions which are strictly administrative or punitive, have been omitted altogether, as lying outside of the necessary limits of a book intended for use as a manual.

Little reference has been made to the Revised Statutes, the object of the compilation not being to present a view of subsisting law at any one period, past or present; but to give the course of legislation, accurately and with sufficient fulness to enable the student to make a thorough examination of it, without the necessity of constant reference to the formidable collection of Statutes at Large.

Besides the acts and resolutions of Congress, treated as above stated, certain, vetoed bills and a few other papers of historical importance have been added, in order to facilitate reference to a class of documents which the student of political and economic history often finds as valuable, for purposes of study, as the measures which actually secure a place on the pages of the statute book.

CHARLES F. DUNBAR.

HARVARD UNIVERSITY,
    March 4, 1891.

CONTENTS.

PART I.

CURRENCY, FINANCE, AND BANKING.

1789–1860.

1789, Chap. V.—*An Act to regulate the Collection of the Duties imposed by law on the tonnage of ships or vessels, and on goods, wares, and merchandises imported into the United States.*

SEC. 30. *And be it further enacted,* That the duties and fees to be collected by virtue of this act, shall be received in gold and silver coin only, at the following rates, that is to say, the gold coins of France, England, Spain and Portugal, and all other gold coin of equal fineness, at eighty-nine cents for every pennyweight. The Mexican dollar at one hundred cents; the crown of France at one dollar and eleven cents; the crown of England at one dollar and eleven cents; and all silver coins of equal fineness at one dollar and eleven cents per ounce.

[Approved, July 31, 1789. 1 Statutes at Large, 45.]

1789, Chap. XII.—*An Act to establish the Treasury Department.*

SECTION 1. *Be it enacted by the Senate and House of Representatives of the United States of America in Congress assembled,* That there shall be a Department of Treasury, in which shall be the following officers, namely: a Secretary of the Treasury, to be deemed head of the department; a Comptroller, an Auditor, a Treasurer, a Register, and an Assistant to the Secretary of the Treasury, which assistant shall be appointed by the said Secretary.

SEC. 2.   *And be it further enacted*, That it shall be the duty of the Secretary of the Treasury to digest and prepare plans for the improvement and management of the revenue, and for the support of public credit; to prepare and report estimates of the public revenue, and the public expenditures; to superintend the collection of the revenue; to decide on the forms of keeping and stating accounts and making returns, and to grant under the limitations herein established, or to be hereafter provided, all warrants for monies to be issued from the Treasury, in pursuance of appropriations by law; to execute such services relative to the sale of the lands belonging to the United States, as may be by law required of him; to make report, and give information to either branch of the legislature, in person or in writing (as he may be required), respecting all matters referred to him by the Senate or House of Representatives, or which shall appertain to his office; and generally to perform all such services relative to the finances, as he shall be directed to perform.

SEC. 3.   *And be it further enacted*, That it shall be the duty of the Comptroller to superintend the adjustment and preservation of the public accounts; to examine all accounts settled by the Auditor, and certify the balances arising thereon to the Register; to countersign all warrants drawn by the Secretary of the Treasury, which shall be warranted by law; to report to the Secretary the official forms of all papers to be issued in the different offices for collecting the public revenue, and the manner and form of keeping and stating the accounts of the several persons employed therein.   He shall moreover provide for the regular and punctual payment of all monies which may be collected, and shall direct prosecutions for all delinquencies of officers of the revenue, and for debts that are, or shall be due to the United States.

SEC. 4.   *And be it further enacted*, That it shall be the duty of the Treasurer to receive and keep the monies of the United States, and to disburse the same upon warrants drawn by the Secretary of the Treasury, countersigned by the Comptroller, recorded by the Register, and not otherwise; he shall take receipts for all monies paid by him, and all receipts for monies received by him shall be endorsed upon warrants signed by the Secretary of the Treasury, without which warrant, so signed, no acknowledgment for money received into the public Treasury shall be valid. And the said Treasurer shall render his accounts to the Comptroller quarterly, (or oftener if required,) and shall transmit a copy thereof, when settled, to the Secretary of the Treasury. . . .

SEC. 5. *And be it further enacted,* That it shall be the duty of the Auditor to receive all public accounts, and after examination to certify the balance, and transmit the accounts with the vouchers and certificate to the Comptroller for his decision thereon: *Provided,* That if any person whose account shall be so audited, be dissatisfied therewith, he may within six months appeal to the Comptroller against such settlement.

SEC. 6. *And be it further enacted,* That it shall be the duty of the Register to keep all accounts of the receipts and expenditures of the public money, and of all debts due to or from the United States; to receive from the Comptroller the accounts which shall have been finally adjusted, and to preserve such accounts with their vouchers and certificates; to record all warrants for the receipt or payment of monies at the Treasury, certify the same thereon, and to transmit to the Secretary of the Treasury, copies of the certificates of balances of accounts adjusted as is herein directed.

SEC. 7. *And be it further enacted,* That whenever the Secretary shall be removed from office by the President of the United States, or in any other case of vacancy in the office of Secretary, the Assistant shall, during the vacancy, have the charge and custody of the records, books, and papers appertaining to the said office.

[Section 8 forbids any person appointed to any office instituted by this act to be concerned in trade, commerce, navigation, or the purchase of public property or public securities, or to take any emolument for transacting business in the department, other than is allowed by law.]

[Approved, September 2, 1789.   1 Statutes at Large, 65.]

1790, Chap. XXXIV. — *An Act making provision for the Debt of the United States.*

WHEREAS, justice and the support of public credit require, that provision should be made for fulfilling the engagements of the United States, in respect to their foreign debt, and for funding their domestic debt upon equitable and satisfactory terms:

SECTION 1. *Be it enacted, . . .* That reserving out of the monies which have arisen since the last day of December last past, and which shall hereafter arise from the duties on goods, wares and merchandise imported into the United States, and on the tonnage of ships or vessels, the yearly sum of six hundred thousand dollars, or so much thereof as may be appropriated from time to time, towards the support of the government of the United States, and their common defence, the residue of the said monies, or so much thereof as may be necessary, as the same shall be received in each year, next after the sum reserved as aforesaid, shall be, and is hereby appropriated to the payment of the interest which shall from time to time become due on the loans heretofore made by the United States in foreign countries; and also to the payment of interest on such further loans as may be obtained for discharging the arrears of interest thereupon, and the whole or any part of the principal thereof; to continue so appropriated until the said loans, as well those already made as those which may be made in virtue of this act, shall be fully satisfied, pursuant to the contracts relating to the same, any law to the contrary notwithstanding. *And provided,* That nothing herein contained, shall be construed to annul or alter any appropriation by law made prior to the passing of this act.

And as new loans are and will be necessary for the payment of the aforesaid arrears of interest, and the instalments of the principal of the said foreign debt due and growing due, and may also be found expedient for effecting an entire alteration in the state of the same:

[Section 2 authorizes the President of the United States to cause not exceeding twelve millions of dollars to be borrowed, for the discharge of said arrears and instalments or for paying off the whole foreign debt, and to make such further contracts respecting said debts as may be expedient, *provided* that no contract shall preclude the United States from reimbursing within fifteen years any sum borrowed.]

And whereas it is desirable to adapt the nature of the provision to be made for the domestic debt to the present circumstances of the United States, as far as it shall be found practicable, consistently with good faith and the rights of the creditors; which can only be done by a voluntary loan on their part:

SEC. 3. *Be it therefore further enacted,* That a loan to the full amount of the said domestic debt be, and the same is hereby proposed; and that books for receiving subscriptions to the said loan be opened at the treasury of the United States, and by a commissioner to be appointed in each of the said states, on the first day of October next, to continue open until the last day of September following, inclusively; and that the sums which shall be subscribed thereto, be payable in certificates issued for the said debt, according to their specie value, and computing the interest upon such as bear interest to the last day of December next, inclusively; which said certificates shall be of these several descriptions, to wit:

Those issued by the register of the treasury.

Those issued by the commissioners of loans in the several states, including certificates given pursuant to the act of Congress of the second of January, one thousand seven hundred and seventy-nine, for bills of credit of the several emissions of the twentieth of May, one thousand seven hundred and seventy-seven, and the eleventh of April, one thousand seven hundred and seventy-eight.

Those issued by the commissioners for the adjustment of the accounts of the quartermaster, commissary, hospital, clothing, and marine departments.

Those issued by the commissioners for the adjustment of accounts in the respective states.

Those issued by the late and present paymaster general, or commissioner of army accounts.

Those issued for the payment of interest, commonly called indents of interest.

And in the bills of credit issued by the authority of the

United States in Congress assembled, at the rate of one hundred dollars in the said bills, for one dollar in specie.

SEC. 4. *And be it further enacted*, That for the whole or any part of any sum subscribed to the said loan, by any person or persons, or body politic, which shall be paid in the principal of the said domestic debt, the subscriber or subscribers shall be entitled to a certificate, purporting that the United States owe to the holder or holders thereof, his, her, or their assigns, a sum to be expressed therein, equal to two-thirds of the sum so paid, bearing an interest of six per centum per annum, payable quarter yearly, and subject to redemption by payments not exceeding in one year, on account both of principal and interest, the proportion of eight dollars upon a hundred of the sum mentioned in such certificate ; and to another certificate purporting that the United States owe to the holder or holders thereof, his, her, or their assigns, a sum to be expressed therein, equal to the proportion of thirty-three dollars and one-third of a dollar upon a hundred of the sum so paid, which after the year one thousand eight hundred shall bear an interest of six per centum per annum, payable quarter yearly, and subject to redemption by payments not exceeding in one year, on account both of principal and interest, the proportion of eight dollars upon a hundred of the sum mentioned in such certificate : *Provided*, That it shall not be understood that the United States shall be bound or obliged to redeem in the proportion aforesaid ; but it shall be understood only that they have a right so to do.

SEC. 5. *And be it further enacted*, That for the whole or any part of any sum subscribed to the said loan by any person or persons, or body politic, which shall be paid in the interest of the said domestic debt, computed to the said last day of December next, or in the said certificates issued in payment of interest, commonly called indents of interest, the subscriber or subscribers shall be entitled to a certificate purporting that the United States owe to the holder or holders thereof, his, her or their assigns, a sum to be specified therein, equal to that by him, her or them so paid, bearing an interest of three per centum per annum, payable quarter yearly, and subject to redemption by payment of the sum specified therein, whenever provision shall be made by law for that purpose.

SEC. 6. *And be it further enacted,* That a commissioner be appointed for each state, to reside therein, whose duty it shall be to superintend the subscriptions to the said loan ; to open books for the same ; to receive the certificates which shall be presented in payment thereof; to liquidate the specie value of such of them as shall not have been before liquidated ; to issue the certificates above mentioned in lieu thereof, according to the terms of each subscription ; to enter in books to be by him kept for that purpose, credits to the respective subscribers to the said loan for the sums to which they shall be respectively entitled ; to transfer the said credits upon the said books from time to time as shall be requisite ; to pay the interest thereupon as the same shall become due, and generally to observe and perform such directions and regulations as shall be prescribed to him by the Secretary of the Treasury, touching the execution of his office.

[Section 7 provides that the stock created in pursuance of this act shall be transferable only on the books of the Treasury or of the commissioners in which it is recorded at the time of transfer, by the owner or by his attorney; but stock may be transferred by the Secretary of the Treasury from the books of one office to those of another, by request of the owner.

Section 8 provides for the payment of the interest, to be made quarterly on the last days of March, June, September, and December in each year.

Sections 9 and 10 provide that nothing in this act shall impair the rights of creditors who do not subscribe to the loan, but that they shall receive to the end of 1791 the same rate of interest as is paid to subscribing creditors, and payable at the same times and places. But as some of the certificates outstanding have not been liquidated to specie value, and as some have been counterfeited, such creditors as do not hold certificates issued by the Register of the Treasury, in order to be entitled to interest, are required to present them before June 1, 1791, to be exchanged for new certificates specifying the specie amounts of debt and otherwise like those heretofore issued by the Register, and made transferable like those issued to subscribers under this act.

Sections 11 and 12 prescribe the salaries to be paid to the commissioners, and provide for their oath of office and official bonds.]

And whereas a provision for the debts of the respective states by the United States, would be greatly conducive to an orderly, economical, and effectual arrangement of the public finances:

SEC. 13. *Be it therefore further enacted*, That a loan be proposed to the amount of twenty-one million and five hundred thousand dollars, and that subscriptions to the said loan be received at the same times and places, and by the same persons, as in respect to the loan herein before proposed concerning the domestic debt of the United States. And that the sums which shall be subscribed to the said loan, shall be payable in the principal and interest of the certificates or notes, which prior to the first day of January last, were issued by the respective states, as acknowledgments or evidences of debts by them respectively owing, except certificates issued by the commissioners of army accounts in the state of North Carolina, in the year one thousand seven hundred and eighty-six.

Provided, That no greater sum shall be received in the certificates of any state than as follows ; that is to say :

In those of New Hampshire, three hundred thousand dollars.

In those of Massachusetts, four million dollars.

In those of Rhode Island and Providence Plantations, two hundred thousand dollars.

In those of Connecticut, one million six hundred thousand dollars.

In those of New York, one million two hundred thousand dollars.

In those of New Jersey, eight hundred thousand dollars.

In those of Pennsylvania, two million two hundred thousand dollars.

In those of Delaware, two hundred thousand dollars.

In those of Maryland, eight hundred thousand dollars.

In those of Virginia, three million five hundred thousand dollars.

In those of North Carolina, two million four hundred thousand dollars.

In those of South Carolina, four million dollars.

In those of Georgia, three hundred thousand dollars.

And provided, That no such certificate shall be received, which from the tenor thereof, or from any public record, act, or document, shall appear or can be ascertained to have been issued for any purpose, other than compensations and expenditures for services or supplies towards the prosecution of the late war, and the defence of the United States, or of some part thereof during the same.

SEC. 14. *Provided also, and be it further enacted,* That if the total amount of the sums which shall be subscribed to the said loan in the debt of any state, within the time limited for receiving subscriptions thereto, shall exceed the sum by this act allowed to be subscribed within such state, the certificates and credits granted to the respective subscribers shall bear such proportion to the sums by them respectively subscribed, as the total amount of the said sums shall bear to the whole sum so allowed to be subscribed in the debt of such state within the same. And every subscriber to the said loan shall, at the time of subscribing, deposit with the commissioners the certificates or notes to be loaned by him.

SEC. 15. *And be it further enacted,* That for two-thirds of any sum subscribed to the said loan, by any person or persons, or body politic, which shall be paid in the principal and interest of the certificates or notes issued as aforesaid by the respective states, the subscriber or subscribers shall be entitled to a certificate, purporting that the United States owe to the holder or holders thereof, or his, her or their assigns, a sum to be expressed therein, equal to two-thirds of the aforesaid two-thirds, bearing an interest of six per centum per annum, payable quarter yearly, and subject to redemption by payments, not exceeding in one year, on account both of principal and interest, the proportion of eight dollars upon a hundred of the sum mentioned in such certificate ; and to another certificate, purporting that the United States owe to the holder or holders thereof, his, her or their assigns, a sum to be expressed therein, equal to the proportion of thirty-three dollars and one-third of a dollar upon a hundred, of the said two-thirds of such sum so subscribed, which, after the year one thousand eight hundred shall bear an interest of six per centum per annum, payable quarter yearly, and subject to redemption by payments, not exceeding in one year, on account both of principal and interest, the proportion of eight dollars upon a hundred of the sum mentioned in such certificate ; and that for the remaining third of any sum so subscribed, the subscriber or subscribers shall be entitled to a certificate, purporting that the United States owe to the holder or holders thereof, his, her or their assigns, a sum to be expressed therein, equal to the said remaining third, bearing an interest of three per centum per annum, payable quarter yearly, and subject to redemption by payment of the sum specified therein whenever provision shall be made by law for that purpose.

SEC. 16. *And be it further enacted*, That the interest upon the certificates which shall be received in payment of the sums subscribed towards the said loan, shall be computed to the last day of the year one thousand seven hundred and ninety-one, inclusively; and the interest upon the stock which shall be created by virtue of the said loan shall commence or begin to accrue on the first day of the year one thousand seven hundred and ninety-two, and shall be payable quarter yearly, at the same time, and in like manner, as the interest on the stock to be created by virtue of the loan above proposed in the domestic debt of the United States.

SEC. 17. *And be it further enacted*, That if the whole sum allowed to be subscribed in the debt or certificates of any state as aforesaid, shall not be subscribed within the time for that purpose limited, such state shall be entitled to receive, and shall receive from the United States, an interest per centum per annum, upon so much of the said sum as shall not have been so subscribed, equal to that which would have accrued on the deficiency, had the same been subscribed in trust for the non-subscribing creditors of such state, who are holders of certificates or notes issued on account of services or supplies towards the prosecution of the late war, and the defence of the United States or of some part thereof, to be paid in like manner as the interest on the stock which may be created by virtue of the said loan, and to continue until there shall be a settlement of accounts between the United States and the individual states; and in case a balance shall then appear in favor of such state, until provision shall be made for the said balance.

But as certain states have respectively issued their own certificates, in exchange for those of the United States, whereby it might happen that interest might be twice payable on the same sums:

SEC. 18. *Be it further enacted*, That the payment of interest whether to states or to individuals, in respect to the debt of any state, by which such exchange shall have been made, shall be suspended, until it shall appear to the satisfaction of the secretary of the treasury, that certificates issued for that purpose by such state have been re-exchanged or redeemed, or until those which shall not have been re-exchanged or redeemed shall be surrendered to the United States.

SEC. 19. *And be it further enacted*, That so much of the debt of each state as shall be subscribed to the said loan, and the monies (if any) that shall be advanced to the same pursuant to this act, shall be a charge against such state, in account with the United States.

SEC. 20. *And be it further enacted*, That the monies arising under the revenue laws, which have been or during the present session of Congress may be passed, or so much thereof as may be necessary, shall be and are hereby pledged and appropriated for the payment of the interest on the stock which shall be created by the loans aforesaid, pursuant to the provisions of this act, first paying that which shall arise on the stock created by virtue of the said first-mentioned loan, to continue so pledged and appropriated, until the final redemption of the said stock, any law to the contrary notwithstanding, subject nevertheless to such reservations and priorities as may be requisite to satisfy the appropriations heretofore made, and which during the present session of Congress may be made by law, including the sums herein before reserved and appropriated: and to the end that the said monies may be inviolably applied in conformity to this act, and may never be diverted to any other purpose, an account shall be kept of the receipts and disposition thereof, separate and distinct from the product of any other duties, imposts, excises and taxes whatsoever, except such as may be hereafter laid, to make good any deficiency which may be found in the product thereof towards satisfying the interest aforesaid.

SEC. 21. *And be it further enacted*, That the faith of the United States be, and the same is hereby pledged to provide and appropriate hereafter such additional and permanent funds as may be requisite towards supplying any such deficiency, and making full provision for the payment of the interest which shall accrue on the stock to be created by virtue of the loans aforesaid, in conformity to the terms thereof respectively, and according to the tenor of the certificates to be granted for the same pursuant to this act.

SEC. 22. *And be it further enacted*, That the proceeds of the sales which shall be made of lands in the western territory, now belonging, or that may hereafter belong to the United States, shall be, and are hereby appropriated towards sinking or discharging the debts, for the payment whereof the United States now are, or by virtue of this act may be holden, and shall be applied solely to that use until the said debts shall be fully satisfied.

[Approved August 4, 1790. 1 Statutes at Large, 138.]

NOTE. — By a series of acts, beginning with that of May 8, 1792, 1 Statutes at Large, 279, the time allowed for subscriptions under section 3 above was extended to December 31, 1797, giving to non-subscribing creditors a rate of interest equal to that which would be payable to them as subscribing creditors. See the act of March 3, 1797, 1 Statutes at Large, 516.

The time for receiving upon loan the debts of the States under section 13 above was also extended by the act of May 8, 1792, to March 1, 1793, "Provided always, that the commissioners of loans for North Carolina shall not be allowed to receive any certificate issued by Patrick Travers, commissioner of Cumberland County, or by the commissioners of army accounts at Warrenton."

1790, Chap. XXXVIII. — *An Act to provide more effectually for the settlement of the Accounts between the United States and the individual States.*

SECTION 1. *Be it enacted*, . . . That a board, to consist of three commissioners, be, and hereby is established to settle the accounts between the United States, and the individual states; and the determination of a majority of the said commissioners on the claims submitted to them, shall be final and conclusive; and they shall have power to employ such number of clerks as they may find necessary.

[Section 2 provides for the oath of office to be taken by the commissioners, and for their payment, at the rate of two thousand two hundred and fifty dollars per annum for each.] *

SEC. 3. *And be it further enacted*, That it shall be the duty of the said commissioners to receive and examine all claims which shall be exhibited to them before the first day of July, one thousand seven hundred and ninety-one, and to determine on all such as shall have accrued for the general or particular defence during the war, and on the evidence thereof, according to the principles of general equity (although such claims may not be sanctioned by the resolves of Congress, or supported by regular vouchers), so as to provide for the final settlement of all accounts between the United States and the states individually; but no evidence of a claim heretofore admitted by a commissioner of the United States for any state or district, shall be subject to such examination; nor shall the claim of any citizen be admitted as a charge against the United States in the account of any state, unless the same was allowed by such state before the twenty-fourth day of September, one thousand seven hundred and eighty-eight.

SEC. 4. *And be it further enacted*, That it shall be the duty of the said commissioners to examine and liquidate to specie value, on principles of equity, the credits and debits of the states already on the books of the treasury for bills of credit subsequent to the eighteenth of March, one thousand seven hundred and eighty.

SEC. 5. *And be it further enacted*, That the commissioners shall debit each state with all advances which have been, or may be made to it by the United States, and with the interest thereon to the last day of the year one thousand seven hundred and eighty-nine, and shall credit each state for its disbursements and advances on the principles contained in the third section of this act, with interest to the day aforesaid, and having struck the balance due to each state, shall find the aggregate of all the balances, which aggregate shall be apportioned between the states agreeably to the rule hereinafter given ; and the difference between such apportionments, and the respective balances, shall be carried in a new account to the debit or credit of the states respectively, as the case may be.

SEC. 6. *And be it further enacted,* That the rule for apportioning to the states the aggregate of the balances first above mentioned, shall be the same that is prescribed by the constitution of the United States, for the apportionment of representation and direct taxes, and according to the first enumeration which shall be made.

SEC. 7. *And be it further enacted,* That the states who shall have balances placed to their credit on the books of the treasury of the United States, shall, within twelve months after the same shall have been so credited, be entitled to have the same funded upon the same terms with the other part of the domestic debt of the United States ; but the balances so credited to any state shall not be transferable.

[Section 8 relates to the compensation of the clerks employed by the commissioners.]

SEC. 9. *And be it further enacted,* That the powers of the said commissioners shall continue until the first day of July, one thousand seven hundred and ninety-two, unless the business shall be sooner accomplished.

[Approved, August 5, 1790.   1 Statutes at Large, 178.]

NOTE. — The time for settling the accounts under this act was extended to July 1, 1793, by the Act of January 23, 1792, 1 Statutes at Large, 229.

1790, Chap. XLVII. — *An Act making Provision for the Reduction of the Public Debt.*

IT being desirable by all just and proper means, to effect a reduction of the amount of the public debt, and as the application of such surplus of the revenue as may remain after satisfying the purposes for which appropriations shall have been made by law, will not only contribute to that desirable end, but will be beneficial to the creditors of the United States, by raising the price of their stock, and be productive of considerable saving to the United States:

SECTION 1. *Be it enacted, . . .* That all such surplus of the product of the duties on goods, wares, and merchandise imported, and on the tonnage of ships or vessels to the last day of December next, inclusively, as shall remain after satisfying the several purposes for which appropriations shall have been made by law to the end of the present session, shall be applied to the purchase of the debt of the United States, at its market price, if not exceeding the par or true value thereof.

SEC. 2. *And be it further enacted,* That the purchases to be made of the said debt, shall be made under the direction of the President of the Senate, the Chief Justice, the Secretary of State, the Secretary of the Treasury, and the Attorney General for the time being; and who, or any three of whom, with the approbation of the President of the United States, shall cause the said purchases to be made in such manner and under such regulations as shall appear to them best calculated to fulfil the intent of this act: *Provided,* That the same be made openly, and with due regard to the equal benefit of the several states : *And provided further,* That to avoid all risk or failure, or delay in the payment of interest stipulated to be paid for and during the year one thousand seven hundred and ninety-one, by the act intituled "An act making provision for the debt of the United States," such reservations shall be made of the surplus as may be necessary to make good the said payments, as they shall respectively become due, in case of deficiency in the amount of the receipts into the treasury during the said year, on account of the duties on goods, wares, and merchandise imported, and the tonnage of ships or vessels, after the last day of December next.

SEC. 3. *And be it further enacted,* That accounts of the application of the said monies shall be rendered for settlement as other public accounts, accompanied with returns of the amount of the said debt purchased therewith, at the end of every quarter of a year, to be computed from the time of commencing the purchases aforesaid : and that a full and exact report of the proceedings of the said five persons, or any . three of them, including a statement of the disbursements and purchases made under their direction, specifying the times thereof, the prices at which, and the parties from whom the same may be made, shall be laid before Congress, within the first fourteen days of each session which may ensue the present, during the execution of their said trust.

SEC. 4.   *And be it further enacted*, That the President of the United States be, and he is hereby authorized to cause to be borrowed, on behalf of the United States, a sum or sums not exceeding in the whole two millions of dollars, at an interest not exceeding five per cent., and that the sum or sums so borrowed be also applied to the purchase of the said debt of the United States, under the like direction, in the like manner, and subject to the like regulations and restrictions with the surplus aforesaid :   *Provided*, That out of the interest arising on the debt to be purchased in manner aforesaid, there shall be appropriated and applied a sum not exceeding the rate of eight per centum per annum on account both of principal and interest towards the repayment of the two millions of dollars so to be borrowed.

[Approved, Aug 12, 1790. 1 Statutes at Large, 186.]

1790–91, Chap. X. — *An Act to incorporate the subscribers to the Bank of the United States.*

WHEREAS it is conceived that the establishment of a bank for the United States, upon a foundation sufficiently extensive to answer the purposes intended thereby, and at the same time upon the principles which afford adequate security for an upright and prudent administration thereof, will be very conducive to the successful conducting of the national finances; will tend to give facility to the obtaining of loans, for the use of the government, in sudden emergencies; and will be productive of considerable advantage to trade and industry in general: Therefore,

SECTION 1.   *Be it enacted*, . . . That a bank of the United States shall be established ; the capital stock whereof shall not exceed ten millions of dollars, divided into twenty-five thousand shares, each share being four hundred dollars ; and that subscriptions, towards constituting the said stock, shall, on the first Monday of April next, be opened at the city of Philadelphia, under the superintendence of such persons, not less than three, as shall be appointed for that purpose by the President of the United States (who is hereby empowered to appoint the said persons accordingly) ; which subscriptions shall continue open, until the whole of the said stock shall have been subscribed.

Sec. 2.   *And be it further enacted,* That it shall be lawful for any person, co-partnership, or body politic, to subscribe for such or so many shares, as he, she, or they shall think fit, not exceeding one thousand, except as shall be hereafter directed relatively to the United States ; and that the sums respectively subscribed, except on behalf of the United States, shall be payable one-fourth in gold and silver, and three-fourths in that part of the public debt, which, according to the loan proposed in the fourth and fifteenth sections of the act entitled "An act making provision for the debt of the United States," shall bear an accruing interest, at the time of payment, of six per centum per annum, and shall also be payable in four equal parts, in the aforesaid ratio of specie to debt, at the distance of six calendar months from each other ; the first whereof shall be paid at the time of subscription.

[Section 3 makes the subscribers a corporation by the name of "The President, Directors and Company of the Bank of the United States," to continue until March 4, 1811; and empowers them to hold property not exceeding fifteen millions of dollars, including the amount of their capital stock, and to make all convenient regulations, and to do all necessary things, subject to the limitations and provisions of this act.

Section 4 provides for the annual election of twenty-five directors, and requires the directors to choose one of their number as president.

Section 5 requires that as soon as four hundred thousand dollars, in gold and silver, shall have been received from the subscribers, a time shall be fixed for the election of directors, and the operations of the bank shall then begin at the city of Philadelphia.

Section 6 empowers the directors to employ the necessary officers, clerks, and servants, and to govern the affairs of the corporation.]

Sec. 7.   *And be it further enacted,* That the following

rules, restrictions, limitations and provisions, shall form and be fundamental articles of the constitution of the said corporation, viz. :

I. The number of votes to which each stockholder shall be entitled, shall be according to the number of shares he shall hold, in the proportions following: That is to say, for one share, and not more than two shares, one vote: for every two shares above two, and not exceeding ten, one vote: for every four shares above ten, and not exceeding thirty, one vote: for every six shares above thirty, and not exceeding sixty, one vote: for every eight shares above sixty, and not exceeding one hundred, one vote: and for every ten shares above one hundred, one vote:—But no person, co-partnership, or body politic shall be entitled to a greater number than thirty votes. And after the first election, no share or shares shall confer a right of suffrage, which shall not have been holden three calendar months previous to the day of election. Stockholders actually resident within the United States, and none other, may vote in elections by proxy.

II. Not more than three-fourths of the directors in office, exclusive of the president, shall be eligible for the next succeeding year: but the director, who shall be president at the time of an election, may always be re-elected.

III. None but a stockholder, being a citizen of the United States, shall be eligible as a director.

IV. No director shall be entitled to any emolument, unless the same shall have been allowed by the stockholders at a general meeting. The stockholders shall make such compensation to the president, for his extraordinary attendance at the bank, as shall appear to them reasonable.

V. Not less than seven directors shall constitute a board for the transaction of business, of whom the president shall always be one, except in case of sickness, or necessary absence; in which case his place may be supplied by any other director, whom he, by writing under his hand, shall nominate for the purpose.

VI. Any number of stockholders, not less than sixty, who, together, shall be proprietors of two hundred shares or up-

wards, shall have power at any time to call a general meeting
of the stockholders, for purposes relative to the institution,
giving at least ten weeks' notice, in two public gazettes of the
place where the bank is kept, and specifying, in such notice,
the object or objects of such meeting.

VII. Every cashier or treasurer, before he enters upon the
duties of his office, shall be required to give bond, with two
or more sureties, to the satisfaction of the directors, in a sum
not less than fifty thousand dollars, with condition for his
good behavior.

VIII. The lands, tenements and hereditaments which it shall
be lawful for the said corporation to hold, shall be only such
as shall be requisite for its immediate accommodation in relation to the convenient transacting of its business, and such
as shall have been *bona fide* mortgaged to it by way of security, or conveyed to it in satisfaction of debts previously contracted in the course of its dealings, or purchased at sales
upon judgments which shall have been obtained for such
debts.

IX. The total amount of the debts, which the said corporation shall at any time owe, whether by bond, bill, note, or
other contract, shall not exceed the sum of ten millions of
dollars, over and above the monies then actually deposited
in the bank for safe-keeping, unless the contracting of any
greater debt shall have been previously authorized by a law
of the United States.   In case of excess, the directors, under
whose administration it shall happen, shall be liable for the
same, in their natural and private capacities ; and an action
of debt may, in such case, be brought against them, or any
of them, their or any of their heirs, executors, or administrators, in any court of record of the United States, or of either
of them, by any creditor or creditors of the said corporation,
and may be prosecuted to judgment and execution ; any condition, covenant, or agreement to the contrary notwithstanding.   But this shall not be construed to exempt the said
corporation, or the lands, tenements, goods or chattels of
the same, from being also liable for and chargeable with the
said excess.   Such of the said directors, who may have been

absent when the said excess was contracted or created, or who may have dissented from the resolution or act whereby the same was so contracted or created, may respectively exonerate themselves from being so liable, by forthwith giving notice of the fact, and of their absence or dissent, to the President of the United States, and to the stockholders, at a general meeting, which they shall have power to call for that purpose.

X. The said corporation may sell any part of the public debt whereof its stock shall be composed, but shall not be at liberty to purchase any public debt whatsoever; nor shall directly or indirectly deal or trade in anything, except bills of exchange, gold or silver bullion, or in the sale of goods really and truly pledged for money lent and not redeemed in due time; or of goods which shall be the produce of its lands. Neither shall the said corporation take more than at the rate of six per centum per annum, for or upon its loans or discounts.

XI. No loan shall be made by the said corporation, for the use or on account of the government of the United States, to an amount exceeding one hundred thousand dollars, or of any particular state, to an amount exceeding fifty thousand dollars, or of any foreign prince or state, unless previously authorized by a law of the United States.

XII. The stock of the said corporation shall be assignable and transferable, according to such rules as shall be instituted in that behalf, by the laws and ordinances of the same.

XIII. The bills obligatory and of credit, under the seal of the said corporation, which shall be made to any person or persons, shall be assignable by indorsement thereupon, under the hand or hands of such person or persons, and of his, her, or their assignee or assignees. and so as absolutely to transfer and vest the property thereof in each and every assignee or assignees successively, and to enable such assignee or assignees to bring and maintain an action thereupon in his, her, or their own name or names. And bills or notes, which may be issued by order of the said corporation, signed by the president, and countersigned by the principal cashier or treasurer thereof, promising the payment of money to any person or persons, his, her, or their order, or to bearer, though not under the seal of the said corporation, shall be binding and obligatory upon the same, in the like manner, and with the like force and effect, as upon any private person or persons, if issued by him or them, in his, her, or their private or natural capacity or capacities; and shall be assignable and negotiable, in like manner as if they were so issued by such private person or persons — that is to say, those which may be payable to any person or persons, his, her, or their order, shall be assignable by indorsement, in like manner, and with the like effect, as foreign bills of exchange now are; and those which are payable to bearer, shall be negotiable and assignable by delivery only.

XIV. Half yearly dividends shall be made of so much of the profits of the bank, as shall appear to the directors advisable; and once in every three years, the directors shall lay before the stockholders, at a general meeting, for their information, an exact and particular statement of the debts which shall have remained unpaid after the expiration of the original credit, for a period of treble the term of that credit; and of the surplus of profit, if any, after deducting losses and dividends. If there shall be a failure in the payment of any part of any sum, subscribed by any person, co-partnership, or body politic, the party failing shall lose the benefit of any dividend, which may have accrued, prior to the time for making such payment, and during the delay of the same.

XV. It shall be lawful for the directors aforesaid, to establish offices wheresoever they shall think fit, within the United States, for the purposes of discount and deposit only, and upon the same terms, and in the same manner, as shall be practised at the bank; and to commit the management of the said offices, and the making of the said discounts, to such persons, under such agreements, and subject to such regulations as they shall deem proper; not being contrary to law, or to the constitution of the bank.

XVI. The officer at the head of the treasury department of

the United States, shall be furnished, from time to time, as often as he may require, not exceeding once a week, with statements of the amount of the capital stock of the said corporation, and of the debts due to the same ; of the monies deposited therein ; of the notes in circulation, and of the cash in hand ; and shall have a right to inspect such general accounts in the books of the bank as shall relate to the said statements. *Provided*, That this shall not be construed to imply a right of inspecting the account of any private individual or individuals with the bank.

SEC. 8. *And be it further enacted*, That if the said corporation, or any person or persons for or to the use of the same, shall deal or trade in buying or selling any goods, wares, merchandise, or commodities whatsoever, contrary to the provisions of this act, all and every person and persons, by whom any order or direction for so dealing or trading shall have been given, and all and every person and persons who shall have been concerned as parties or agents therein, shall forfeit and lose treble the value of the goods, wares, merchandises, and commodities, in which such dealing and trade shall have been ; one half thereof to the use of the informer, and the other half thereof to the use of the United States, to be recovered with costs of suit.

SEC. 9. *And be it further enacted*, That if the said corporation shall advance or lend any sum, for the use or on account of the government of the United States, to an amount exceeding one hundred thousand dollars ; or of any particular state to an amount exceeding fifty thousand dollars ; or of any foreign prince or state, (unless previously authorized thereto by a law of the United States,) all and every person and persons, by and with whose order, agreement, consent, approbation, or connivance, such unlawful advance or loan shall have been made, upon conviction thereof, shall forfeit and pay, for every such offence, treble the value or amount of the sum or sums which shall have been so unlawfully advanced or lent ; one-fifth thereof to the use of the informer, and the residue thereof to the use of the United States ; to be disposed of by law and not otherwise.

SEC. 10. *And be it further enacted*, That the bills or notes of the said corporation, originally made payable, or which shall have become payable on demand, in gold and silver coin, shall be receivable in all payments to the United States.

SEC. 11. *And be it further enacted*, That it shall be lawful for the President of the United States, at any time or times, within eighteen months after the first day of April next, to cause a subscription to be made to the stock of the said corporation, as part of the aforesaid capital stock of ten millions of dollars, on behalf of the United States, to an amount not exceeding two millions of dollars ; to be paid out of the monies which shall be borrowed by virtue of either of the acts, the one entitled "An act making provision for the debt of the United States ; " and the other entitled "An act making provision for the reduction of the public debt ; " borrowing of the bank an equal sum, to be applied to the purposes for which the said monies shall have been procured ; reimbursable in ten years, by equal annual instalments ; or at any time sooner, or in any greater proportions, that the government may think fit.

SEC. 12. *And be it further enacted*, That no other bank shall be established by any future law of the United States, during the continuance of the corporation hereby created ; for which the faith of the United States is hereby pledged.

[Approved, February 25, 1791. 1 Statutes at Large, 191.]

1790–91, Chap. XI. — *An Act supplementary to the act intituled " An act to incorporate the subscribers to the Bank of the United States."*

SECTION 1. *Be it enacted*, . . . That the subscriptions to the stock of the Bank of the United States, as provided by the act, intituled " An act to incorporate the subscribers to the bank of the United States," shall not be opened until the first Monday in July next.

SEC. 2. *And be it further enacted*, That so much of the first payment as by the said act is directed to be in the six per cent. certificates of the United States, may be deferred until the first Monday in January next.

Sec. 3. *And be it further enacted*, That no person, corporation, or body politic, except in behalf of the United States, shall, for the space of three months after the said first Monday in July next, subscribe in any one day, for more than thirty shares.

Sec. 4. *And be it further enacted*, That every subscriber shall, at the time of subscribing, pay into the hands of the persons who shall be appointed to receive the same, the specie proportion required by the said act to be then paid. And if any such subscriber shall fail to make any of the future payments, he shall forfeit the sum so by him first paid, for the use of the corporation.

Sec. 5. *And be it further enacted*, That such part of the public debt, including the assumed debt, as is funded at an interest of three per cent. may be paid to the bank, in like manner with the debt funded at six per cent., computing the value of the former at one half the value of the latter, and reserving to the subscribers who shall have paid three per cent. stock, the privilege of redeeming the same with six per cent. stock, at the above rate of computation, at any time before the first day of January, one thousand seven hundred and ninety-three; unless the three per cent. stock shall have been previously disposed of by the directors.

[Approved, March 2, 1791. 1 Statutes at Large, 196.]

1790-91, Chap. XV. — *An Act repealing, after the last day of June next, the duties heretofore laid upon Distilled Spirits imported from abroad, and laying others in their stead; and also upon Spirits distilled within the United States, and for appropriating the same.*

Sec. 60. *And be it further enacted*, That the nett product of the duties herein before specified, which shall be raised, levied and collected by virtue of this act, or so much thereof as may be necessary, shall be, and is hereby pledged and appropriated for the payment of the interest of the several and respective loans which had been made in foreign countries, prior to the fourth day of August last; and also upon all and every the loan and loans which have been and shall be made, and obtained pursuant to the act intituled "An act making provision for the debt of the United States;" and according to the true intent and meaning of the said act, and of the several provisions and engagements therein contained and expressed, and subject to the like priorities and reservations as are made and contained in and by the said act, in respect to the monies therein appropriated, and subject to this farther reservation, that is to say—Of the nett amount or product during the present year, of the duties laid by this act, in addition to those heretofore laid upon spirits imported into the United States, from any foreign port or place, and of the duties laid by this act on spirits distilled within the United States, and on stills; to be disposed of towards such purposes for which appropriations shall be made during the present session. And to the end that the said monies may be inviolably applied in conformity to the appropriation hereby made, and may never be diverted to any other purpose until the final redemption, or reimbursement of the loans or sums for the payment of the interest whereof they are appropriated, an account shall be kept of the receipts and disposition thereof, separate and distinct from the product of any other duties, impost, excise, and taxes whatsoever, except those heretofore laid and appropriated to the same purposes.

SEC. 61. *And be it further enacted*, That the unappropriated surplus, if any there shall be, of the revenue arising under this act, at the end of this and every succeeding year, shall be applied to the reduction of the public debt, in like manner as is directed by the act, intituled "An act making provision for the reduction of the public debt," and provided by the act, intituled "An act making provision for the debt of the United States;" unless the said surplus, or any part thereof, shall be required for the public exigencies of the United States, and shall, by special acts of Congress, be appropriated thereto.

SEC. 62. *And be it further enacted*, That the several duties imposed by this act, shall continue to be collected and paid, until the debts and purposes for which they are pledged and appropriated shall be fully discharged and satisfied, and

no longer. *Provided always*, That nothing herein contained
'shall be construed to prevent the legislature of the United
States from substituting other duties or taxes of equal value
to all or any of the said duties and imposts.

[Approved, March 3, 1791. 1 Statutes at Large, 213.]

1791-92, Chap. XXXVIII. — *An Act supplementary to the
act making provision for the Debt of the United States.*

[Sections 1, 2, 3, and 4 provide for extending the time allowed for receiving on loan the domestic debt of the United States, and the debt of
the respective states, under the Act of August 4, 1790. See *Note* on p. 18.

Section 5 authorizes the President of the United States to discharge
the principal and interest of the debt due to foreign officers, out of any
monies borrowed under the aforesaid act and not needed to fulfil its
purposes.]

SEC. 6. *And be it further enacted.* That the President of
the Senate, the Chief Justice, the Secretary of State, the Secretary of the Treasury, and the Attorney General, for the
time being, shall be commissioners, who, or any three of
whom, are hereby authorized, with the approbation of the
President of the United States, to purchase the debt of the
United States, at its market price, if not exceeding the par
or true value thereof; for which purchase the interest on so
much of the public debt, as has already been, or may hereafter
be purchased for the United States, or as shall be paid into
the treasury, and so much of the monies appropriated for the
payment of the interest on the foreign and domestic debt, as
shall exceed what may be sufficient for the payment of such
interest to the creditors of the United States, shall be and are
hereby appropriated. And it shall be the duty of the said
commissioners to render to the legislature, within two months
after the commencement of the first session thereof in every
year, a full and precise account of all such purchases made,
and public debt redeemed, in pursuance of this act.

SEC. 7. And whereas it is expedient to establish a fund for
the gradual reduction of the public debt: *Be it further enacted*, That the interest on so much of the debt of the United
States, as has been or shall be purchased or redeemed for or

by the United States, or as shall be paid into the treasury
thereof in satisfaction of any debt or demand, and the surplus
of any sum or sums appropriated for the payment of the interest upon the said debt, which shall remain after paying such
interest, shall be, and hereby are appropriated and pledged
firmly and inviolably for and to the purchase and redemption of the said debt, to be applied under the direction of the
President of the Senate, the Chief Justice, the Secretary of
State, the Secretary of the Treasury, and the Attorney-Gen-
eral for the time being, or any three of them, with the approbation of the President of the United States, for the time
being, in manner following, that is to say: First, to the purchase of the several species of stock constituting the debt of the
United States, at their respective market prices, not exceeding the par or true value thereof, and as nearly as may be, in
equal proportions, until the annual amount of the said funds,
together with any other provisions which may be made by law,
shall be equal to two per centum of the whole amount of the
outstanding funded stock bearing a present interest of six per
centum.   Thenceforth, secondly, to the redemption of the
said last mentioned stock, according to the right for that purpose reserved to the United States, until the whole amount
thereof shall have been redeemed.   And lastly, after such
redemption, to the purchase, at its market price, of any other
stock consisting of the debt of the United States, which may
then remain unredeemed: and such purchase, as far as the
fund shall at any time extend, shall be made within thirty
days next after each day, on which a quarterly payment of
interest on the debt of the United States shall become due,
and shall be made by a known agent, to be named by the
said commissioners.

SEC. 8.   *And be it further enacted,* That all future purchases of public debt on account of the United States, shall
be made at the lowest price, at which the same can be obtained
by open purchase, or by receiving sealed proposals, to be
opened in the presence of the commissioners, or persons authorized by them to make purchases, and the persons making
such proposals.

SEC. 9. *And be it further enacted,* That quarter yearly accounts of the application of the said fund shall be rendered for settlement, as ꝛother public accounts, accompanied with returns of the sums of the said debt, which shall have been from time to time purchased or redeemed ; and a full and exact report of the proceedings of the said commissioners, including a statement of the disbursements, which shall have been made, and of the sums which shall have been purchased or redeemed under their direction, and specifying dates, prices, parties, and places, shall be laid before Congress, within the first fourteen days of each session which may ensue the present, during the execution of the said trust.

[Approved, May 8, 1792.　1 Statutes at Large, 281.]

1793–94, Chap. XXXVII. — *An Act making provision for the payment of the interest on the balances due to certain States, upon a final settlement of the accounts between the United States and the individual States.*

SECTION 1. *Be it enacted,* . . . That interest upon the balances reported to be due to certain states, by the commissioners for settling accounts between the United States and individual states, be allowed, from the last day of December, one thousand seven hundred and eighty-nine, and to be computed to the last day of December, one thousand seven hundred and ninety-four, at the rate of four per centum per annum : And that the amount of such interest be placed to the credit of the state, to which the same shall be found due, upon the books of the treasury of the United States, and shall bear an interest of three per centum per annum, from and after the said last day of December, one thousand seven hundred and ninety-four.

[Section 2 provides for the quarterly payment of the interest due to any state, beginning on the last day of March, 1795; and pledges for the payment of the interest so much of the duties arising from imports and tonnage, after December 31, 1794, as may be necessary and not otherwise appropriated, also pledging the faith of the United States to provide for any deficiency.]

[Approved, May 31, 1794.　1 Statutes at Large, 371.]

NOTE. — By the act of January 2, 1795, 1 Statutes at Large, 409, any state is authorized, within two years, to transfer stock thus created to creditors of the state who were such prior to July 1, 1793. This authority was continued to March 4, 1799, by the act of July 6, 1797. See *ibid*. 533.

1794–95, Chap. XLV. — *An Act making further provision for the support of Public Credit, and for the redemption of the Public Debt.*

[Section 1 authorizes the commissioners of the sinking fund to borrow not exceeding one million dollars in any one year, in anticipation of the revenue, for the payment of interest on the public debt, and appropriates for the interest on such temporary loan the proceeds of duties on goods imported, on tonnage, and upon spirits distilled within the United States, and stills.

Sections 2–4 authorize a loan to be issued in exchange for equal amounts of the foreign debt, to bear an interest equal to the interest payable on the foreign debt exchanged, with an addition of one-half of one per cent. per annum, and the principal to be reimbursable at pleasure. The new loan is to be entered on the books of the treasury in like manner as the domestic funded debt, and to be transferable in like manner; and the interest and principal of loans authorized by this act are to be payable at the treasury only, so far as relates to the principal and interest of the domestic debt.

Section 5 provides that so much of the duties on goods imported, on tonnage, and upon spirits distilled and stills as may be set free by subscriptions to the new loan, with such further part of the proceeds as may be necessary, shall remain appropriated for the payment of interest on the said loan until the principal thereof is reimbursed : provided that nothing herein contained shall alter any existing contract concerning the foreign debt except as to such holders as may subscribe to the new loan.|

SEC. 6.   *And be it further enacted,* That the several and respective duties laid and contained in and by the act, intituled "An act laying additional duties on goods, wares, and merchandise imported into the United States," passed the seventh day of June, one thousand seven hundred and ninety-four, shall, together with the other duties heretofore charged with the payment of interest on the public debt, continue to be levied, collected and paid, until the whole of the capital or principal of the present debt of the United States, and future loans which may be made, pursuant to law, for the exchange, reimbursement or redemption thereof, or of any part thereof, shall be reimbursed or redeemed, and shall be, and hereby are, pledged and appropriated for the payment of interest upon the said debt and loans, until the same shall be so reimbursed or redeemed.

[Section 7 annuls the reservation made by § 4 of the act of August 12, 1790, and makes other provision for the same purpose.]

SEC. 8. *And be it further enacted,* That the following appropriations, in addition to those heretofore made, be made to the fund constituted by the seventh section of the act, intituled "An act supplementary to the act making provision for the debt of the United States," passed the eighth day of May, one thousand seven hundred and ninety-two, to be hereafter denominated "The Sinking Fund," to wit: First, So much of the proceeds of the duties on goods, wares and merchandise imported; on the tonnage of ships or vessels, and on spirits distilled within the United States and stills, as, together with the monies which now constitute the said fund, and shall accrue to it, by virtue of the provisions herein before made, and by the interest upon each instalment, or part of principal, which shall be reimbursed, will be sufficient, yearly and every year, commencing the first day of January next, to reimburse and pay so much as may rightfully be reimbursed and paid, of the principal of that part of the debt or stock which, on the said first day of January next, shall bear an interest of six per centum per annum, redeemable by payments on account both of principal and interest, not exceeding, in one year, eight per centum, excluding that which shall stand to the credit of the commissioners of the sinking fund, and that which shall stand to the credit of certain states, in consequence of the balances reported in their favour, by the commissioners for settling accounts between the United States and individual states: Secondly, — The dividends, which shall be, from time to time, declared on so much of the stock of the Bank of the United States, as belongs to the United States (deducting thereout such sums, as will be requisite to pay interest on any part remaining unpaid

of the loan of two millions of dollars, had of the Bank of the
United States, pursuant to the eleventh section of the act, by
which the said bank is incorporated) : Thirdly, — So much
of the duties on goods, wares, and merchandise imported, on
the tonnage of ships or vessels, and on spirits distilled within
the United States and stills, as, with the said dividends, after
such deduction, will be sufficient, yearly and every year, to
pay the remaining instalments of the principal of the said
loan, as they shall become due, and as, together with any
monies, which, by virtue of provisions in former acts, and
herein before made, shall, on the first day of January, in the
year one thousand eight hundred and two, belong to the said
sinking fund, not otherwise specially appropriated ; and with
the interest on each instalment, or part of principal, which
shall, from time to time, be reimbursed, or paid, of that part
of the debt or stock, which, on the first day of January, in
the year one thousand eight hundred and one, shall begin to
bear an interest of six per centum per annum, will be sufficient, yearly and every year, commencing on the first day of
January, in the year one thousand eight hundred and two,
to reimburse and pay so much, as may rightfully be reimbursed and paid, of the said principal of the said debt or
stock, which shall so begin to bear an interest of six per centum per annum, on the said first day of January, in the year
one thousand eight hundred and one, excluding that, which
shall stand to the credit of the commissioners of the sinking
fund, and that, which shall stand to the credit of certain
states, as aforesaid : Fourthly, — The net proceeds of the
sales of lands belonging, or which shall hereafter belong to
the United States, in the western territory thereof : Fifthly,
— All monies, which shall be received into the treasury, on
account of debts due to the United States, by reason of any
matter prior to their present constitution ; And lastly, — all
surpluses of the revenues of the United States, which shall
remain, at the end of any calendar year, beyond the amount
of the appropriations charged upon the said revenues, and
which, during the session of Congress next thereafter, shall
not be otherwise specially appropriated or reserved by law.

SEC. 9. *And be it further enacted*, That as well the monies which shall accrue to the said sinking fund, by virtue of the provisions of this act, as those which shall have accrued to the same, by virtue of the provisions of any former act or acts, shall be under the direction and management of the commissioners of the sinking fund, or the officers designated in and by the second section of the act, intituled " An act making provision for the reduction of the public debt," passed the twelfth day of August, one thousand seven hundred and ninety, and their successors in office ; and shall be, and continue appropriated to the said fund, until the whole of the present debt of the United States, foreign and domestic, funded and unfunded, including future loans, which may be made for reimbursing or redeeming any instalments or parts of principal of the said debt, shall be reimbursed and redeemed ; and shall be, and are hereby declared to be vested in the said commissioners, in trust, to be applied, according to the provisions of the aforesaid act of the eighth day of May, in the year one thousand seven hundred and ninety-two, and of this act, to the reimbursement and redemption of the said debt, including the loans aforesaid, until the same shall be fully reimbursed and redeemed.   And the faith of the United States is hereby pledged, that the monies or funds aforesaid, shall inviolably remain, and be appropriated and vested, as aforesaid, to be applied to the said reimbursement and redemption, in manner aforesaid, until the same shall be fully and completely effected.

SEC. 10. *And be it further enacted*, That all reimbursements of the capital, or principal of the public debt, foreign and domestic, shall be made under the superintendence of the commissioners of the sinking fund, who are hereby empowered and required, if necessary, with the approbation of the President of the United States, as any instalments or parts of the said capital or principal become due, to borrow, on the credit of the United States, the sums requisite for the payment of the said instalments, or parts of principal : *Provided*, That any loan which may be made by the said commissioners, shall be liable to reimbursement at the pleasure

of the United States ; and that the rate of interest thereupon
shall not exceed six per centum per annum ; and for greater
caution, it is hereby declared that it shall be deemed a good
execution of the said power to borrow, for the said commissioners, with the approbation of the President, to cause to be
· constituted certificates of stock, signed by the Register of the
Treasury for the sums to be respectively borrowed, bearing
an interest of six per centum per annum, and redeemable at
the pleasure of the United States ; and to cause the said
certificates of stock to be sold in the market of the United
States or elsewhere ; *Provided*, That no such stock be sold
under par. And for the payment of interest on any sum or
sums which may be so borrowed, either by direct loans, or by
the sale of certificates of stock, the interest on the sum or
sums which shall be reimbursed by the proceeds thereof (except that upon the funded stock, bearing, and to bear an
interest of six per centum, redeemable by payments, not
exceeding in one year, eight per centum on account of both
principal and interest), and so much of the duties on goods,
wares and merchandise imported, on the tonnage of ships or
vessels, and upon spirits distilled within the United States,
and upon stills, as may be necessary, shall be, and hereby
are pledged and appropriated.

Sec. 11. *And be it further enacted*, That it shall be the
duty of the commissioners of the sinking fund, to cause to be
applied and paid, out of the said fund, yearly and every
year, at the treasury of the United. States, the several and
respective sums following, to wit : First, such sum and sums
as, according to the right for that purpose reserved, may
rightfully be paid for, and towards the reimbursement or
redemption of such debt or stock of the United States, as, on
the first day of January next, shall bear an interest of six
per centum per annum, redeemable by payments, not exceeding in one year, eight per centum, on account both of principal and interest, excluding that standing to the credit of
the commissioners of the sinking fund, and that standing to
the credit of certain states, as aforesaid, commencing the
said reimbursement or redemption, on the said first day of

January next: Secondly, such sum and sums as, according to
the conditions of the aforesaid loan, had of the Bank of the
United States, shall be henceforth payable towards the reimbursement thereof, as the same shall respectively accrue :
Thirdly, such sum and sums as, according to the right for
that purpose reserved, may rightfully be paid for and towards
the reimbursement or redemption of such debt or stock of the
United States as, on the first day of January, in the year one
thousand eight hundred and one, shall begin to bear an interest of six per centum per annum, redeemable by payments,
not exceeding, in one year, eight per centum, on account both
of principal and interest, excluding that standing to the
credit of the commissioners of the sinking fund, and that
standing to the credit of certain states, as aforesaid, commencing the said reimbursement or redemption, on the first
day of January, in the year one thousand eight hundred and
two : and, also to cause to be applied all such surplus of the
said fund, as may at any time exist, after satisfying the
purposes aforesaid, towards the further and final redemption
of the present debt of the United States, foreign and domestic, funded and unfunded, including loans for the reimbursement thereof, by payment or purchase, until the said debt
shall be completely reimbursed or redeemed.

SEC. 12. *Provided always, and be it further enacted*,
That nothing in this act shall be construed to vest in the
commissioners of the sinking fund a right to pay, in the purchase or discharge of the unfunded domestic debt of the
United States, a higher rate than the market price or value
of the funded debt of the United States : *And provided
also*, That if after all the debts and loans aforesaid, now due,
and that shall arise under this act, excepting the said debt
or stock bearing an interest of three per cent., shall be fully
paid and discharged, any part of the principal of the said
debt or stock bearing an interest of three per cent. as aforesaid, shall be unredeemed, the government shall have liberty,
if they think proper, to make other and different appropriations of the said funds.

SEC. 13. *And be it further enacted*, That all priorities

heretofore established in the appropriations by law, for the interest on the debt of the United States, as between the different parts of the said debt, shall, after the year one thousand seven hundred and ninety-six, cease, with regard to all creditors of the United States, who do not, before the expiration of the said period, signify, in writing, to the Comptroller of the Treasury, their dissent therefrom; and that thenceforth, with the exception only of the debts of such creditors who shall so signify their dissent, the funds or revenues charged with the said appropriations shall, together, constitute a common or consolidated fund, chargeable indiscriminately, and without priority, with the payment of the said interest.

[Section 14 requires that all outstanding loan office certificates, final settlements, and indents of interest shall be presented before January 1, 1797, to the Auditor of the Treasury, to be exchanged for new certificates, or registered and returned, at the option of the holder; and all certificates, not so presented, shall be forever barred.

Section 15 enacts that any transfer of stock standing to the credit of a state, made after December 31, 1795, shall be upon condition that it shall be lawful to reimburse so much of the principal of the stock transferred as will make its reimbursement equal to that of the same stock transferred previous to the said day.]

SEC. 16. *And be it further enacted*, That in regard to any sum which shall have remained unexpended upon any appropriation other than for the payment of interest on the funded debt; for the payment of interest upon, and reimbursement, according to contract, of any loan or loans made on account of the United States; for the purposes of the sinking fund; or for a purpose, in respect to which, a longer duration is specially assigned by law, for more than two years after the expiration of the calendar year in which the act of appropriation shall have been passed, such appropriation shall be deemed to have ceased and been determined; and the sum so unexpended shall be carried to an account on the books of the treasury, to be denominated "THE SURPLUS FUND." But no appropriation shall be deemed to have so ceased and been determined, until after the year one thousand seven hundred and ninety-five, unless it shall appear to the Secretary of the Treasury, that the object thereof hath been fully satisfied, in which case, it shall be lawful for him to cause to be carried the unexpended residue thereof, to the said account of "the surplus fund."

[By sections 17, 18, and 19, the treasury is required to establish rules for the execution of this act; all restrictions and regulations heretofore imposed by law upon the commissioners of the sinking fund are made applicable in analogous cases under this act, and an account of all sales of stock or loans made is required to be laid before Congress within fourteen days after its next meeting; and in every case it is made lawful to borrow from the Bank of the United States, whatever the amount of the loan.]

[Approved, March 3, 1795. 1 Statutes at Large, 433.]

1795–96, Chap. XVI.—*An Act in addition to an act intituled " An act making further provision for the support of Public Credit, and for the redemption of the Public Debt."*

SECTION 1. *Be it enacted,* . . . That it shall be lawful for the commissioners of the sinking fund, and they are hereby required, to cause the funded stock of the United States bearing a present interest of six per centum per annum, to be reimbursed and paid, in manner following, to wit: First, by dividends to be made on the last days of March, June, and September for the present year, and from the year one thousand seven hundred and ninety-seven, to the year one thousand eight hundred and eighteen inclusive, at the rate of one and one half per centum upon the original capital. Secondly, by dividends to be made on the last day of December for the present year, and from the year one thousand seven hundred and ninety-seven, to the year one thousand eight hundred and seventeen inclusive, at the rate of three and one half per centum upon the original capital; and by a dividend to be made on the last day of December, in the year one thousand eight hundred and eighteen, of such a sum, as will then be adequate, according to the contract, for the final redemption of the said stock.

[Section 2 makes similar provision for the reimbursement of the stock bearing six per cent after the year 1800, by a like series of dividends beginning March 31, 1801, and ending December 31, 1824.

Section 3 extends these provisions to all balances of stock, bearing a present or deferred interest of six per cent, standing to the credit of the states, under the act of May 31, 1794; and Section 4 appropriates, in addition to sums already appropriated, such a sum of the duties on goods imported, on tonnage, and on spirits distilled in the United States and on stills, as shall be sufficient, with monies already applicable, to reimburse the said balances, in the manner directed.]

[Approved, April 28, 1796. 1 Statutes at Large, 458.]

1795–96, Chap. XLIV. — *An Act making provision for the payment of certain Debts of the United States.*

[Sections 1 and 2 authorize the commissioners of the sinking fund to borrow a sum not exceeding five millions of dollars, to be used in paying the capital of any debt due by the United States to the Bank of the United States, or to the Bank of New York, or any instalment of foreign debt, the loan to bear an interest of six per cent, payable quarteryearly, and to be redeemable at the pleasure of the United States after the close of the year 1819. The Bank of the United States is authorized to lend the whole sum and to sell the stock received therefor. Credits for the sums borrowed are to be entered on the books of the treasury, and certificates "for sums not less than one hundred dollars" are to be issued by the Register, and are to be transferable and the interest thereon is to be payable, as provided in sections 7 and 8 of the act of August 4, 1790.]

SEC. 3. *And be it further enacted,* That it shall be deemed a good execution of the power to borrow, herein granted, for the said commissioners of the sinking fund to cause to be constituted certificates of stock, of the description herein mentioned, and to cause the same to be sold in the United States, or elsewhere: *Provided,* That no more than one moiety of the said stock shall be sold under par. And it shall be lawful for the commissioners of the sinking fund, if they shall find the same to be most advantageous, to sell such and so many of the shares of the stock of the Bank of the United States, belonging to the United States, as they may think proper; and that they apply the proceeds thereof to the payment of the said debts, instead of selling certificates of stock, in the manner prescribed in this act. And such of the revenues of the United States, heretofore appropriated for the payment of interest of debts, thus discharged, shall be, and the same are hereby pledged and appropriated, towards the payment of the interest and instalments of the principal which shall hereafter become due on the loan obtained of the Bank of the United States, pursuant to the eleventh section of the act for incorporating the subscribers to the said bank.

SEC. 4. *And be it further enacted,* That such of the revenues of the United States, heretofore appropriated for the payment of interest on such debts as may be liberated or set free, by payments from the proceeds of the loan herein proposed, together with such further sums of the proceeds of the duties on goods, wares, and merchandise imported; on the tonnage of ships or vessels; and upon spirits distilled in the United States, and stills; as may be necessary, shall be, and the same are hereby, pledged and appropriated for the payment of the interest, which shall be payable upon the sums subscribed to the said loan; and shall continue so pledged and appropriated, until the principal of the said loan shall be fully reimbursed and redeemed.

[Approved May 31, 1796. 1 Statutes at Large, 488.]

1796–97, Chap. XIV. — *An Act to authorize the receipt of evidences of the Public Debt, in payment for the Lands of the United States.*

Be it enacted, . . . That the evidences of the public debt of the United States shall be receivable in payment for any of the lands which may be hereafter sold in conformity to the act intituled "An Act providing for the sale of the lands of the United States in the territory northwest of the river Ohio, and above the mouth of Kentucky River," at the following rates, viz.: the present foreign debt of the United States, and such debt, or stock, as, at the time of payment, shall bear an interest of six per centum per annum, shall be received at their nominal value; and the other species of debt, or stock, of the United States, shall be received at a rate bearing the same proportion to their respective market price, at the seat of government, at the time of payment, as the nominal value of the above mentioned six per centum stock shall, at the same time, bear to its market price at the same place; the Secretary of the Treasury, in all cases, determining what such market price is.

[Approved, March 3, 1797. 1 Statutes at Large, 507.]

NOTE. — This provision is also made applicable under the act of May 10, 1800, amending the acts providing for the sale of public lands. 2 Statutes at Large, 74.

1797-98, Chap. LI. — *An Act respecting loan office and final settlement certificates, indents of interest, and the unfunded or registered debt credited in the books of the Treasury.*

[By section 1 the time fixed by section 14 of the act of March 3, 1795, for the presentation of loan office certificates, final settlements, and indents of interest, is extended for one year.

Sections 2 and 3 provide that on the settlement of such certificates and indents of interest, the creditors may receive three per cent. stock of the United States, to the amount of the indents and of arrearages of interest on certificates accruing prior to January 1, 1791; and that the principal sums of the certificates, with interest since January 1, 1791, shall be discharged by reimbursement equal to the sum which would have been payable if the certificates had been subscribed, and by payment of the market value of the remaining funded stock which would have been created by such subscription.

The remaining sections forbid the officers of the treasury to issue any further certificates of registered or unfunded debt; require the commissioners of the sinking fund to reimburse the principal sums of the unfunded or registered debt; and authorize the creditors of the unfunded or registered debt to receive three per cent. stock equal to the arrearages of interest due to them prior to January 1, 1791.]

[Approved, June 12, 1798. 1 Statutes at Large, 562.]

1797-98, Chap. LXXIX. — *An Act to enable the President of the United States to borrow money for the Public Service.*

[Section 1 authorizes the President to borrow from the Bank of the United States, or from any other body, or from any person, upon such terms as he shall think most advantageous, a sum not exceeding five millions of dollars, *provided* that no contract shall be made precluding the reimbursement of such loan at any time after fifteen years from its date.]

SEC. 2. *And be it further enacted,* That so much as may be necessary of the surplus of the duties on imports and tonnage beyond the permanent appropriations heretofore charged upon them by law, shall be and hereby is pledged and appropriated for paying the interest of all such monies as may be borrowed, pursuant to this act, according to the terms and conditions on which the loan or loans, respectively, may be effected ; and also for paying and discharging the principal sum or sums of any such loan or loans, according to the terms and conditions to be fixed, as aforesaid. And the faith of the United States shall be and hereby is pledged, to establish sufficient permanent revenues for making up any deficiency that may hereafter appear in the provisions for paying the said interest and principal sums, or any of them, in manner aforesaid.

SEC. 3. *And be it further enacted*, That the sums to be borrowed, pursuant to this act, shall be paid into the treasury of the United States, and there separately accounted for ; and that the same shall be, and hereby are appropriated in manner following : First, to make up any deficiency in any appropriation heretofore made by law, or to be made, during the present session of Congress ; and, secondly, to defray the expenses which may be incurred before the end of the next session of Congress, by calling into actual service any part of the militia of the United States, or by raising, equipping, and calling into actual service, any regular troops, or volunteers, pursuant to authorities vested or to be vested in the President of the United States, by law.

[Approved, July 16, 1798. 1 Statutes at Large, 607.]

NOTE. — By an act with the same title, approved May 7, 1800, 2 Statutes at Large, 60, provision is made in identical terms for borrowing, for the same purposes, the further sum of three millions five hundred thousand dollars.

1797–98, Chap. LXXXIV. — *An Act making certain appropriations ; and to authorize the President to obtain a Loan on the credit of the direct tax.*

SEC. 2. *And be it further enacted*, That the President of the United States shall be, and he is hereby authorized to

borrow of the Bank of the United States, who are hereby
enabled to lend the same, or of any other corporation, persons or person, the sum of two millions of dollars, upon the
credit, and in anticipation of the direct tax, laid and ' to
be collected within the United States ; which tax shall be,
and is hereby pledged for the repayment of any loan which
shall be obtained thereon, as aforesaid ; and the faith of the
United States shall be, and is hereby pledged to make good
any deficiency : *Provided*, that the interest to be allowed
for such loan shall not exceed six per centum per annum,
and that the principal shall be reimbursed at the pleasure of
the United States.

[Approved, July 16, 1798. 1 Statutes at Large, 609.]

1798–99, Chap. III. — *An Act respecting Balances reported
against certain States, by the Commissioners appointed
to settle the Accounts between the United States and the
several States.*

SECTION 1. *Be it enacted,* . . . That if any state, against
which a balance was reported by the commissioners appointed
to settle the accounts between the United States and the
several states, shall, on or before the first day of April, one
thousand eight hundred, by a legislative act, engage to pay
into the treasury of the United States within five years after
passing such legislative act, or to expend, within the time
last mentioned, in erecting, enlarging or completing any for-
tifications for the defence of the United States at such place
or places the jurisdiction whereof, having been, previously to
such expenditure, ceded by such state to the United States,
with reservation that process civil and criminal issuing under
authority of such state, may be served and executed therein,
and according to such plan or plans as shall be approved by
the President of the United States, a sum in money, or in
stock of the United States, equal to the balance reported as
aforesaid, against such state, or to the sum assumed by the
United States in the debt of such state, such payment or
expenditure, when so made, shall be accepted by the United

States as a full discharge of all demands on account of said balance; and the President of the United States shall be, and hereby is authorized to cause credit to be given to such state on the books of the treasury of the United States accordingly: *Provided however*, that no more than one third part of the whole payment or expenditure that may be made by any such state shall be made in three per cent. stock, nor more than one third part of the remaining two thirds shall be made in deferred stock: *And provided also*, that any such state may obtain a full discharge, as aforesaid, by the payment or expenditure of a sum of money, sufficient in the opinion of the Secretary of the Treasury, to purchase, at market price, the different species of stock, the payment or expenditure of which would be accepted as a full discharge, as aforesaid.

SEC. 2. *Provided always, and be it further enacted,* That if any such state as is aforesaid shall have expended, since the establishment of the present government of the United States, any sum of money in fortifying any place since ceded by such state to the United States, or which may be so ceded, within one year after the passage of this act, such expenditure having been ascertained and proved to the satisfaction of the Secretary of the Treasury, shall be taken and allowed as part of the expenditure intended by this act.

[Approved, February 15, 1799.   1 Statutes at Large, 616.]

1799–1800, Chap. LVIII. — *An Act supplementary to the act entitled "an Act to establish the Treasury Department."*

Be it enacted . . . That it shall be the duty of the Secretary of the Treasury to digest, prepare and lay before Congress at the commencement of every session, a report on the subject of finance, containing estimates of the public revenue and public expenditures, and plans for improving or increasing the revenues, from time to time, for the purpose of giving information to Congress in adopting modes of raising the money requisite to meet the public expenditures.

[Approved, May 10, 1800.   2 Statutes at Large, 79.]

1801-2, Chap. XXXII. — *An Act making provision for the redemption of the whole of the Public Debt of the United States.*

Be it enacted . . . That so much of the duties on merchandise and tonnage as, together with the monies, other than surpluses of revenue, which now constitute the sinking fund, or shall accrue to it by virtue of any provisions heretofore made, and together with the sums annually required to discharge the annual interest and charges accruing on the present debt of the United States, including temporary loans heretofore obtained, and also future loans which may be made for reimbursing, or redeeming, any instalments, or parts of the principal of the said debt, will amount to an annual sum of seven millions three hundred thousand dollars, be, and the same hereby is yearly appropriated to the said fund ; and the said sums are hereby declared to be vested in the commissioners of the sinking fund, in the same manner as the monies heretofore appropriated to the said fund, to be applied by the said commissioners to the payment of interest and charges, and to the reimbursement or redemption of the principal of the public debt, and shall be and continue appropriated until the whole of the present debt of the United States, and the loans which may be made for reimbursing or redeeming any parts or instalments of the principal of the said debt shall be reimbursed and redeemed : *Provided,* that after the whole of the said debt, the old six per cent. stock, the deferred stock, the seventeen hundred and ninety six six per cent stock and three per cent. stock excepted, shall have been reimbursed or redeemed, any balance of the sums annually appropriated by this act, which may remain unexpended at the end of six months next succeeding the end of the calendar year to which such annual appropriation refers, shall be carried to the surplus fund, and cease to be vested by virtue of this act in the commissioners of the sinking fund, and the appropriation, so far as relates to such unexpended balance, shall cease and determine.

SEC. 2. *And be it further enacted,* That it shall be the duty of the Secretary of the Treasury annually, and in each

4

year, to cause to be paid to the commissioners of the sinking fund the said sum of seven millions three hundred thousand dollars, in such payments, and at such times, in each year as the situation of the treasury will permit : *Provided*, that all such payments as may be necessary to enable the said commissioners to discharge, or reimburse, any demands against the United States, on account of the principal or interest of the debt, which shall be actually due, in conformity to the engagements of the said states, shall be made at such time and times, in each year as will enable the said commissioners faithfully and punctually to comply with such engagement.

Sec. 3. *And be it further enacted*, That all reimbursements of the capital, or principal of the present debt of the United States, including future loans which may be made for reimbursing or redeeming any instalments, or parts of the same, and all payments on account of the interest and charges accruing upon the said debt shall be made under the superintendence of the commissioners of the sinking fund. And it shall be the duty of the said commissioners to cause to be applied and paid out of the said fund, yearly and every year, at the treasury of the United States, the several and respective sums following, to wit: first, such sum and sums as by virtue of any act or acts, they have heretofore been directed to apply and to pay : secondly, such sum and sums as may be annually wanted to discharge the annual interest and charges accruing on any other part of the present debt of the United States, including the interest and charges which may accrue on future loans which may be made for reimbursing or redeeming any instalments, or parts of the principal of the said debt : thirdly, such sum and sums as may annually be required to discharge any instalment or part of the principal of the present debt of the United States, and of any future loans which may be made for reimbursing, or discharging the same, which shall be actually due and demandable, and which shall not by virtue of this, or any other act, be renewed or prolonged, or reimbursed, out of the proceeds of a new loan : and also it shall be the duty

of the said commissioners to cause to be applied the surplus
of such fund as may at any time exist, after satisfying the
purposes aforesaid, towards the further and final redemption, by payment, or purchase, of the present debt of the
United States, including loans for the reimbursement thereof,
temporary loans heretofore obtained from the Bank of the
United States, and those demands against the United States,
under any treaty, or convention, with a foreign power, for
the payment of which the faith of the United States has
been, or may hereafter be pledged by Congress : *Provided,
however,* that the whole, or any part, of such demands, arising under a treaty, or convention, with a foreign power,
and of such temporary loans, may, at any time, be reimbursed, either out of the sinking fund, or, if the situation of
the treasury will permit, out of any other monies which have
been, or may hereafter be, appropriated to that purpose.

[Section 4 empowers the commissioners to borrow, at home or
abroad, the sums requisite for payment of the instalments of the Dutch
debt, falling due in the years from 1803 to 1800, and requires that a
like sum shall be laid out in the payment or redemption of the present
debt of the United States, so as to effect the annual payment of seven
million three hundred thousand dollars agreeably to the provision made
above ; but any loan thus made shall be reimbursable within six years
from its date, and the rate of interest thereon shall not exceed five per
cent., nor shall the charges exceed five per cent of the capital borrowed. The power thus given is not to diminish or affect the power
to borrow given to the commissioners by section 10 of the Act of
March 3, 1795, on page 88, or the power to sell the shares of the Bank
of the United States belonging to the government, given by section 8
of the Act of May 31, 1796, on page 43.

Sections 5 and 6 authorize the commissioners, with the approbation
of the President, to contract with any bank or individual for the payment, in Holland, of any part of the Dutch debt and its interest, or to
employ an agent for procuring remittances for the discharge of said
debt or its interest, allowing therefor a compensation not exceeding one
fourth of one per cent. on the remittances procured. And the commissioners are empowered, in like manner, to employ an agent in
Europe, for the transaction of any business relative to the discharge of
the Dutch debt, or of any loan authorized for the discharge thereof.]

SEC. 7. *And be it further enacted,* That nothing in this
act contained shall be construed to repeal, alter, or affect

any of the provisions of any former act pledging the faith of the United States to the payment of the interest, or principal, of the public debt; and that all such payments shall continue to be made at the time heretofore prescribed by law; and the surplus only of the appropriations made by this act beyond the sums payable by virtue of the provisions of any former act, shall be applicable to the reimbursement, redemption, or purchase of the public debt .in the manner provided by this act.

SEC. 8. *And be it further enacted,* That all the restrictions and regulations heretofore established by law, for regulating the execution of the duties enjoined upon the commissioners of the sinking fund, shall apply to and be in as full force for the execution of the analogous duties enjoined by this act, as if they were herein particularly repeated and re-enacted. *Provided, however,* that the particular annual account of all sales of stock, of loans, and of payments, by them made, shall, hereafter, be laid before Congress on the first week of February, in each year; and so much of any former act as directed such account to be laid before Congress within fourteen days after their meeting, is hereby repealed.

[Approved, April 29, 1802. 2 Statutes at Large, 167.]

1803-4, Chap. II. — *An Act authorizing the creation of a stock, to the amount of eleven millions two hundred and fifty thousand dollars, for the purpose of carrying into effect the convention of the thirtieth of April, one thousand eight hundred and three, between the United States of America and the French Republic; and making provision for the payment of the same.*

Be it enacted, . . . That for the purpose of carrying into effect the convention of the thirtieth day of April, one thousand eight hundred and three, between the United States of America and the French Republic, the Secretary of the Treasury be, and he is hereby authorized, to cause to be constituted, certificates of stock, signed by the register of the treasury, in favor of the French Republic, or of its assignees, for the sum of eleven millions two hundred and fifty thousand dollars, bearing an interest of six per centum per annum, from the time when possession of Louisiana shall have been obtained, in conformity with the treaty of the thirtieth day of April, one thousand eight hundred and three, between the United States of America and the French Republic, and in other respects conformable with the tenor of the convention aforesaid; and the President of the United States is authorized to cause the said certificates of stock to be delivered to the government of France, or to such person or persons as shall be authorized to receive them, in three months at most, after the exchange of the ratifications of the treaty aforesaid, and after Louisiana shall be taken possession of in the name of the government of the United States; and credit, or credits, to the proprietors thereof, shall thereupon be entered and given on the books of the treasury, in like manner as for the present domestic funded debt, which said credits or stock shall thereafter be transferable only on the books of the treasury of the United States, by the proprietor or proprietors of such stock, his, her, or their attorney: and the faith of the United States is hereby pledged for the payment of the interest, and for the reimbursement of the principal of the said stock, in conformity with the provisions of the said convention: *Provided, however*, that the Secretary of the Treasury may, with the approbation of the President of the United States, consent to discharge the said stock in four equal annual instalments, and also shorten the periods fixed by the convention for its reimbursement: *And provided also*, that every proprietor of the said stock may, until otherwise directed by law, on surrendering his certificate of such stock, receive another to the same amount, and bearing an interest of six per centum per annum, payable quarter-yearly at the treasury of the United States.

[By the Act of July 1, 1812, the stock created as above is made transferable like other stocks of the United States, from the books of the treasury to those of any commissioner, and from the books of one commissioner to those of another or to those of the treasury. 2 Statutes at Large, 771.]

SEC. 2. *And be it further enacted*, That the annual interest accruing on the said stock, which may, in conformity with the convention aforesaid, be payable in Europe, shall be paid at the rate of four shillings and sixpence sterling for each dollar, if payable in London, and at the rate of two guilders and one half of a guilder, current money of Holland, for each dollar, if payable in Amsterdam.

SEC. 3. *And be it further enacted*, That a sum equal to what will be necessary to pay the interest which may accrue on the said stock to the end of the present year, be, and the same is hereby appropriated for that purpose, to be paid out of any monies in the treasury not otherwise appropriated.

SEC. 4. *And be it further enacted*, That from and after the end of the present year (in addition to the annual sum of seven millions three hundred thousand dollars yearly appropriated to the sinking fund, by virtue of the act intituled "An act making provision for the redemption of the whole of the public debt of the United States"), a further annual sum of seven hundred thousand dollars, to be paid out of the duties on merchandise and tonnage, be, and the same hereby is, yearly appropriated to the said fund, making in the whole, an annual sum of eight millions of dollars, which shall be vested in the commissioners of the sinking fund in the same manner, shall be applied by them for the same purposes, and shall be, and continue appropriated, until the whole of the present debt of the United States, inclusively of the stock created by virtue of this act, shall be reimbursed and redeemed, under the same limitations as have been provided by the first section of the above-mentioned act, respecting the annual appropriation of seven millions three hundred thousand dollars, made by the same.

SEC. 5. *And be it further enacted*, That the Secretary of the Treasury shall cause the said further sum of seven hundred thousand dollars to be paid to the commissioners of the sinking fund, in the same manner as was directed by the above-mentioned act respecting the annual appropriation of seven millions three hundred thousand dollars ; and it shall be the duty of the commissioners of the sinking fund to cause

to be applied and paid out of the said fund, yearly, and
every year, at the treasury of the United States, such sum
and sums as may be annually wanted to discharge the annual
interest and charges accruing on the stock created by virtue
of this act, and the several instalments, or parts of principal of the said stock, as the same shall become due and may
be discharged, in conformity to the terms of the convention
aforesaid, and of this act.

[Approved, November 10, 1803. 2 Statutes at Large, 245.]

1805-6, Chap. L. — *An Act to repeal so much of any act or
acts as authorize the receipt of evidences of the public
debt, in payment for lands of the United States; and
for other purposes, relative to the public debt.*

Be it enacted, . . . That so much of any act or acts as
authorize the receipt of evidences of the public debt, in payment for the lands of the United States, shall from and after
the thirtieth day of April, one thousand eight hundred and
six, be repealed: *Provided,* that the right of all persons
who may have purchased public lands previous to the passage of this act, to pay for the same in stock, shall in no
wise be affected or impaired : *And provided further*, that
there shall be allowed on every payment made in money, at
or before the same shall fall due, for lands purchased before
the thirtieth day of April, one thousand eight hundred and
six, in addition to the discounts now allowed by law, a deduction equal to the difference at the time of such payment,
between the market price of six per cent. stock and the
nominal value of its unredeemed amount, which market price
shall, from time to time, be stated by the Secretary of the
Treasury to the officers of the several land-offices.

SEC. 2. *And be it further enacted,* That the commissioners of the sinking fund shall not be authorized to purchase
any of the several species of the public debt, at a higher
price than at the rates following, that is to say ; they shall
not pay more for three per cent. stock than sixty per cent.
of its nominal value ; nor for any other species of the public
debt more than the nominal value of its unredeemed amount,

the eight per cent. stock only excepted; for which they
shall be authorized, in addition thereto, to give at the rate
of one half of one per cent. on the said nominal value, for
each quarterly dividend which may be payable on such purchased stock, from the time of such purchase to the first day
of January, one thousand eight hundred and nine.

SEC. 3. *And be it further enacted*, That so much of any
act as directs that purchases of the public debt, by the commissioners of the sinking fund, shall be made within the
thirty days next ensuing after each day on which a quarterly
payment of interest on the debt of the United States shall
become due : and also so much of any act as directs that the
said purchases shall be made by open purchase or by sealed
proposals, be, and the same hereby is repealed. And the
said commissioners are hereby authorized to make such purchases, under the restrictions laid by the preceding section,
in such manner, and at such times and places as they shall
deem most eligible ; and for that purpose to appoint a known
agent or agents, to whom they may allow a commission, not
exceeding one fourth of one per cent. on the respective purchases of such agents.

[Approved, April 18, 1806.   2 Statutes at Large, 405.]

1806-7, Chap. XII. — *An Act supplementary to the act, intituled " An act making provision for the redemption
of the whole of the public debt of the United States."*

WHEREAS it is desirable to adapt the nature of the provision for
the redemption of the public debt to the present circumstances
of the United States, which can only be done by a voluntary
subscription on the part of the creditors :

Be it enacted, . . . That a subscription to the full amount
of the old six per cent. deferred and three per cent. stocks
be, and the same is hereby proposed ; for which purpose
books shall be opened at the treasury of the United States,
and by the several commissioners of loans, on the first day
of July next, to continue open until the seventeenth day of
March next following, inclusively, the fourteen last days of

each quarter excepted, for such parts of the above mentioned descriptions of stock, as shall, on the day of subscription, stand on the books of the treasury, and of the several commissioners of loans, respectively; which subscription shall be effected by a transfer to the United States, in the manner provided by law for such transfers, of the credit or credits standing on the said books, and by a surrender of the certificates of the stock subscribed.

Sec. 2. *And be it further enacted,* That for the whole or any part of any sum which shall thus be subscribed, in old six per cent. or deferred stock, credits shall be entered to the respective subscribers, and the subscriber or subscribers shall be entitled to a certificate, or certificates, purporting that the United States owe to the holder or holders thereof, his, her, or their assigns, a sum to be expressed therein, equal to the amount of principal of the stock thus subscribed, which shall remain unredeemed on the day of such subscription, bearing an interest of six per centum per annum, payable quarter yearly, from the first day of the quarter, during which such subscription shall have been made, transferable in the same manner as is provided by law for the transfers of the stock subscribed, and subject to redemption at the pleasure of the United States : *Provided,* that no single certificate shall be issued for an amount greater than ten thousand dollars : *And provided further,* that no reimbursement shall be made except for the whole amount of any such new certificate, nor till after at least six months' previous public notice of such intended reimbursement.

Sec. 3. *And be it further enacted,* That for the whole or any part of any sum which shall thus be subscribed in three per cent. stock, credits shall likewise be entered to the respective subscribers ; and the subscriber, or subscribers, shall be entitled to a certificate, purporting that the United States owe to the holder or holders thereof, his, her, or their assigns, a sum to be expressed therein, equal to sixty-five per centum of the amount of the principal of the stock thus subscribed, bearing an interest of six per centum, per annum, payable quarter yearly, from the first day of the quarter, during which such subscription shall have been made, and transferable and subject to redemption in the same manner, and under the same regulations and restrictions, as the stock created by the preceding section of this act: *Provided*, that no part of the stock thus created, shall be reimbursable without the assent of the holder, or holders of such stock, until after the whole of the eight per cent. and four and a half per cent. stocks, as well as all the six per cent. stock which may be created by virtue of the preceding section, shall have been redeemed.

[Section 4 authorizes the commissioners of the sinking fund to appoint an agent in London and another in Amsterdam, to receive subscriptions and transfers and to issue new certificates in favor of stockholders residing in Europe.

Section 5 provides that stockholders subscribing either in the United States or in Europe, but resident in Europe, may at their option receive the interest on the new stock either in the United States or in London or Amsterdam; if in London, at the rate of four shillings and sixpence sterling for the dollar, and if in Amsterdam at the rate of two and a half guilders for the dollar, credits therefor being entered and transferable only on the books of the treasury: *provided*, that the interest thus payable abroad shall not be payable until six months after the day for payment in the United States, and shall be subject to a deduction of one half of one per cent. on its amount for commission; *and provided also*, that the certificates of stock thus held may be exchanged for others bearing interest payable in the United States.]

SEC. 6. *And be it further enacted*, That the same funds which heretofore have been, and now are, pledged, by law, for the payment of the interest, and for the redemption or reimbursement of the stock which may be subscribed by virtue of the provisions of this act, shall remain pledged for the payment of interest accruing on the stock created by reason of such subscription, and for the redemption or reimbursement of the principal of the same. It shall be the duty of the commissioners of the sinking fund to cause to be applied, and paid out of the said fund, yearly, and every year, such sum, and sums, as may be annually wanted to discharge the annual interest and charges accruing on the stock which may be created by virtue of this act. The said commissioners are hereby authorized to apply, from time to time, such sum and sums, out of the said fund, as they may think proper, towards redeeming, by purchase, or by reimbursement, in conformity with the provisions of this act, the principal of the said stock. And the annual sum of eight millions of dollars, vested by law in the said commissioners, shall be, and continue appropriated to the payment of interest and redemption of the public debt, until the whole of the stock which may be created by the preceding sections of this act, shall have been redeemed, or reimbursed.

SEC. 8. *And be it further enacted,* That whensoever notice of reimbursement shall be given, as prescribed by the second and third sections of this act, the certificates intended to be reimbursed, shall be designated therein. In every reimbursement the preference shall be given to such holders of certificates as, previous to the said notice, shall have notified in writing to the treasury department their wish to be reimbursed. If there should not be applications to the treasury sufficient to require the payment of the whole sum to be applied to that purpose, the Secretary of the Treasury, after paying off all sums for the payment of which application shall have been made, shall determine, by lot, what other certificates shall be reimbursed so as to make up the whole amount to be discharged: and in case the applications shall exceed the amount to be discharged, the Secretary of the Treasury shall proceed to determine, by lot, what applications shall be entitled to priority of payment.

SEC. 10. *And be it further enacted,* That nothing in this act contained shall be construed, in any wise, to alter, abridge, or impair the rights of those creditors of the United States, who shall not subscribe to the loan created by virtue of this act.

[Approved, February 11, 1807. 2 Statutes at Large, 415.]

1808-9, Chap. XXVIII. — *An Act further to amend the several acts for the establishment and regulation of the Treasury, War, and Navy departments.*

[Section 4 provides that disbursing agents for the army and navy " shall, whenever practicable, keep the public monies in their hands, in

some incorporated bank, to be designated for the purpose by the President of the United States," and shall make monthly returns thereof.]

[Approved, March 3, 1809. 2 Statutes at Large, 535.]

1809, Chap. X. — *An Act supplementary to the act, intituled
"An Act making further provision for the support
of public credit, and for the redemption of the public
debt."*

Be it enacted, . . . That the powers vested in the commissioners of the sinking fund, by the tenth section of the
act to which this act is a supplement, shall extend to all
the cases of reimbursement of any instalments or parts of
the capital, or principal, of the public debt now existing,
which may become payable according to law. And in every
case in which a loan may be made accordingly, it shall be
lawful for such loan to be made of the Bank of the United
States, anything in any act of Congress to the contrary
notwithstanding.

[Approved, June 28, 1809. 2 Statutes at Large, 551.]

1809-10, Chap. XLV. — *An Act authorizing a loan of
money, for a sum not exceeding the amount of the
principal of the public debt, reimbursable during the
year one thousand eight hundred and ten.*

Be it enacted, . . . That the President of the United
States be, and he is hereby empowered to borrow, on the
credit of the United States, a sum not exceeding the amount
of the principal of the public debt, which will be reimbursed,
according to law, during the present year, by the commissioners of the sinking fund, at a rate of interest, payable
quarter yearly, not exceeding six per centum per annum, and
reimbursable at the pleasure of the United States, or at such
period as may be stipulated by contract, not exceeding six
years from the first day of January next; to be applied, in
addition to the monies now in the treasury, or which may be
received therein from other sources during the present year,
to defray any of the public expenses which are, or may be
authorized by law. The stock thereby created, shall be

transferable in the same manner as is provided by law for
the transfer of the funded debt. It shall be lawful for the
Bank of the United States to lend the said sum, or any part
thereof; and it is further hereby declared, that it shall be
deemed a good execution of the said power to borrow, for
the Secretary of the Treasury, with the approbation of the
President of the United States, to cause to be constituted .
certificates of stock, signed by the register of the treasury,
or by a commissioner of loans, for the sum to be borrowed,
or for any part thereof, bearing an interest of six per cent.
per annum, transferable and reimbursable as aforesaid; and
to cause the said certificates of stock to be sold: *Provided*,
that no such stock be sold under par.

[By section 2 the Secretary of the Treasury is authorized, with the
approbation of the President, to give the preference, among subscribers
to the loan here provided for, to the holders of exchanged six per cent
stock issued under the act of February 11, 1807, to an amount not exceeding for any stockholder the amount of such exchanged stock held
by him: *provided*, that the sum thus borrowed from holders of the
exchanged stock shall be reimbursable at the pleasure of the United
States.]

SEC. 3. *And be it further enacted*, That so much of the
funds constituting the annual appropriation of eight millions
of dollars for the payment of the principal and interest of
the public debt of the United States, as may be wanted for
that purpose, is hereby pledged and appropriated for the
payment of the interest and for the reimbursement of the
principal of the stock, which may be created by virtue of
this act. It shall accordingly be the duty of the commissioners of the sinking fund, to cause to be applied and paid
out of the said fund yearly, and every year, such sum and
sums as may be annually wanted to discharge the interest
accruing on the said stock, and to reimburse the principal,
as the same shall become due, and may be discharged in
conformity with the terms of the loan; and they are further
authorized to apply, from time to time, such sum or sums
out of the said fund as they may think proper, towards redeeming by purchase, and at a price not above par, the prin-

cipal of the said stock or any part thereof. And the faith of the United States is hereby pledged to establish sufficient revenues for making up any deficiency that may hereafter take place in the funds hereby appropriated for paying the said interest and principal sums, or any of them, in manner aforesaid.

[Approved, May 1, 1810. 2 Statutes at Large, 610.]

1810–11, Chap. XXXII. — *An Act authorizing a loan of money, for a sum not exceeding five millions of dollars.*

[Section 1 empowers the President to borrow on the credit of the United States a sum not exceeding five millions of dollars at a rate of interest, payable quarter-yearly, not exceeding six per cent., and to be reimbursed at pleasure or at periods not exceeding six years from January 1, 1812. This loan is to be applied to defray any authorized public expense, the stock to be transferable like the funded debt, and not to be sold under par.

Section 2 is identical with section 3 of the Act of May 1, 1810, above.]

[Approved, March 2, 1811. 2 Statutes at Large, 656.]

1811–12, Chap. XLI. — *An Act authorizing a loan for a sum not exceeding eleven millions of dollars.*

[By sections 1 and 2 the President is authorized to borrow on the credit of the United States, in order to defray expenses authorized by law during the present session of Congress, a sum not exceeding eleven millions of dollars, at an interest not exceeding six per cent. per annum, payable quarter-yearly. No contract is to be made precluding reimbursement at any time after the expiration of twelve years from January 1, 1813, and none of the stock is to be sold under par.]

SEC. 3. *And be it further enacted,* That so much of the funds constituting the annual appropriation of eight millions of dollars, for the payment of the principal and interest of the public debt of the United States, as may be wanted for that purpose, after satisfying the sums necessary for the payment of the interest and such part of the principal of the said debt as the United States are now pledged annually to pay or reimburse, is hereby pledged and appropriated for the payment of the interest, and for the reimbursement of the principal of the stock which may be created by virtue of this act; it shall accordingly be the duty of the commissioners of the sinking fund, to cause to be applied and paid out of the said fund yearly, such sum and sums as may be annually wanted to discharge the interest accruing on the said stock, and to reimburse the principal as the same shall become due, and may be discharged in conformity with the terms of the loan; and they are further authorized to apply, from time to time, such sum or sums out of the said fund as they may think proper, towards redeeming by purchase, and at a price not above par, the principal of the said stock, or any part thereof. And the faith of the United States is hereby pledged to establish sufficient revenues for making up any deficiency that may hereafter take place in the funds hereby appropriated for paying the said interest and principal sums, or any of them, in manner aforesaid.

[Approved, March 14, 1812.   2 Statutes at Large, 694.]

NOTE. — By the Act of July 6, 1812, authority is given for the employment of agents for the purpose of selling any part of the stock authorized above, and a commission not exceeding one eighth of one per cent is allowed. 2 Statutes at Large, 784.

1811-12, Chap. XLIII. — *An Act repealing the tenth section of the act to incorporate the subscribers to the Bank of the United States.*

Be it enacted, . . . That the tenth section of the act entituled "An act to incorporate the subscribers to the Bank of the United States," shall be, and the same is hereby repealed.

[Approved, March 19, 1812.   2 Statutes at Large, 695.]

1811-12, Chap. CXI. — *An Act to authorize the issuing of Treasury Notes.*

Be it enacted, . . . That the President of the United States be, and he is hereby authorized to cause treasury notes for such sum or sums as he may think expedient, but not exceeding in the whole the sum of five millions of dol-

lars, to be prepared, signed and issued in the manner herein
after provided.

SEC. 2. *And be it further enacted,* That the said treasury
notes shall be reimbursed by the United States, at such
places, respectively, as may be expressed on the face of the
said notes, one year, respectively, after the day on which
the same shall have been issued: from which day of issue
they shall bear interest, at the rate of five and two fifths per
centum a year, payable to the owner and owners of such notes,
at the treasury, or by the proper commissioner of loans, at
the places and times respectively designated on the face of
said notes for the payment of principal.

[Section 3 provides for the signing and countersigning of the notes,
and for the compensation of the persons employed for this purpose.]

SEC. 4. *And be it further enacted,* That the Secretary of
the Treasury be, and he is hereby authorized, with the approbation of the President of the United States, to cause to
be issued such portion of the said treasury notes as the President may think expedient in payment of supplies, or debts
due by the United States, to such public creditors, or other
persons, as may choose to receive such notes in payment,
as aforesaid, at par: and the Secretary of the Treasury is
further authorized, with the approbation of the President of
the United States, to borrow, from time to time, not under
par, such sums as the President may think expedient, on the
credit of such notes. And it shall be a good execution of
this provision to pay such notes to such bank or banks as
will receive the same at par and give credit to the treasurer
of the United States for the amount thereof, on the day on
which the said notes shall thus be issued and paid to such
bank or banks respectively.

SEC. 5. *And be it further enacted,* That the said treasury
notes shall be transferable by delivery and assignment endorsed thereon by the person to whose order the same shall,
on the face thereof, have been made payable.

SEC. 6. *And be it further enacted,* That the said treasury
notes, wherever made payable, shall be everywhere received

in payment of all duties and taxes laid by the authority of
the United States, and of all public lands sold by the said
authority. On every such payment, credit shall be given for
the amount of both the principal and the interest which, on
the day of such payment, may appear due on the note or
notes thus given in payment. And the said interest shall, on
such payments, be computed at the rate of one cent and one
half of a cent per day on every hundred dollars of principal, and each month shall be computed as containing thirty
days.

[Section 7 provides that any public officer who may receive such
treasury notes shall, on payment of the same into the treasury or into
any bank where public monies are deposited, be credited with the principal of the notes so paid in, and the interest which may then have
accrued, and shall be charged with the interest accruing on the notes
while in his hands. But no such charge for accruing interest shall be
made against any bank receiving payment for the United States from
individuals or public officers, which shall receive such notes as specie
and shall credit the treasurer of the United States with the amount
thereof, including the interest due on the day of receipt.]

SEC. 8. *And be it further enacted,* That the commissioners of the sinking fund be, and they are hereby authorized
and directed to cause to be reimbursed and paid the principal and interest of the treasury notes which may be issued
by virtue of this act, at the several time and times when
the same, according to the provisions of this act, should be
thus reimbursed and paid. And the said commissioners are
further authorized to make purchases of the said notes, in
the same manner as of other evidences of the public debt,
and at a price not exceeding par, for the amount of the
principal and interest due at the time of purchase on such
notes. So much of the funds constituting the annual appropriation of eight millions of dollars, for the principal and
interest of the public debt of the United States, as may be
wanted for that purpose, after satisfying the sums necessary
for the payment of the interest and such part of the principal of the said debt as the United States are now pledged
annually to pay and reimburse, is hereby pledged and appropriated for the payment of the interest, and for the reim-

bursement or purchase of the principal of the said notes. And so much of any monies in the treasury not otherwise appropriated as may be necessary for that purpose, is hereby appropriated for making up any deficiency in the funds thus pledged and appropriated for paying the principal and interest as aforesaid.

[Sections 9 and 10 provide for the expense of preparing the notes for issue, and fix the penalties for counterfeiting and for uttering counterfeited notes.]

[Approved, June 30, 1812. 2 Statutes at Large, 766.]

1811–12, Chap. CXXXV. — *An Act authorizing a subscription for the old six per cent. and deferred stocks, and providing for an exchange of the same.*

[By section 1 a subscription to the full amount of the old six per cent. and deferred stocks is proposed, to remain open from October 1, 1812 to March 17, 1813, inclusively, the last fourteen days of each quarter excepted, in terms identical with those of section 1 of the Act of February 11, 1807 on page 56.]

SEC. 2. *And be it further enacted*, That for such part of the amount of old six per cent. or deferred stock, thus subscribed, as shall remain unredeemed on the day of such subscription, credits shall be entered to the respective subscribers, on the books of the treasury or of the commissioners of loans where such subscription shall have been made, and the subscriber or subscribers shall be entitled to receive a certificate or certificates purporting that the United States owe to the holder or holders thereof, his, her, or their assigns, a sum to be expressed therein, equal to the unredeemed amount of the principal of the old six per cent. or deferred stocks, subscribed as aforesaid, bearing an interest of six per centum per annum, payable quarter yearly, from the first day of the quarter during which such subscription shall have been made, transferable in the same manner as is provided by law for the transfers of the stock subscribed, and subject to redemption at the pleasure of the United States at any time after the thirty-first day of December, one thousand eight hundred and twenty-four: *Provided,*

That no reimbursement shall be made except for the whole amount of the stock standing at the time, to the credit of any proprietor, on the books of the treasury or of the commissioners of loans respectively, nor till after at least six months' previous public notice of such intended reimbursement.

[Section 3 is identical with section 6 of the Act of February 11, 1807, except that, in the concluding sentence, only "such part of the annual sum of eight millions as may be necessary and wanting for the above purposes," to wit, the payment of interest and reimbursement of principal of the stock now to be created, is to continue appropriated until the redemption of the stock.]

SEC. 4. *And be it further enacted*, That nothing in this act contained shall be construed in anywise to alter, abridge or impair the rights of those creditors of the United States who shall not subscribe to the loan to be opened by virtue of this act.

[Approved, July 6, 1812.   2 Statutes at Large, 783.]

1812-13, Chap. XXI. — *An Act authorizing a Loan for a sum not exceeding sixteen millions of dollars.*

[Section 1 empowers the President to borrow, on the credit of the United States, a sum not exceeding sixteen millions of dollars, to be applied to defray expenses authorized during the present session of Congress; but no engagement is to be entered into which shall preclude the reimbursement of the loan at any time after twelve years from January 1, 1814.]

SEC. 2. *And be it further enacted*, That the President of the United States do cause to be laid before Congress, on the first Monday in February, eighteen hundred and fourteen, or as soon thereafter as Congress may be in session, an account of all the monies obtained by the sale of the certificates of stock, by virtue of the power given him by the preceding section, together with a statement of the rate at which the same may have been sold.

[Section 3 authorizes the employment of agents, to procure subscriptions to the stock or to sell the same, and allows a commission not exceeding one quarter of one per cent on the amount disposed of by them.

Section 4, pledging for the support of this loan the requisite amount of the sinking fund, and prescribing the duties of the commissioners of the sinking fund, is identical with section 3 of the Act of March 14, 1812, on page 62.]

[Approved, February 8, 1813. 2 Statutes at Large, 798.]

1812–13, Chap. XXVII.— *An Act authorizing the issuing of Treasury notes for the service of the year one.thousand eight hundred and thirteen.*

Be it enacted, . . . That the President of the United States be, and he is hereby authorized to cause treasury notes for such sum or sums as he may think expedient, but not exceeding in the whole the sum of five millions of dollars, to be prepared, signed, and issued, in the manner hereinafter provided.

SEC. 2. *And be it further enacted*, That the President of the United States be, and he is hereby authorized, in addition to the amount authorized by the next preceding section of this act, to cause treasury notes, for such sum or sums as he may think expedient, but not exceeding in the whole the further sum of five millions of dollars, to be prepared, signed, and issued in the manner hereinafter provided : *Provided*, that the amount of money borrowed or obtained, by virtue of the notes which may be issued by virtue of this section, shall be deemed and held to be in part of the sum of sixteen millions of dollars, authorized to be borrowed by virtue of the act to that effect, passed during the present session of Congress.

SEC. 3. *And be it further enacted*, That the said treasury notes shall be reimbursed by the United States, at such places respectively as may be expressed on the face of the said notes, one year respectively after the day on which the same shall have been issued ; from which day of issue they shall bear interest, at the rate of five and two-fifths per centum a year, payable to the owner and owners of such notes, at the treasury, or by the proper commissioner of loans, or by the officer designated for that purpose, at the places and times respectively designated on the face of said notes, for the payment of principal.

[Sections 4 and 5, providing for the signing of the notes and authorizing their issue in any of several methods, are nearly identical with sections 3 and 4 of the Treasury Note Act of June 30, 1812, on page 64; but to section 5 of the present act is added a provision that the Secretary may "sell, not under par, such portion of the said notes as the President may think expedient."

Section 6 authorizes the employment of agents for the purpose of selling any of the notes now to be issued, and allows a commission not exceeding one quarter of one per cent. on the amount thus sold.

Sections 7, 8, and 9, relating to the transfer of the notes, their receipt for public dues, and the manner of crediting public officers and banks with the interest accruing on them, are identical with the sections 5, 6 and 7 of the Act of June 30, 1812.]

SEC. 10. *And be it further enacted*, That the commissioners of the sinking fund be, and they are hereby authorized and directed to cause to be reimbursed and paid the principal and interest of the treasury notes which may be issued by virtue of this act, at the several time and times when the same, according to the provisions of this act, should be thus reimbursed and paid ; and the said commissioners are further authorized to make purchases of the said notes, in the same manner as of other evidences of the public debt, and at a price not exceeding par, for the amount of the principal and interest due at the time of purchase of such notes. So much of the funds constituting the annual appropriation of eight millions of dollars, for the payment of the principal and interest of the public debt of the United States, as may be wanted for that purpose, after satisfying the sums necessary for the payment of the interest and such part of the principal of the said debt, as the United States are now pledged annually to pay and reimburse, including therein the interest and principal which may become payable upon any loan or loans which may be contracted by virtue of any law passed during the present session of Congress, is hereby pledged and appropriated for the payment of the interest, and for the reimbursement or purchase of the principal of the said notes ; and so much of any monies in the treasury not otherwise appropriated, as may be necessary for that purpose, is hereby appropriated for making up any deficiency in the funds thus pledged and appropriated, for paying the principal and interest as aforesaid ; and the Secretary of the Treasury is hereby authorized and directed for that purpose to cause to be paid to the commissioners of the sinking fund such sum or sums of money, and at such time and times as will enable the said commissioners faithfully and punctually to pay the principal and interest of the said notes.

[Sections 11 and 12, providing for the expense of preparing the notes for issue, and fixing the penalties for counterfeiting, and for uttering counterfeited notes, follow closely the corresponding sections of the Act of June 30, 1812.]

[Approved, February 25, 1813. 2 Statutes at Large, 801.]

1813, Chap. LI. — *An Act authorizing a loan for a sum not exceeding seven millions five hundred thousand dollars.*

[Section 1 empowers the President to borrow on the credit of the United States a sum not exceeding seven million five hundred thousand dollars, to be applied to defray expenses for the years 1813 and 1814, but provides that no contract shall be entered into precluding the reimbursement of the sum thus borrowed, at any time after twelve years from January 1, 1814.

Section 2 authorizes the sale of certificates of the stock thus to be created: "*Provided*, that no such certificate shall be sold at a rate less than eighty-eight per centum, or eighty-eight dollars in money for one hundred dollars in stock ; " and requires that an account of moneys obtained by such sales and a statement of the rate obtained shall be laid before Congress on the first Monday in February, 1814, or as soon thereafter as Congress shall be in session.

Section 3, authorizing the employment of agents in disposing of the stock, follows the terms of section 3 of the Act of February 8, 1813, on page 67.

Section 4, pledging for the support of this loan the requisite amount of the sinking fund and prescribing the duties of the commissioners of the sinking fund, is identical with section 3 of the Act of March 14, 1812, on page 62.]

[Approved, August 2, 1813. 3 Statutes at Large, 75.]

1813–14, Chap. XVIII. — *An Act to authorize the issuing of treasury notes for the service of the year one thousand eight hundred and fourteen.*

Be it enacted, . . . That the President of the United States be, and he is hereby authorized to cause treasury notes, for a sum not exceeding five millions of dollars, to be prepared, signed, and issued, in the manner hereinafter provided.

SEC. 2. *And be it further enacted*, That the President of the United States be, and he is hereby authorized to cause treasury notes for a further and additional sum not exceeding in the whole five millions of dollars, or such part thereof as he shall deem expedient, to be prepared, signed, and issued, in the manner hereinafter provided : but the amount of money borrowed or obtained for the notes which may be issued by virtue of this section, shall be deemed and held to be in part of the sum which may be authorized to be borrowed by virtue of any act authorizing a loan which may be passed during the present session of Congress.

SEC. 3. *And be it further enacted*, That the said treasury notes shall be reimbursed by the United States at such places respectively, as may be expressed on the face of such notes, one year respectively after the day on which the same shall have been issued; from which day of issue they shall bear interest at the rate of five and two-fifths per centum a year, payable to the owner or owners of such notes, at the treasury, or by the proper commissioner of loans, or by the officer designated for that purpose, at the places and times respectively designated on the face of said notes for the payment of principal.

[Sections 4, 5 and 6, providing for the signing of the notes and for their issue or sale, and for the employment and compensation of agents in their sale, follow the language of the corresponding sections 4, 5 and 6 of the Act of February 25, 1813, on page 69.

Sections 7, 8 and 9, relating to the transfer of the notes, their receipt for public dues, and the manner of crediting public officers and banks with interest accruing on them, are identical with the sections 5, 6 and 7 of the Act of June 30, 1812, on page 64.

Section 10, containing the sinking fund provisions, is identical with section 10 of the Treasury Note Act of February 25, 1813.

Sections 11 and 12, providing for the expense of preparing the notes for issue and fixing the penalties for counterfeiting and for uttering counterfeited notes, follow the language of the corresponding sections of the Act of June 30, 1812.]

[Approved, March 4, 1814. 3 Statutes at Large, 100.]

1813-14, Chap. XXIX. — *An Act to authorize a loan for a sum not exceeding twenty-five millions of dollars.*

[Section 1 empowers the President to borrow, on the credit of the United States, a sum not exceeding twenty-five millions of dollars, to be applied to defray any expenses authorized by law, during the present year : *provided*, that no contract shall be made to preclude the reimbursement of the sum thus borrowed, at any time after twelve years from December 31, 1814.

Section 2 authorizes the sale of the stock thus to be created, but fixes no limit as to the rate, and requires the Secretary of the Treasury to lay before Congress during the first week of February, 1815, an account of the moneys procured by sale of the stock and a statement of the rate obtained.

Section 3, authorizing the employment of agents in disposing of the stock, follows the terms of section 3 of the Act of February 8, 1813, on page 67.

Section 4, containing the sinking fund provisions, is identical with section 3 of the Act of March 14, 1812, on page 62.]

[Approved, March 24, 1814.   3 Statutes at Large, 111.]

1814-15, Chap. IV. — *An Act to authorize a loan for a sum not exceeding three millions of dollars.*

[Section 1 authorizes the President to borrow, on the credit of the United States, a sum not exceeding three millions of dollars, to be applied to defray any expenses authorized by law during the present year : *provided*, that no contract shall be entered into precluding the reimbursement of the sum thus borrowed, at any time after twelve years from December 31, 1814.

Section 2 authorizes the Secretary of the Treasury to sell the stock thus to be created, but fixes no limit as to the rate of sale, requiring him to lay before Congress an account of the moneys thus procured and the rate obtained.

Section 3 authorizing the employment of agents in. disposing of the stock follows the terms of section 3 of the Act of February 8, 1813.]

SEC. 4. *And be it further enacted*, That it shall be lawful to receive in payment of any loan obtained under this act, or under any other act of Congress authorizing a loan, treasury notes which have been issued according to law, and which shall become due and payable on or before the first day of January next, at the par value of such treasury notes, together with the interest thereon accrued, at the time of the payment on account of the loan.

SEC. 5. *And be it further enacted*, That so much of the funds constituting the annual appropriation of eight millions of dollars, for the payment of the principal and interest of the public debt of the United States as may be wanted for that purpose, after satisfying the sums necessary for the payment of the interest and such part of the principal of said debt, as the United States are now pledged annually to pay or reimburse, is hereby pledged and appropriated for the payment of the interest, and for the reimbursement of the principal of the stock which may be created by virtue of this act. It shall accordingly be the duty of the commissioners of the sinking fund, to cause to be applied and paid out of the said fund, yearly, such sum and sums as may be annually wanted to discharge the interest accruing on the said stock, and to reimburse the principal, as the same shall become due, and may be discharged in conformity with the terms of the loan; and they are further authorized to apply, from time to time, such sum or sums out of the said fund, as they may think proper, towards redeeming, by purchase, and at a price not above par, the principal of the said stock, or any part thereof.

SEC. 6. *And be it further enacted*, That in addition to the annual sum of eight millions of dollars, heretofore appropriated to the sinking fund, adequate and permanent funds shall during the present session of Congress, be provided and appropriated, for the payment of the interest and reimbursement of the principal of said stock created by this act.

SEC. 7. *And be it further enacted*, That an adequate and permanent sinking fund, gradually to reduce and eventually to extinguish the public debt, contracted and to be contracted during the present war, shall also be established during the present session of Congress.

[Approved, November 15, 1814. 3 Statutes at Large, 144.]

1814-15, Chap. XII. — *An Act to provide additional revenues for defraying the expenses of government, and
maintaining the public credit, by duties on carriages,
and the harness used therefor.*

SEC. 10. *And be it further enacted,* That towards establishing an adequate revenue to provide for the payment of
the expenses of government, for the punctual payment of the
public debt, principal and interest, contracted and to be contracted, according to the terms of the contracts respectively,
and for creating an adequate sinking fund, gradually to reduce and eventually to extinguish the public debt, contracted
and to be contracted, the internal duties laid and imposed
by this act, (and those laid and imposed by the "Act laying
duties on carriages for the conveyance of persons," passed
twenty-fourth July, one thousand eight hundred and thirteen,
so far as the same are not hereby abolished,) shall be laid,
levied, and collected, during the present war between the
United States and Great Britain, and until the purposes
aforesaid shall be completely accomplished, anything in any
act of Congress to the contrary thereof in any wise notwithstanding.   And for effectual application of the revenue to
be raised by and from the said internal duties to the purposes aforesaid, in due form of law, the faith of the United
States is hereby pledged ; *Provided always,* That whenever
Congress shall deem it expedient to alter, reduce, or change
the said internal duties, or any or either of them, it shall
be lawful so to do, upon providing and substituting by law,
at the same time, and for the same purposes, other duties
which shall be equally productive with the duties so altered,
reduced, or changed : And, *Provided further,* that nothing
in this act contained shall be deemed or construed in any
wise to rescind or impair any specific appropriation of the
said duties, or any or either of them, heretofore made by
law, but such appropriation shall remain and be carried into
effect according to the true intent and meaning of the laws
making the same, anything in this act to the contrary thereof
in any wise notwithstanding.

[Approved, December 15, 1814.   3 Statutes at Large, 148.]

NOTE. — This provision, without substantial change, is embodied in section 23 of the Act of December 21, 1814, laying duties on distilled spirits and on licenses to distillers ; in section 5 of the Act of December 23, 1814, laying duties on sales by auction and on licenses to retailers of wines and liquors and increasing rates of postage; in section 41 of the Act of January 9, 1815, levying an annual direct tax; and in all these cases was made applicable to previous acts on the same subject matter. It is also embodied in section 23 of the Act of January 18, 1815, laying excise duties on manufactures ; and in section 25 of the Act of the same day laying duties on household furniture and watches. See 3 Statutes at Large, 158, 161, 179, 186, 191.

1814–15, Chap. XV. — *An Act to provide additional revenues for defraying the expenses of government and maintaining the public credit, by laying duties on spirits distilled within the United States, and territories thereof, and by amending the acts laying duties on licenses to distillers of spirituous liquors.*

[Section 25 authorizes the anticipation of the duties laid by this act, by a loan upon the pledge of the said duties for its reimbursement, for an amount not exceeding six millions of dollars and at a rate not above six per cent., the money so obtained to be applied only to the purposes to which the duties pledged are applicable by law. The same provision is embodied in the act of January 9, 1815, laying a direct tax. See 3 Statutes at Large, 179.]

[Approved, December 21, 1814. 3 Statutes at Large, 158.]

1814–15, Chap. XVII. — *An Act supplementary to the acts authorizing a loan for the several sums of twenty-five millions of dollars and three millions of dollars.*

Be it enacted, . . . That the Secretary of the Treasury be and he is hereby authorized, with the approbation of the President of the United States, to cause treasury notes to be prepared, signed and issued, for and in lieu of so much of the sum authorized to be borrowed on the credit of the United States, by the act of Congress, entitled " An Act to authorize a loan for a sum not exceeding twenty-five millions of dollars," passed on the twenty-fourth day of March, in the year one thousand eight hundred and fourteen, and also for, and in lieu of so much of the sum authorized to be borrowed on the credit of the United States by the act of Congress, entitled " An act authorizing a loan for [a] sum of three millions of dollars," passed on the fifteenth day of November, in the year one thousand eight hundred and fourteen, as has not been borrowed or otherwise employed in the issue of treasury notes according to law : *Provided always*, That the whole amount of treasury notes issued by virtue of this act, for and in lieu of the residue of the said two sums as aforesaid, shall not exceed the sum of seven millions five hundred thousand dollars : and further, that the treasury notes so issued shall be applied to the same uses to which the said two loans authorized as aforesaid were respectively by law made applicable.

[Section 8 provides that the treasury notes issued under this act shall be prepared and issued in the same form, and reimbursable, transferable and receivable in the same manner, as the notes issued under the Act of March 4, 1814 ; and that the Secretary of the Treasury shall have the same powers to sell or pay out the notes, or to borrow money on the pledge thereof, and to employ agents for the purpose of making sales of the same.]

SEC. 4. *And be it further enacted*, That a sum equal to the whole amount of the treasury notes issued by virtue of this act, to be paid out of any money in the treasury not otherwise appropriated, shall be and the same is hereby appropriated for the payment and reimbursement of the principal and interest of such treasury notes, according to contract, and the faith of the United States is hereby pledged to provide adequate funds for any deficiency in the appropriation hereby made.

[Section 5 and 6 provide, as in previous acts, for the expense of preparing the notes and for the punishment of counterfeiting or uttering counterfeited notes.]

[Approved, December 26, 1814.   3 Statutes at Large, 161.]

1814–1815, Chap. LVI. — *An Act to authorize the issuing of treasury notes for the service of the year one thousand eight hundred and fifteen.*

Be it enacted, . . . That the Secretary of the Treasury, with the approbation of the President of the United States, be, and he is hereby authorized to cause treasury notes for a sum not exceeding twenty-five millions of dollars, to be prepared, signed, and issued, at the treasury of the United States, in the manner hereinafter provided.

[Section 2 provides for the signing and countersigning of the notes.]

SEC. 3. *And be it further enacted*, That the said treasury notes shall be prepared of such denominations as the Secretary of the Treasury, with the approbation of the President of the United States, shall, from time to time, direct; and such of the said notes as shall be of a denomination less than one hundred dollars, shall be payable to bearer and be transferable by delivery alone, and shall bear no interest; and such of the said notes as shall be of the denomination of one hundred dollars, or upwards, may be made payable to order, and transferable by delivery and assignment, endorsed on the same, and bearing an interest from the day on which they shall be issued, at the rate of five and two-fifths per centum per annum; or they may be made payable to bearer, and transferable by delivery alone, and bearing no interest, as the Secretary of the Treasury, with the approbation of the President of the United States, shall direct.

SEC. 4. *And be it further enacted*, That it shall be lawful for the holders of the aforesaid treasury notes, not bearing an interest, and of the treasury notes bearing an interest at the rate of five and two-fifths per centum per annum, to present them at any time, in sums not less than one hundred dollars, to the treasury of the United States, or to any commissioner of loans; and the holders of the said treasury notes not bearing an interest, shall be entitled to receive therefor, the amount of the said notes, in a certificate or certificates of funded stock, bearing interest at seven per centum per annum, and the holders of the aforesaid treasury notes bearing an interest at the rate of five and two-fifths per centum, shall be entitled to receive therefor the amount of the said notes including the interest due on the same, in a like certificate or certificates of funded stock, bearing an interest of six per centum per annum, from the first day of the calendar month next ensuing that in which the said notes shall thus be respectively presented, and payable quarter-yearly, on the same days whereon the interest of the funded debt is now payable. And the stock thus to be issued shall be transferable in the same manner as the other funded stock of [the] United States; the interest on the same, and its eventual reimbursement, shall be effected out of such fund as has been or shall be established by law for the payment and reimbursement of the funded public debt contracted since the declaration of war against Great Britain. And the faith of the United States is hereby pledged to establish sufficient revenues and to appropriate them as an addition to the said fund, if the same shall, at any time hereafter, become inadequate for effecting the purpose aforesaid: *Provided however, And be it further enacted,* That it shall be lawful for the United States to reimburse the stock thus created, at any time after the last day of December, one thousand eight hundred and twenty-four.

SEC. 5. *And be it further enacted,* That it shall be lawful for the Secretary of the Treasury to cause the treasury notes which, in pursuance of the preceding section, shall be delivered up and exchanged for funded stock, and also the treasury notes which shall have been paid to the United States for taxes, duties, or demands, in the manner hereinafter provided, to be reissued, and applied anew, to the same purposes, and in the same manner, as when originally issued.

SEC. 6. *And be it further enacted,* That the treasury notes authorized to be issued by this act, shall be everywhere received in all payments to the United States. On every such payment the note or notes shall be received for the amount of both the principal and the interest, which, on the day of such payment, may appear due on such of the notes as shall bear interest, thus given in payment; and the interest on the said notes bearing an interest, shall, on such payments, be computed at the rate of one cent and one half of a cent per day, on every hundred dollars of principal; and each month shall be computed as containing thirty days.

[Section 7 provides for crediting collectors and other receivers of public moneys with the principal of the notes received by them in payment, and makes the same provisions for crediting and charging interest, in case the notes so received bear interest, as are made in the Treasury Note Act of June 30, 1812, on page 65, and in subsequent acts.]

SEC. 8. *And be it further enacted*, That the Secretary of the Treasury be, and he is hereby authorized, with the approbation of the President of the United States, to cause the said treasury notes to be issued at the par value thereof, in payment of services, of supplies, or of debts, for which the United States are or may be answerable by law, to such person and persons as shall be willing to accept the same in payment; and to deposit portions of the said notes in the loan offices, or in state banks, for the purpose of paying the same to the public creditors as aforesaid; and to borrow money on the credit of the said notes; or to sell the same, at a rate not under par; and it .shall be a good execution of this provision, to pay such notes to such bank or banks as will receive the same at par, and give credit to the Treasurer of the United States for the amount thereof, on the day on which the said notes shall thus be issued and paid to such bank or banks respectively.

SEC. 9. *And be it further enacted*, That it shall and may be lawful for the holder of any treasury notes issued, or authorized to be issued, under any laws heretofore passed, to convert the same into certificates of funded debt, upon the same terms, and in the same manner hereinbefore provided, in relation to the treasury notes authorized by this act, bearing an interest of five and two-fifths per centum.

[Sections 10 and 11 provide, as in previous acts, for the expense of preparing the notes and for the punishment of counterfeiting or uttering counterfeited notes.]

[Approved, February 24, 1815. 3 Statutes at Large, 213.]

1814–15, Chap. LXXXVII. — *An Act to authorize a loan for a sum not exceeding eighteen millions four hundred and fifty-two thousand eight hundred dollars.*

[Section 1 authorizes the President to borrow, on the credit of the United States, a sum not exceeding eighteen million four hundred and fifty-two thousand eight hundred dollars, to be applied to defray any expenses authorized by law during the present year : *provided,* that no contract shall be made precluding the United States from reimbursing the sum thus borrowed at any time after twelve years from December 31, 1815.

Section 2 authorizes the Secretary of the Treasury to sell the stock thus to be created, but without fixing any limit of rate, and requires an account of the moneys thus procured and of the rate obtained for the stock, to be laid before Congress during the first week of February, 1816.

Section 3, authorizing the employment of agents in disposing of the stock, follows the terms of section 3 of the Act of February 8, 1813, on page 67.

Section 4, containing the sinking fund provisions, is identical with section 3 of the Act of March 14, 1812, on page 62.]

SEC. 6. *And be it further enacted,* That it shall be lawful for the Secretary of the Treasury to accept in payment of any loan obtained in virtue of this act, such treasury notes as have been actually issued, before the passing of this act, and which were made by law a charge upon the sinking fund, such treasury notes to be credited for the principal thereof, and the amount of interest actually accrued at the time of the payment.

SEC. 7. *And be it further enacted,* That it shall be lawful for the Secretary of the Treasury to cause to be paid, the interest upon treasury notes which have become due, and remain unpaid, as well with respect to the time elapsed before they become due, as with respect to the time that shall elapse after they become due, and until funds shall be assigned for the payment of the said treasury notes, and notice thereof shall be given by the Secretary of the Treasury.

[Approved, March 3, 1815. 3 Statutes at Large, 227.]

1815-16, Chap. XLIV. — *An Act to incorporate the subscribers to the Bank of the United States.*

Be it enacted, . . . That a bank of the United States of America shall be established, with a capital of thirty-five millions of dollars, divided into three hundred and fifty thousand shares, of one hundred dollars each share.

Seventy thousand shares, amounting to the sum of seven millions of dollars, part of the capital of the said bank, shall be subscribed and paid for by the United States, in the manner hereinafter specified; and two hundred and eighty thousand shares, amounting to the sum of twenty-eight millions of dollars, shall be subscribed and paid for by individuals, companies, or corporations, in the manner hereinafter specified.

SEC. 2. *And be it further enacted*, That subscriptions for the sum of twenty-eight millions of dollars, towards constituting the capital of the said bank, shall be opened on the first Monday in July next. . . .

[The places at which subscriptions are to be received are then named, provision is made for the appointment of commissioners to receive them and for the time and manner of receiving, and directions are given as to the course of proceeding in case the amount subscribed exceeds or falls short of the twenty-eight millions to be raised.]

SEC. 3. *And be it further enacted*, That it shall be lawful for any individual, company, corporation, or state, when the subscriptions shall be opened as herein before directed, to subscribe for any number of shares of the capital of the said bank, not exceeding three thousand shares, and the sums so subscribed shall be payable, and paid, in the manner following; that is to say, seven millions of dollars thereof in gold or silver coin of the United States, or in gold coin of Spain, or the dominions of Spain, at the rate of one hundred cents for every twenty-eight grains and sixty-hundredths of a grain of the actual weight thereof, or in other foreign gold or silver coin at the several rates prescribed by the first section of an act regulating the currency of foreign coins in the United States, passed tenth day of April, one thousand eight hundred and six, and twenty-one millions of dollars thereof in like gold or silver coin, or in the funded debt of the United States contracted at the time of the subscriptions respectively. And the payments made in the funded debt of the United States, shall be paid and received at the following rates: that is to say, the funded debt bearing an interest of six per centum per annum, at the nominal or par value thereof; the funded

debt bearing an interest of three per centum per annum, at
the rate of sixty-five dollars for every sum of one hundred
dollars of the nominal amount thereof; and the funded debt
bearing an interest of seven per centum per annum, at the
rate of one hundred and six dollars and fifty-one cents, for
every sum of one hundred dollars of the nominal amount
thereof; together with the amount of the interest accrued on
the said several denominations of funded debt, to be computed and allowed to the time of subscribing the same to the
capital of the said bank as aforesaid. And the payments of
the said subscriptions shall be made and completed by the
subscribers, respectively, at the times and in the manner following; that is to say, at the time of subscribing there shall
be paid five dollars on each share, in gold or silver coin as
aforesaid, and twenty-five dollars more in coin as aforesaid,
or in funded debt as aforesaid; at the expiration of six
calendar months after the time of subscribing, there shall be
paid the further sum of ten dollars on each share, in gold or
silver coin as aforesaid, and twenty-five dollars more in coin
as aforesaid, or in funded debt as aforesaid; at the expiration of twelve calendar months from the time of subscribing,
there shall be paid the further sum of ten dollars on each
share, in gold or silver coin as aforesaid, and twenty-five
dollars more, in coin as aforesaid, or in funded debt as
aforesaid.

[Section 4 provides for the payment in coin, to be made to the commissioners by subscribers at the time of subscription, for the transfer of
certificates of funded debt subscribed by them, and for the delivery of
coin and certificates by the commissioners to the president and directors,
after the organization of the bank.]

SEC. 5. *And be it further enacted*, That it shall be lawful
for the United States to pay and redeem the funded debt
subscribed to the capital of the said bank at the rates aforesaid, in such sums, and at such times, as shall be deemed
expedient, anything in any act or acts of Congress to the
contrary thereof notwithstanding. And it shall also be lawful for the president, directors, and company, of the said bank,
to sell and transfer for gold and silver coin, or bullion, the

funded debt subscribed to the capital of the said bank as aforesaid : *Provided always*, That they shall not sell more thereof than the sum of two millions of dollars in any one year ; nor sell any part thereof at any time within the United States, without previously giving notice of their intention to the Secretary of the Treasury, and offering the same to the United States for the period of fifteen days, at least, at the current price, not exceeding the rates aforesaid.

SEC. 6. *And be it further enacted*, That at the opening of subscription to the capital stock of the said bank, the Secretary of the Treasury shall subscribe, or cause to be subscribed, on behalf of the United States, the said number of seventy thousand shares, amounting to seven millions of dollars as aforesaid, to be paid in gold or silver coin, or in stock of the United States, bearing interest at the rate of five per centum per annum ; and if payment thereof, or of any part thereof, be made in public stock, bearing interest as aforesaid, the said interest shall be payable quarterly, to commence from the time of making such payment on account of the said subscription, and the principal of the said stock shall be redeemable in any sums, and at any periods, which the government shall deem fit. And the Secretary of the Treasury shall cause the certificates of such public stock to be prepared, and made in the usual form, and shall pay and deliver the same to the president, directors, and company, of the said bank on the first day of January, one thousand eight hundred and seventeen, which said stock it shall be lawful for the said president, directors, and company, to sell and transfer for gold and silver coin or bullion at their discretion : *Provided*, They shall not sell more than two millions of dollars thereof in any one year.

SEC. 7. *And be it further enacted*, That the subscribers to the said bank of the United States of America, their successors and assigns, shall be, and are hereby, created a corporation and body politic, by the name and style of "The president, directors, and company, of the bank of the United States," and shall so continue until the third day of March, in the year one thousand eight hundred and thirty-six, and by that name shall be, and are hereby, made able and capable, in law, to have, purchase, receive, possess, enjoy, and retain, to them and their successors, lands, rents, tenements, hereditaments, goods, chattels and effects, of whatsoever kind, nature, and quality, to an amount not exceeding, in the whole, fifty-five millions of dollars, including the amount of the capital stock aforesaid ; and the same to sell, grant, demise, alien or dispose of; to sue and be sued, plead and be impleaded, answer and be answered, defend and be defended, in all state courts having competent jurisdiction, and in any circuit court of the United States : and also to make, have, and use, a common seal, and the same to break, alter, and renew, at their pleasure : and also to ordain, establish, and put in execution, such by-laws, and ordinances, and regulations, as they shall deem necessary and convenient for the government of the said corporation, not being contrary to the Constitution thereof, or to the laws of the United States; and generally to do and execute all and singular the acts, matters, and things, which to them it shall or may appertain to do; subject, nevertheless, to the rules, regulations, restrictions, limitations, and provisions, hereinafter prescribed and declared.

SEC. 8. *And be it further enacted*, That for the management of the affairs of the said corporation, there shall be twenty-five directors, five of whom, being stockholders, shall be annually appointed by the President of the United States, by and with the advice and consent of the Senate, not more than three of whom shall be residents of any one state ; and twenty of whom shall be annually elected at the banking house in the city of Philadelphia, on the first Monday of January, in each year, by the qualified stockholders of the capital of the said bank, other than the United States, and by a plurality of votes then and there actually given, according to the scale of voting hereinafter prescribed : *Provided always*, That no person, being a director in the bank of the United States, or any of its branches, shall be a director of any other bank; and should any such director act as a director in any other bank, it shall forthwith vacate his

appointment in the direction of the bank of the United
States. . . .

[The directors are annually to elect one of their number to be president of the corporation, and in case of his death, resignation, or removal, to elect another. Any vacancy occurring among the directors is
to be supplied by the President of the United States or by the stockholders, as the case may be ; "but the President of the United States
alone shall have power to remove any of the directors appointed by him
as aforesaid."]

SEC. 9. *And be it further enacted,* That as soon as the
sum of eight millions four hundred thousand dollars in gold
and silver coin, and in the public debt, shall have been actually received on account of the subscriptions to the capital
of the said bank (exclusively of the subscription aforesaid,
on the part of the United States) notice thereof shall be
given, . . .

[and the subscribers shall then proceed to elect directors and the President of the United States to appoint five directors on behalf of the government, "though not stockholders," and the bank shall thereupon be
organized and commence its operations, the directors so elected and appointed serving until the end of the first Monday in January next.

Section 10 authorizes the directors to appoint and govern such officers, clerks, and servants as may be necessary for executing their
business.]

SEC. 11. *And be it further enacted,* That the following
rules, restrictions, limitations, and provisions, shall form
and be fundamental articles of the constitution of the said
corporation, to wit :

1. The number of votes to which the stockholders shall
be entitled, in voting for directors, shall be according to
the number of shares he, she, or they, respectively, shall
hold, in the proportions following, that is to say ; for one
share and not more than two shares, one vote ; for every
two shares above two, and not exceeding ten, one vote ; for
every four shares above ten, and not exceeding thirty, one
vote ; for every six shares above thirty, and not exceeding
sixty, one vote ; for every eight shares above sixty, and not
exceeding one hundred, one vote ; and for every ten shares
above one hundred, one vote ; but no person, copartner-

ship, or body politic, shall be entitled to a greater number
than thirty votes; and after the first election, no share or
shares shall confer a right of voting, which shall not have
been holden three calendar months previous to the day of
election. And stockholders actually resident within the
United States, and none other, may vote in elections by
proxy.

Second. Not more than three-fourths of the directors
elected by the stockholders, and not more than four-fifths
of the directors appointed by the President of the United
States, who shall be in office at the time of an annual election, shall be elected or appointed for the next succeeding
year; and no director shall hold his office more than three
years out of four in succession: but the director who shall
be the president at the time of an election may always be reappointed, or re-elected, as the case may be.

Third. None but a stockholder, resident citizen of the
United States, shall be a director; nor shall a director be
entitled to any emoluments; but the directors may make such
compensation to the president for his extraordinary attendance at the bank, as shall appear to them reasonable.

Fourth. Not less than seven directors shall constitute a
board for the transaction of business, of whom the president
shall always be one, except in case of sickness or necessary
absence: in which case his place may be supplied by any
other director whom he, by writing, under his hand, shall
depute for that purpose. And the director so deputed may
do and transact all the necessary business, belonging to
the office of the president of the said corporation, during
the continuance of the sickness or necessary absence of the
president.

Fifth. A number of stockholders, not less than sixty,
who, together, shall be proprietors of one thousand shares
or upwards, shall have power at any time to call a general
meeting of the stockholders, for purposes relative to the
institution, giving at least ten weeks' notice in two public
newspapers of the place where the bank is seated, and specifying in such notice the object or objects of such meeting.

Sixth. Each cashier or treasurer, before he enters upon the duties of his office, shall be required to give bond, with two or more sureties, to the satisfaction of the directors, in a sum not less than fifty thousand dollars, with a condition for his good behavior, and the faithful performance of his duties to the corporation.

Seventh. The lands, tenements, and hereditaments, which it shall be lawful for the said corporation to hold, shall be only such as shall be requisite for its immediate accommodation in relation to the convenient transacting of its business, and such as shall have been *bona fide* mortgaged to it by way of security, or conveyed to it in satisfaction of debts previously contracted in the course of its dealings, or purchased at sales, upon judgments which shall have been obtained for such debts.

Eighth. The total amount of debts which the said corporation shall at any time owe, whether by bond, bill, note, or other contract, over and above the debt or debts due for money deposited in the bank, shall not exceed the sum of thirty-five millions of dollars, unless the contracting of any greater debt shall have been previously authorized by law of the United States. In case of excess, the directors under whose administration it shall happen, shall be liable for the same in their natural and private capacities : and an action of debt may in such case be brought against them, or any of them, their or any of their heirs, executors, or administrators, in any court of record of the United States, or either of them, by any creditor or creditors of the said corporation, and may be prosecuted to judgment and execution, any condition, covenant, or agreement to the contrary notwithstanding. But this provision shall not be construed to exempt the said corporation or the lands, tenements, goods, or chattels of the same from being also liable for, and chargeable with, the said excess.

Such of the said directors, who may have been absent when the said excess was contracted or created, or who may have dissented from the resolution or act whereby the same was so contracted or created, may respectively exonerate themselves from being so liable, by forthwith giving notice of the fact, and of their absence or dissent, to the President of the United States, and to the stockholders, at a general meeting, which they shall have power to call for that purpose.

Ninth. The said corporation shall not, directly or indirectly, deal or trade in anything except bills of exchange, gold or silver bullion, or in the sale of goods really and truly pledged for money lent and not redeemed in due time, or goods which shall be the proceeds of its lands. It shall not be at liberty to purchase any public debt whatsoever, nor shall it take more than at the rate of six per centum per annum for or upon its loans or discounts.

Tenth. No loan shall be made by the said corporation, for the use or on account of the government of the United States, to an amount exceeding five hundred thousand dollars, or of any particular state, to an amount exceeding fifty thousand dollars, or of any foreign prince or state, unless previously authorized by a law of the United States.

Eleventh. The stock of the said corporation shall be assignable and transferable, according to such rules as shall be instituted in that behalf, by the laws and ordinances of the same.

Twelfth. The bills, obligatory and of credit, under the seal of the said corporation, which shall be made to any person or persons, shall be assignable by endorsement thereupon, under the hand or hands of such person or persons, and his, her, or their executors or administrators, and his, her or their assignee or assignees, and so as absolutely to transfer and vest the property thereof in each and every assignee or assignees successively, and to enable such assignee or assignees, and his, her or their executors or administrators, to maintain an action thereupon in his, her, or their own name or names: *Provided,* That said corporation shall not make any bill obligatory, or of credit, or other obligation under its seal for the payment of a sum less than five thousand dollars. And the bills or notes which may be issued by order of the said corporation, signed by the president, and countersigned by the principal cashier or treasurer thereof, promising the payment of money to any person or persons, his, her or their order, or, to bearer, although not under the seal of the said corporation, shall be binding and obligatory upon the same, in like manner, and with like force and effect, as upon any private person or persons, if issued by him, her or them, in his, her or their private or natural capacity or capacities, and shall be assignable and negotiable in like manner as if they were so issued by such private person or persons ; that is to say, those which shall be payable to any person or persons, his, her or their order, shall be assignable by endorsement, in like manner, and with the like effect as foreign bills of exchange now are ; and those which are payable to bearer shall be assignable and negotiable by delivery only : *Provided*, That all bills or notes, so to be issued by said corporation, shall be made payable on demand, other than bills or notes for the payment of a sum not less than one hundred dollars each, and payable to the order of some person or persons, which bills or notes it shall be lawful for said corporation to make payable at any time not exceeding sixty days from the date thereof.

Thirteenth. Half yearly dividends shall be made of so much of the profits of the bank as shall appear to the directors advisable ; and once in every three years the directors shall lay before the stockholders, at a general meeting, for their information, an exact and particular statement of the debts which shall have remained unpaid after the expiration of the original credit, for a period of treble the term of that credit, and of the surplus of the profits, if any, after deducting losses and dividends. If there shall be a failure in the payment of any part of any sum subscribed to the capital of the said bank, by any person, copartnership or body politic, the party failing shall lose the benefit of any dividend which may have accrued prior to the time for making such payment, and during the delay of the same.

Fourteenth. The directors of the said corporation shall establish a competent office of discount and deposit in the District of Columbia, whenever any law of the United

States shall require such an establishment; also one such
office of discount and deposit in any state in which two
thousand shares shall have been subscribed or may be held,
whenever, upon application of the legislature of such state,
Congress may, by law, require the same: *Provided*, the
directors aforesaid shall not be bound to establish such office
before the whole of the capital of the bank shall have been
paid up. And it shall be lawful for the directors of the said
corporation to establish offices of discount and deposit,
wheresoever they shall think fit, within the United States
or the territories thereof, and to commit the management of
the said offices, and the business thereof, respectively to
such persons, and under such regulations as they shall deem
proper, not being contrary to law or the constitution of the
bank. Or, instead of establishing such offices, it shall be
lawful for the directors of the said corporation, from time
to time, to employ any other bank or banks, to be first approved by the Secretary of the Treasury, at any place or
places that they may deem safe and proper, to manage and
transact the business proposed as aforesaid, other than for
the purposes of discount, to be managed and transacted by
such offices, under such agreements, and subject to such regulations, as they shall deem just and proper. Not more than
thirteen nor less than seven managers or directors, of every
office established as aforesaid, shall be annually appointed
by the directors of the bank, to serve one year; they shall
choose a president from their own number; each of them
shall be a citizen of the United States, and a resident of the
state, territory or district, wherein such office is established;
and not more than three-fourths of the said managers or
directors, in office at the time of an annual appointment,
shall be reappointed for the next succeeding year; and no
director shall hold his office more than three years out
of four, in succession; but the president may be always
reappointed.

Fifteenth. The officer at the head of the Treasury Department of the United States shall be furnished, from time
to time, as often as he may require, not exceeding once a

week, with statements of the amount of capital stock of the said corporation and of the debts due to the same; of the moneys deposited therein; of the notes in circulation, and of the specie in hand; and shall have a right to inspect such general accounts in the books of the bank as shall relate to the said statement: *Provided*, That this shall not be construed to imply a right of inspecting the account of any private individual or individuals with the bank.

Sixteenth. No stockholder, unless he be a citizen of the United States, shall vote in the choice of directors.

Seventeenth. No note shall be issued of less amount than five dollars.

[Sections 12 and 13 prescribe the penalties to be imposed in case the corporation, or any person to its use, shall deal in goods, wares, or merchandise contrary to the provisions of this act, or shall lend any sum of money for the use of the government of the United States, or of any particular state, or any foreign prince or state, except as allowed above, and without being previously authorized thereto by law.]

SEC. 14. *And be it further enacted*, That the bills or notes of the said corporation originally made payable, or which shall have become payable on demand, shall be receivable in all payments to the United States, unless otherwise directed by act of Congress.

SEC. 15. *And be it further enacted*, That during the continuance of this act, and whenever required by the Secretary of the Treasury, the said corporation shall give the necessary facilities for transferring the public funds from place to place, within the United States, or the territories thereof, and for distributing the same in payment of the public creditors, without charging commissions or claiming allowance on account of difference of exchange, and shall also do and perform the several and respective duties of the commissioners of loans for the several states, or of any one or more of them, whenever required by law.

SEC. 16. *And be it further enacted*, That the deposits of the money of the United States, in places in which the said bank and branches thereof may be established, shall be made in said bank or branches thereof, unless the Secretary of the

Treasury shall at any time otherwise order and direct; in which case the Secretary of the Treasury shall immediately lay before Congress, if in session, and if not, immediately after the commencement of the next session, the reasons of such order or direction.

SEC. 17. *And be it further enacted*, That the said corporation shall not at any time suspend or refuse payment in gold and silver, of any of its notes, bills or obligations; nor of any moneys received upon deposit in said bank, or in any of its offices of discount and deposit. And if the said corporation shall at any time refuse or neglect to pay on demand any bill, note or obligation issued by the corporation, according to the contract, promise or undertaking therein expressed; or shall neglect or refuse to pay on demand any moneys received in said bank, or in any of its offices aforesaid, on deposit, to the person or persons entitled to receive the same, then, and in every such case, the holder of any such note, bill, or obligation, or the person or persons entitled to demand and receive such moneys as aforesaid, shall respectively be entitled to receive and recover interest on the said bills, notes, obligations or moneys, until the same shall be fully paid and satisfied, at the rate of twelve per centum per annum from the time of such demand as aforesaid: *Pro- vided*, That Congress may at any time hereafter enact laws enforcing and regulating the recovery of the amount of the notes, bills, obligations or other debts, of which payment shall have been refused as aforesaid, with the rate of interest above mentioned, vesting jurisdiction for that purpose in any courts, either of law or equity, of the courts of the United States, or territories thereof, or of the several states, as they may deem expedient.

[Sections 18 and 19 prescribe the penalties for forging, counterfeiting, or altering bills or notes of the bank or checks drawn upon it, and for passing any forged, counterfeited, or altered bill, note, or check, and also for engraving any plate to be used in forging or counterfeiting, or having in possession any such plate, or blank notes in the similitude of those issued by the corporation, or any paper for use in counterfeiting.]

SEC. 20. *And be it further enacted*, That in consideration of the exclusive privileges and benefits conferred by this act, upon the said bank, the president, directors, and company thereof, shall pay to the United States, out of the corporate funds thereof, the sum of one million and five hundred thousand dollars, in three equal payments; that is to say: five hundred thousand dollars at the expiration of two years; - five hundred thousand dollars at the expiration of three years; and five hundred thousand dollars at the expiration of four years after the said bank shall be organized, and commence its operations in the manner herein before provided.

SEC. 21. *And be it further enacted*, That no other bank shall be established by any future law of the United States during the continuance of the corporation hereby created, for which the faith of the United States is hereby pledged. *Provided*, Congress may renew existing charters for banks in the District of Columbia, not increasing the capital thereof, and may also establish any other bank or banks in said district, with capitals not exceeding, in the whole, six millions of dollars, if they shall deem it expedient. And, notwithstanding the expiration of the term for which the said corporation is created, it shall be lawful to use the corporate name, style, and capacity, for the purpose of suits for the final settlement and liquidation of the affairs and accounts of the corporation, and for the sale and disposition of their estate, real, personal, and mixed: but not for any other purpose, or in any other manner whatsoever, nor for a period exceeding two years after the expiration of the said term of incorporation.

SEC. 22. *And be it further enacted*, That if the subscriptions and payments to said bank shall not be made and completed so as to enable the same to commence its operations, or if the said bank shall not commence its operations on or before the first Monday in April next, then, and in that case, Congress may, at any time, within twelve months thereafter, declare, by law, this act null and void.

SEC. 23. *And be it further enacted*, That it shall, at all

times, be lawful, for a committee of either House of Congress, appointed for that purpose, to inspect the books, and to examine into the proceedings of the corporation hereby created, and to report whether the provisions of this charter have been, by the same, violated or not; and whenever any committee, as aforesaid, shall find and report, or the President of the United States shall have reason to believe that the charter has been violated, it may be lawful for Congress to direct, or the President to order a scire facias to be sued out of the circuit court of the district of Pennsylvania, in the name of the United States, (which shall be executed upon the president of the corporation for the time being, at least fifteen days before the commencement of the term of said court,) calling on the said corporation to show cause wherefore the charter hereby granted, shall not be declared forfeited; and it shall be lawful for the said court, upon the return of the said scire facias, to examine into the truth of the alleged violation, and if such violation be made appear, then to pronounce and adjudge that the said charter is forfeited and annulled. *Provided, however,* Every issue of fact which may be joined between the United States and the corporation aforesaid, shall be tried by a jury. And it shall be lawful for the court aforesaid to require the production of such of the books of the corporation as it may deem necessary for the ascertainment of the controverted facts: and the final judgment of the court aforesaid, shall be examinable in the Supreme Court of the United States, by writ of error, and may be there reversed or affirmed, according to the usages of law.

[Approved, April 10, 1816. 3 Statutes at Large, 266.]

NOTE. — By the Act of March 3, 1819, 3 Statutes at Large, 508, the provisions of the above act which relate to the right of voting for directors are enforced, by prescribing, in every case where more than thirty votes are offered by any one person, oaths as to the actual ownership of the shares, to be taken by the person offering the votes and by the signer of any proxy. And the same act provides against the bribery by gift or promise of the president or either of the directors of the bank, or of either of its branches, in any matter coming before the said president and directors for decision, by making the briber and the person bribed punishable on conviction by fine and imprisonment at the discretion of the court, and further disqualifies them from holding any office of trust or profit under the corporation, or any office of honor, trust, or profit under the United States.

1815–16, Resolution No. VIII.— *A Resolution relative to the more effectual collection of the public revenue.*

Resolved by the Senate and House of Representatives . . . That the Secretary of the Treasury be, and he hereby is, required and directed to adopt such measures as he may deem necessary to cause, as soon as may be, all duties, taxes, debts, or sums of money, accruing or becoming payable to the United States, to be collected and paid in the legal currency of the United States, or treasury notes, or notes of the bank of the United States as by law provided and declared, or in notes of banks which are payable and paid on demand in the said legal currency of the United States, and that from and after the twentieth day of February next, no such duties, taxes, debts, or sums of money accruing or becoming payable to the United States as aforesaid, ought to be collected or received otherwise than in the legal currency of the United States, or treasury notes, or notes of the bank of the United States, or in notes of banks which are payable and paid on demand in the said legal currency of the United States.

[Approved, April 30, 1816.   3 Statutes at Large, 343.]

1816–17, Chap. XXXVIII.— *An Act transferring the duties of commissioners of loans to the Bank of the United States, and abolishing the office of commissioner of loans.*

[This act requires the Bank of the United States and its branches to perform the duties of commissioners of loans for the several states, and provides that all acts now performed by the said commissioners in transferring stock from the books of one loan office to another, or to the books of the treasury, or from the books of the treasury to the books of the loan offices, shall be performed by the president of the Bank of the United States, the presidents of the several branches of the said bank, and by the presidents of such state banks as the Bank of the United States may employ in states where it has no branches.

It is further made the duty of the commissioners of loans and of the agent for military pensions, where there is no such commissioner, and in states where there is a bank established by law, to deliver up the records and papers of their respective offices to the president of the Bank of the United States, or of a branch thereof, or of such state bank as may be employed; and the office of commissioner of loans is accordingly abolished upon such delivery.]

[Approved, March 3, 1817.　3 Statutes at Large, 360.]

1816-17, Chap. LXXXV. — *An Act to repeal so much of any acts now in force as authorize a loan of money, or an issue of Treasury notes.*

[Sections 1 and 2 repeal so much of any acts of Congress as authorizes the President to borrow money on the credit of the United States, and to cause certificates of stock to be issued therefor, or to cause treasury notes to be prepared and issued : *provided*, that no securities for money already borrowed shall thus be invalidated, nor shall the right of the holders of treasury notes already issued be affected.]

SEC. 3. *And be it further enacted,* That so much of the act, entitled " An act to authorize the issuing of treasury notes for the service of the year one thousand eight hundred and fifteen," as makes it lawful for the Secretary of the Treasury to cause the treasury notes, [in] cases therein mentioned, to be re-issued and applied anew to the same purposes, and in the same manner, as when originally issued, be, and the same is hereby repealed.

SEC. 4. *And be it further enacted,* That all treasury notes which are now, or shall hereafter become, the property of the United States, (from reimbursement, purchase, exchange, or receipts, on account of taxes, duties, and demands,) shall be cancelled or destroyed at such times, and under such regulations and securities, as the commissioners of the sinking fund, with the approbation of the President, shall establish and determine.

[Approved, March 3, 1817.　3 Statutes at Large, 377.]

1816–17, Chap. LXXXVII. — *An Act to provide for the redemption of the public debt.*

Be it enacted, . . . That so much of any act or acts of Congress, as makes appropriations for the purchase or reimbursement of the principal, or for the payment of the interest, of the funded debt of the United States be, and the same is hereby repealed.

SEC. 2. *And be it further enacted,* That from the proceeds of the duties on merchandise imported, and on the tonnage of vessels, and from the proceeds of the internal duties, and of the sales of western lands, now belonging, or which may hereafter belong, to the United States, the annual sum of ten millions of dollars be, and the same is yearly, appropriated to the sinking fund ; and the said sum is hereby declared to be vested in the commissioners of the sinking fund, in the same manner as the moneys heretofore appropriated to the said fund, to be applied by the said commissioners to the payment of interest and charges, and to the reimbursement or purchase of the principal of the public debt; and it shall be the duty of the Secretary of the Treasury annually to cause to be paid to the commissioners of the sinking fund, the said sum of ten millions of dollars, in such payments, and at such times in each year, as the situation of the treasury will best admit: *Provided,* That all such payments as may be necessary to enable the said commissioners to discharge or reimburse any demands against the United States, on account of the principal or interest of the debt which shall be actually due in conformity to the engagements of the said United States, shall [and] may be made at such times in each year as will enable the said commissioners faithfully and punctually to comply with such engagement: *Provided, also,* That any money which may have been paid, before the passage of this act, to the commissioners of the sinking fund for the year one thousand eight hundred and seventeen, as a part of the annual appropriation heretofore made by law to that fund, shall be held to be a payment for the year one thousand eight hundred and seventeen, on

7

account of the appropriation of ten millions hereinbefore
directed.

Sec. 3. *And be it further enacted*, That in addition to
the sum of ten millions of dollars, hereinbefore annually
appropriated to the sinking fund, there shall be appropriated for the year one thousand eight hundred and seventeen,
to the sinking fund, the further sum of nine millions of dollars, to be paid out of any moneys in the treasury not otherwise appropriated, at such time within the year as the
Secretary of the Treasury shall deem most conducive to
the public interest, to be applied by the commissioners of
the sinking fund to the purchase or redemption of the public
debt: and it shall be lawful for the Secretary of the Treasury, at any time during the year one thousand eight hundred
and seventeen, if he shall deem it expedient to do so, to
cause to be paid to the commissioners of the sinking fund
a further sum, not exceeding four millions of dollars, which
shall be considered as an advance to that amount, on the
appropriation of ten millions, payable in the next year, and
the said amount shall also be applied by the said commissioners to the purchase or redemption of the public debt,
and the commissioners aforesaid are authorized and directed
to apply the sums by this act appropriated to the purchase
and redemption of the public debt, holden by the Bank of
the United States, if not otherwise to be obtained on the
terms stated in this act.

Sec. 4. *And be it further enacted*, That after the year
one thousand eight hundred and seventeen, whenever there
shall be, at any time after an adjournment of Congress, in
any year, a surplus of money in the treasury, above the
sums appropriated for the service of such year, the payment
of which to the commissioners of the sinking fund, will yet
leave in the treasury, at the end of the year, a balance equal
to two millions of dollars, then such surplus shall be, and
the same is hereby, appropriated to the sinking fund, to be
paid at such times as the situation of the treasury will best
permit; and shall be applied, by the commissioners thereof,
to the purchase or redemption of the public debt.

SEC. 5. *And be it further enacted,* That whenever, in any year, there shall be a surplus in the sinking fund, beyond the amount of interest and principal, which may be actually due and payable to [by] the United States, in such year, in conformity with their engagements, the commissioners of the sinking fund shall be, and they are hereby, authorized, with the approbation of the President of the United States, to purchase the debt of the United States, at its market price, if such price shall not exceed the following rates, viz: for stock of the United States, bearing an interest of three per centum per annum, there shall not be paid more than sixty-five dollars for every hundred dollars of the principal thereof: for stock bearing an annual interest of six per centum per annum, there shall not be paid more than the par or true value thereof; and for stock bearing an annual interest of seven per centum, there shall not be paid an advance above the par value thereof, which shall exceed, for every hundred dollars of stock, the computed value of an annuity of one dollar for a number of years, equal to that during which the stock so purchased will not be reimbursable at the pleasure of government, estimating, in such computation, the interest of money at six per centum per annum.

SEC. 6. *And be it further enacted,* That all certificates of public debt which, by payment or purchase, have become, or hereafter shall become, the property of the United States, shall be cancelled or destroyed, at such times, and under such regulations and securities, as the commissioners of the sinking fund, with the approbation of the President, shall establish and determine. And no interest shall be considered as accruing, and no further payment shall be made, on account of such debt, the certificates of which have been so cancelled and destroyed.

SEC. 7. *And be it further enacted,* That nothing in this act contained shall be construed to prevent the Congress of the United States, if war shall occur with any foreign power, from applying, to any object of public service, any surplus of the amount herein appropriated to the sinking fund, which may be left in any year after paying the interest and princi-

pal which may be actually due and payable by the United
States, in conformity with their engagements. Nor shall
anything in this act be construed to repeal, alter, or affect,
any of the provisions of any former act, pledging the faith
of the United States to the payment of the interest or principal of the public debt, but' all such payments shall continue
to be made at the time heretofore prescribed by law, excepting only as before provided, that no payments shall be made
on certificates which have become the property of the United
States.

[Approved, March 3, 1817.   3 Statutes at Large, 379.]

1817–18, Chap. LVI. —*An Act to authorize the payment of certain certificates.*

[This act suspends for the term of two years from its passage, so much
of the acts of March 3, 1795, and June 12, 1798, on page 44, as bar from
settlement loan office and final settlement certificates and indents of interest; and provides that, upon the presentation at the Treasury and adjustment of such claims, they shall be paid, with interest at the rate of six per
cent. from the date of the last payment of interest endorsed thereon.]

[Approved, April 13, 1818.   3 Statutes at Large, 425.]

NOTE. — By the Act of May 7, 1822, having the same title as the above'
the provisions of the acts of 1795 and 1798 are further suspended for the
the term of two years and from thence until the end of the next session
of Congress. 3 *ibid*. 697.   And by the Act of July 14, 1832, the act of 1822
is revived and continued in force for the term of four years and from
thence until the end of the next session of Congress. 4 *ibid*. 602.

1819–20, Chap. CIII. — *An Act to authorize the President of the United States to borrow a sum not exceeding three millions of dollars.*

[Section 1 empowers the President to borrow, on the credit of the
United States, a sum not exceeding three millions of dollars, at a rate
not exceeding five per cent., and reimbursable at any time after January 1, 1832, or at a rate not exceeding six per cent., and reimbursable
at pleasure, to be applied in defraying any public expenses authorized
by law.

Section 2 authorizes the Bank of the United States to lend the sum or
any part thereof, and further authorizes the sale of certificates of the
stock, "*provided*, that no stock shall be sold under par."

Section 3, authorizing the employment of agents in disposing of the stock, follows the terms of section 8 of the Act of February 8, 1813, on page 67.

Section 4 makes the same sinking fund provisions as section 3 of the Act of March 14, 1812, on page 62, with the substitution of "ten millions of dollars" for eight millions, as the amount of the total annual appropriation for the public debt.]

[Approved, May 15, 1820. 3 Statutes at Large, 582.]

1820-21, Chap. XXXVIII. — *An Act to authorize the President of the United States to borrow a sum not exceeding five millions of dollars.*

[Section 1 empowers the President to borrow, on the credit of the United States, a sum not exceeding five millions of dollars, at a rate not exceeding five per cent., and reimbursable at any time after January 1, 1835, to be applied in defraying any public expenses authorized by law.

Sections 2, 3, and 4 are identical with sections 2, 3, and 4 of the Act of May 15, 1820, above.]

[Approved, March 3, 1821. 3 Statutes at Large, 635.]

1821-22, Chap. VIII. — *An Act authorizing the transfer of certain certificates of the funded debt of the United States.*

Be it enacted, . . . That the certificates of the funded debt of the United States, which, upon the assumption of the debts of the several creditor states, were issued in their favor, respectively, be, and hereby are, made transferable, according to the rules and forms instituted for the purpose of transfers of the public debt.

[Approved, February 19, 1822. 3 Statutes at Large, 651.]

1821-22, Chap. XXVIII. — *An Act to authorize the Secretary of the Treasury to exchange a stock bearing an interest of five per cent. for certain stocks bearing an interest of six and seven per cent.*

Be it enacted . . . That a subscription, to the amount of twelve millions of dollars, of the seven per cent. stock, and of the six per cent. stock of the year eighteen hundred and twelve, and also for fourteen millions of the six per cent. stock of the years eighteen hundred and thirteen, fourteen,

and fifteen, be, and the same is hereby, proposed : for which
purpose books shall be opened at the Treasury of the United
States, and at the several loan offices, on the first day of
May, one thousand eight hundred and twenty-two, to continue open until the first day of July next thereafter, for such
parts of the above-mentioned description of stocks as shall,
on the day of subscription, stand on the books of the treasury, and on those of the several loan offices, respectively ;
which subscription shall be effected by a transfer to the United
States, in the manner provided by law for such transfers, of
the credit or credits standing on the said books, and by a
surrender of the certificates of the stock so subscribed.

[Section 2 provides that for any sum thus subscribed of the six per
cent. stocks of 1812 and 1813, the subscribers shall be entitled to an equal
amount of stock bearing interest at five per cent. and payable quarterly
from June 30, 1822, and redeemable at the pleasure of the United States,
one third after December 31, 1830, one third after December 31, 1831, and
one third after December 31, 1832; and that for any sum subscribed of
the seven per cent. stock, the subscribers shall be entitled to an equal
amount of five per cent. stock, bearing interest and dated as above, and
redeemable in like manner after December 31, 1833: *provided,* that no
reimbursement shall be made of any new certificate, except for its whole
amount, nor until after six months' notice.

Section 3 provides that if the subscription authorized by section 1 is
not completed by July 1, 1822, the remainder of the amount may be subscribed at any time before October 1, 1822; and that for so much as may
be subscribed of the six per cent. stocks of 1812, 1813, 1814, and 1815, the
subscribers shall be entitled to an equal amount of stock, bearing interest at five per cent. and payable quarterly from September 30, 1822, and
redeemable after 1830, 1831, and 1832 as above ; and that for so much of
the seven per cent. stock as may be subscribed, the subscribers shall be
entitled to an equal amount of five per cent. stock, with interest payable
as above, and redeemable in like manner after 1833, the same proviso
being made as to the conditions of reimbursement.]

SEC. 4. *And be it further enacted,* That the same funds
which have heretofore been, and now are, pledged by law, for
the payment of the interest, and for the redemption or reimbursement of the stock which may be subscribed by virtue of
the provisions of this act, shall remain pledged for the payment of the interest accruing on the stock created by reason
of such subscription, and for the redemption or reimbursement

of the principal of the same. It shall be the duty of the commissioners of the sinking fund to cause to be applied and paid, out of the said fund, yearly and every year, such sum and sums as may be annually wanted to discharge the interest accruing on the stock which may be created by virtue of this act. The said commissioners are hereby authorized to apply, from time to time, such sum and sums, out of the said fund, as they may think proper, towards redeeming, by purchase or by reimbursement, in conformity with the provisions of this act, the principal of the said stock. And such part of the annual sum of ten millions of dollars, vested by law in the said commissioners, as may be necessary and wanting for the above purposes, shall be and continue appriated [appropriated] to the payment of interest and redemption of the public debt, until the whole of the stock which may be created under the provisions of this act shall have been redeemed or reimbursed.

SEC. 5. *And be it further enacted,* That nothing in this act contained shall be construed in any wise to alter, abridge, or impair, the rights of those creditors of the United States who shall not subscribe to the loan to be opened by virtue of this act.

[Approved, April 20, 1822. 3 Statutes at Large, 663.]

1821-22, Chap. XLVII.—*An Act relating to treasury notes.*

Be it enacted, . . . That, from and after the passage of this act, no treasury note shall be received in payment on account of the United States, or paid, or funded, except at the treasury of the United States.

[Approved, May 3, 1822. 3 Statutes at Large, 675.]

1823-24, Chap. XVI.—*An Act authorizing the commissioners of the sinking fund to purchase the seven per cent. stock of the United States, in the year one thousand eight hundred and twenty-four.*

Be it enacted, . . . That the commissioners of the sinking fund be, and they are hereby, authorized to purchase, during the year one thousand eight hundred and twenty-four, any stock of the United States, bearing an interest of seven per centum per annum, not exceeding the sum of eight millions six hundred and ten thousand dollars, upon such terms as they may think proper, not exceeding the following rates above the principal sum purchased, that is to say:

For all such stock as they may purchase before the first day of April next, at a rate not exceeding two dollars for every sum of one hundred dollars, in addition to the interest which would have accrued on that day upon the said stock:

For all such stock which they may purchase between the first day of April and the first day of July next, at a rate not exceeding seventy-five cents on every sum of one hundred dollars, in addition to the interest which would have accrued on the day last mentioned:

For all such stock which they may purchase between the first day of July and the first day of October next, at a rate not exceeding, on every sum of one hundred dollars, the amount of interest which would have accrued on the day last mentioned: and

For all such stock which they may purchase between the first day of October next, and the first day of January, one thousand eight hundred and twenty-five, at a rate not exceeding the principal and the interest which shall have accrued at the day of purchase.

Sec. 2. *And be it further enacted*, That the said commissioners are hereby authorized to make such purchases, under the foregoing restrictions, at such times and places as they may deem most expedient, out of any moneys in the treasury, heretofore appropriated for the redemption of the public debt, or out of any money in the treasury not otherwise appropriated.

[Approved, January 22, 1824. 4 Statutes at Large, 4.]

1823–24, Chap. CXL. — *An act to authorize the creation of a stock to an amount not exceeding five millions of dollars, to provide for the awards of the commissioners under the treaty with Spain, of the twenty-second of February, one thousand eight hundred and nineteen.*

Be it enacted, . . . That, for the purpose of providing funds to discharge the awards of the commissioners under the treaty with Spain, of the twenty-second day of February, in the year of our Lord one thousand eight hundred and nineteen, the Secretary of the Treasury be, and he is hereby, authorized, with the approbation of the President of the United States, to cause to be issued and sold to the Bank of the United States, or others, at a sum not less than the par value thereof, certificates of stock of the United States, to any amount not exceeding the sum of five millions of dollars, and bearing an interest of not exceeding four and one half per centum per annum, from the period of the sale thereof; which stock, so created, shall be redeemable at the pleasure of the United States, at any time after the first day of January, in the year one thousand eight hundred and thirty-two. And, upon the sale of such stock, in manner aforesaid, credit or credits to the proprietors thereof, shall thereupon be entered and given on the books of the treasury, in like manner as for the present funded debt; which said credits or stock shall thereafter be transferable as other public stock of the United States.

[Section 2 provides for the award and application of the moneys thus borrowed.]

[Approved, May 24, 1824. 4 Statutes at Large, 33.]

1823–24, Chap. CXCII. — *An Act to authorize the Secretary of the Treasury to exchange a stock, bearing an interest of four and one-half per cent., for certain stocks bearing an interest of six per cent.*

Be it enacted, . . . That the President of the United States be, and he is hereby, empowered to borrow, on or before the first day of April next, on the credit of the United

States, a sum not exceeding five millions of dollars, at a rate of interest, payable quarter-yearly, not exceeding four and one-half per centum per annum, and reimbursable at the pleasure of the government, at any time after the thirty-first day of December, one thousand eight hundred and thirty-one, to be applied in addition to the moneys which may be in the treasury at the time of borrowing the same, to pay off and discharge such part of the six per cent. stock of the United States, of the year one thousand eight hundred and twelve, as may be redeemable after the first day of January next.

[Section 2 authorizes the Bank of the United States to lend the sum or any part thereof, and further authorizes the sale of certificates of the new stock : "*provided*, that no stock be sold under par."

Sections 3 and 4 provide that a subscription, to the amount of fifteen million dollars of the six per cent. stock of 1813 shall be opened on July 1, 1824, to continue open until October 1 following; and that for so much as shall be thus subscribed, the subscribers shall be entitled to an equal amount of stock, bearing interest at the rate of four and one-half per cent. and payable quarterly from September 30, 1824, and redeemable at the pleasure of the United States, one half after December 31, 1832, and one half after December 31, 1833: *provided* that no reimbursement shall be made of any new certificate except for its whole amount, nor until after six months' notice.

Sections 5 and 6 contain the same provisions for the sinking fund and for saving the rights of non-subscribing creditors as those contained in sections 4 and 5 of the Act of April 20, 1822, on page 102.]

[Approved, May 26, 1824.   4 Statutes at Large, 73.]

1824–25, Chap. C. — *An Act authorizing the Secretary of the Treasury to borrow a sum not exceeding twelve millions of dollars, or to exchange a stock of four and one-half per cent. for a certain stock bearing an interest of six per cent.*

Be it enacted. . . . That the President of the United States be, and he is hereby, authorized to borrow, on or before the first day of January next, on the credit of the United States, a sum not exceeding twelve millions of dollars, at a rate of interest payable quarterly, not exceeding four and one-half per centum per annum, six millions whereof reimbursable at the pleasure of the government, at any time after the thirty-first day of December, in the year eighteen hundred and twenty-eight; and six millions at any time after the thirty-first day of December, in the year eighteen hundred and twenty-nine, to be applied, in addition to the moneys which may be in the treasury at the time of borrowing the same, to pay off and discharge such part of the six per cent. stock of the United States, of the year one thousand eight hundred and thirteen, as may be redeemable after the first day of January next.

[Section 2 is identical with section 2 of the Act of May 26, 1824, *above.*

Sections 3 and 4 provide that a subscription to the amount of twelve million dollars of the six per cent. stock of 1813 shall be opened on April 1, 1825, to continue open until October 1 following, all thus subscribed to be considered as part of the twelve millions authorized by section 1; and that for so much as shall be thus subscribed, the subscribers shall be entitled to an equal amount of stock bearing interest not exceeding four and one half per cent. and payable quarterly from December 31, 1825, and redeemable at the pleasure of the United States, one half after December 31, 1828, and one half after December 31, 1829: *provided,* that no reimbursement shall be made of any new certificate except for its whole amount, nor until after six months' notice.

Sections 5 and 6 contain the same provisions for the sinking fund, and for saving the rights of non-subscribing creditors, as those contained in sections 4 and 5 of the Act of April 20, 1822, on page 102.]

[Approved, March 3, 1825. 4 Statutes at Large, 129.]

1829-30, Chap. LXXVIII. — *An Act to authorize the commissioners of the sinking fund to redeem the public debt of the United States.*

Be it enacted, . . . That whenever in the opinion of the Secretary of the Treasury, the state of the treasury will admit of the application of a greater sum than ten millions of dollars in any one year, to the payment of interest and charges, and to the reimbursement or purchase of the principal of the public debt, it shall be lawful for him, with the approbation of the President of the United States, to cause such surplus to be placed at the disposal of the commissioners of the sinking fund, and the same shall be applied by them to the reimbursement or purchase of the principal of the public debt, at such times as the state of the treasury will best admit.

SEC. 2. *And be it further enacted*, That, whenever, in any year, there shall be a surplus in the sinking fund beyond the amount of interest and principal of the debt which may be actually due and payable by the United States in such year, in conformity with their engagements, it shall be lawful for the commissioners of the sinking fund to apply such surplus to the purchase of any portion of the public debt, at such rates as, in their opinion, may be advantageous to the United States ; anything in any act of Congress to the contrary notwithstanding.

SEC. 3. *And be it further enacted*, That the fourth and fifth sections of the act, entitled " An act to provide for the redemption of the public debt," approved on the third of March, one thousand eight hundred and seventeen, are hereby repealed.

[Approved, April 24, 1830.   4 Statutes at Large, 396.]

1833–34, Chap. XCII. — *An Act making appropriations for the civil and diplomatic expenses of government for the year one thousand eight hundred and thirty-four.*

SEC. 3. *And be it further enacted*, That no payment of the money, appropriated by this act, or any other act passed at the present session of Congress, shall be made in the note or notes of any bank which shall not be at par value at the place where such payment may be made, provided that nothing herein contained shall be construed to make anything but gold and silver a tender in payment of any debt due from the United States to individuals.

[Approved, June 27, 1834.   4 Statutes at Large, 699.]

NOTE. — The above provision is repeated without change as section 4 of the appropriation act of March 3, 1835, 4 *ibid.*, 771.

1835–36, Chap. L. — *An Act to repeal so much of the act entitled "An act transferring the duties of Commissioner of Loans to the Bank of the United States, and abolishing the office of Commissioner of Loans," as requires the Bank of the United States to perform the duties of Commissioner of Loans for the several States.*

[Section 1 repeals the provisions of the act of March 3, 1817, which transfer the duties of commissioner of loans to the United States Bank, its branches and state banks employed by it, and requires the immediate transfer of all papers and records relating to said duties to the Secretary of the Treasury.]

SEC. 2. *And be it further enacted*, That the Bank of the United States and its several branches, and the State Banks employed by the Bank of the United States, performing the duties of Commissioners of Loans, shall be, and they are hereby required to pay into the Treasury of the United States, within three months after the passing of this act, all the money in their possession for the redemption of the public debt of the United States, and the interest thereon remaining in their hands, which has not been applied for by the person or persons entitled to receive the same.

SEC. 3. *And be it further enacted*, That it shall be the duty of the Secretary of the Treasury to pay over to the person or persons entitled to receive the same, the amount so received into the Treasury by virtue of the second section of this act, out of any money in the Treasury not otherwise appropriated.

SEC. 4. *And be it further enacted*, That nothing contained in this act shall be construed to authorize the appointment of a Commissioner or Commissioners of loans in any State, District, or Territory of the United States.

[Approved, April 11, 1836. 5 Statutes at Large, 8.]

NOTE. — By the Act of April 20, 1836, 5 Statutes at Large, 10, it is also provided that all acts and parts of acts enabling the Bank of the United States or its branches to pay pensions granted under the authority of the United States are repealed, and that payments of pensions shall be made by such persons and corporations as the Secretary of War may direct.

1835–36, Chap. LII. — *An Act making appropriations for the payment of the revolutionary and other pensioners of the United States, for the year one thousand eight hundred and thirty-six.*

SEC. 2. *And be it further enacted*, That hereafter, no bank note of less denomination than ten dollars, and that from and after the third day of March, anno Domini, eighteen hundred and thirty-seven, no bank note of less denomination than twenty dollars shall be offered in payment in any case whatsoever in which money is to be paid by the United States or the Post Office Department, nor shall any bank note, of any denomination, be so offered, unless the same shall be payable, and paid on demand, in gold or silver coin, at the place where issued, and which shall not be equivalent to specie at the place where offered, and convertible into gold or silver upon the spot, at the will of the holder, and without delay or loss to him ; *Provided*, That nothing herein contained shall be construed to make anything but gold or silver a legal tender by any individual, or by the United States.

[Approved, April 14, 1836. 5 Statutes at Large, 9.]

1835–36, Chap. XCVII. — *An Act repealing the fourteenth section of the "Act to incorporate the subscribers to the Bank of the United States," approved April tenth, eighteen hundred and sixteen.*

Be it enacted, . . . That the fourteenth section of the act entitled "An act to incorporate the subscribers to the Bank of the United States," approved April tenth, eighteen hundred and sixteen, shall be, and the same is hereby, repealed.

[Approved, June 15, 1836. 5 Statutes at Large, 48.]

1835–36, Chap. CXV. — *An Act to regulate the deposites of the public money.*

Be it enacted, . . . That it shall be the duty of the Secretary of the Treasury to select as soon as may be practicable and employ as the depositories of the money of the United

States, such of the banks incorporated by the several States, by Congress for the District of Columbia, or by the Legislative Councils of the respective Territories for those Territories, as may be located at, adjacent or convenient to the points or places at which the revenues may be collected, or disbursed, and in those States, Territories or Districts in which there are no banks, or in which no bank can be employed as a deposite bank, and within which the public collections or disbursements require a depository, the said Secretary may make arrangements with a bank or banks, in some other State, Territory or District, to establish an agency, or agencies, in the States, Territories or Districts so destitute of banks, as banks of deposite; and to receive through such agencies such deposites of the public money, as may be directed to be made at the points designated, and to make such disbursements as the public service may require at those points; the duties and liabilities of every bank thus establishing any such agency to be the same in respect to its agency, as are the duties and liabilities of deposite banks generally under the provisions of this act: *Provided*, That at least one such bank shall be selected in each State and Territory, if any can be found in each State and Territory willing to be employed as depositories of the public money, upon the terms and conditions hereinafter prescribed, and continue to conform thereto; and that the Secretary of the Treasury shall not suffer to remain in any deposite bank, an amount of the public moneys more than equal to three-fourths of the amount of its capital stock actually paid in, for a longer time than may be necessary to enable him to make the transfers required by the twelfth section of this act; and that the banks so selected, shall be, in his opinion, safe depositories of the public money, and shall be willing to undertake to do and perform the several duties and services, and to conform to the several conditions prescribed by this act.

[Under sections 2 and 3 it is provided that if at any place there is no bank in safe condition or having sufficient capital to become a depository of the moneys collected, or willing to act as such, the Secretary of the Treasury may order such moneys to be deposited in banks in the same State or in adjacent States; but nothing shall prevent Congress from ordering the removal of public money at any time, or from changing the terms of deposit, or prevent the banks from declining to act further as depositories, upon making tender of all public moneys on hand. And no bank shall be employed until it shall have given to the Secretary of the Treasury a statement of its condition and of the current price of its stock, a list of its directors, a copy of its charter, and the other information necessary to form a judgment of its safety.]

SEC. 4. *And be it further enacted,* That the said banks, before they shall be employed as the depositories of the public money, shall agree to receive the same, upon the following terms and conditions, to wit:

First. Each bank shall furnish to the Secretary of the Treasury, from time to time, as often as he may require, not exceeding once a week, statements setting forth its condition and business, as prescribed in the foregoing section of this act, except that such statements need not, unless requested by the said Secretary, contain a list of the directors, or a copy of the charter. And the said banks shall furnish to the Secretary of the Treasury, and to the Treasurer of the United States, a weekly statement of the condition of his account upon their books. And the Secretary of the Treasury shall have the right, by himself, or an agent appointed for that purpose, to inspect such general accounts in the books of the bank, as shall relate to the said statements: *Provided,* That this shall not be construed to imply a right of inspecting the account of any private individual or individuals with the bank.

Secondly. To credit as specie, all sums deposited therein to the credit of the Treasurer of the United States, and to pay all checks, warrants, or drafts, drawn on such deposites, in specie if required by the holder thereof.

Thirdly. To give, whenever required by the Secretary of the Treasury, the necessary facilities for transferring the public funds from place to place, within the United States, and the Territories thereof, and for distributing the same in payment of the public creditors, without charging commissions or claiming allowance on account of difference of exchange.

Fourthly. To render to the Government of the United States all the duties and services heretofore required by law to be performed by the late Bank of the United States and its several branches or offices.

SEC. 5. *And be it further enacted,* That no bank shall be selected or continued as a place of deposite of the public money which shall not redeem its notes and bills on demand in specie; nor shall any bank be selected or continued as aforesaid, which shall after the fourth of July, in the year one thousand eight hundred and thirty-six, issue or pay out any note or bill of a less denomination than five dollars; nor shall the notes or bills of any bank be received in payment of any debt due to the United States which shall, after the said fourth day of July, in the year one thousand eight hundred and thirty-six, issue any note or bill of a less denomination than five dollars.

[By sections 6 and 7 the Secretary of the Treasury is authorized, if necessary, to require from any bank collateral security for the safe keeping of public moneys deposited, and the due performance of duties required by this act, and to enter into contracts with the banks for the performance of such duties and services.

Section 8 provides that no bank employed as a place of deposit shall be discontinued as a depository, nor shall the public moneys be withdrawn from it, unless the bank shall fail to perform some duty, or refuse to pay its notes in specie, or fail to keep on hand such amount of specie as the Secretary of the Treasury deems necessary for its safety as a depository. In every such case it is made the duty of the Secretary to discontinue the bank as a depository, to withdraw from it all public moneys, and to report the facts immediately to Congress; and he is authorized to deposit the moneys withdrawn in other banks; or, in default of any bank to receive them, the moneys shall be kept by the Treasurer of the United States, subject to disbursement according to law.

Sections 9 and 10 provide that until the Secretary shall have employed banks as depositories under this act, the several State and District banks now employed shall continue to be depositories upon the same conditions as heretofore; and it is made his duty to lay before Congress at the beginning of every annual session a statement of the number and names of the banks employed, their condition, and the amount deposited in each; and whenever any bank is selected as depository, he is required to report its name and condition at once, if Congress is in session, and if not, then during the first week of the next session.]

8

SEC. 11. *And be it further enacted,* That whenever the amount of public deposites to the credit of the Treasurer of the United States, in any bank shall, for a whole quarter of a year, exceed the one-fourth part of the amount of the capital stock of such bank actually paid in, the banks shall allow and pay to the United States, for the use of the excess of the deposites over the one-fourth part of its capital, an interest at the rate of two per centum per annum, to be calculated for each quarter, upon the average excesses of the quarter; and it shall be the duty of the Secretary of the Treasury, at the close of each quarter, to cause the amounts on deposite in each deposite bank for the quarter, to be examined and ascertained, and to see that all sums of interest accruing under the provisions of this section, are, by the banks respectively passed to the credit of the Treasurer of the United States in his accounts with the respective banks.

SEC. 12. *And be it further enacted,* That all warrants or orders for the purpose of transferring the public funds from the banks in which they now are, or may hereafter be deposited, to other banks, whether of deposite or not, for the purpose of accommodating the banks to which the transfer may be made, or to sustain their credit, or for any other purpose whatever, except it be to facilitate the public disbursements, and to comply with the provisions of this act, be, and the same are hereby, prohibited and declared to be illegal; and in cases where transfers shall be required for purposes of equalization under the provisions of this act, in consequence of too great an accumulation of deposites in any bank, such transfers shall be made to the nearest deposite banks which are considered safe and secure, and which can receive the moneys to be transferred under the limitations in this act imposed.: *Provided,* That it may be lawful for the President of the United States to direct transfers of public money to be made from time to time to the mint and branch mints of the United States, for supplying metal for coining.

[The supplementary act of July 4, 1836, declares that nothing herein contained shall be construed to prevent the making of transfers from banks in one State or Territory to banks in another, whenever required in order to prevent inconvenient accumulations, or to produce a ,due equality and just proportion. 5 Statutes at Large, 115.]

SEC. 13. *And be it further enacted,* That the money which shall be in the Treasury of the United States, on the first day of January, eighteen hundred and thirty-seven, reserving the sum of five millions of dollars, shall be deposited with such of the several States, in proportion to their respective representation in the Senate and House of Representatives of the United States, as shall, by law, authorize their Treasurers, or other competent authorities to receive the same on the terms hereinafter specified ; and the Secretary of the Treasury shall deliver the same to such Treasurers, or other competent authorities, on receiving certificates of deposite therefor, signed by such competent authorities, in such form as may be prescribed by the Secretary aforesaid ; which certificates shall express the usual and legal obligations, and pledge the faith of the State, for the safe keeping and repayment thereof, and shall pledge the faith of the States receiving the same, to pay the said moneys, and every part thereof, from time to time, whenever the same shall be required, by the Secretary of the Treasury, for the purpose of defraying any wants of the public treasury, beyond the amount of the five millions aforesaid : *Provided,* That if any State declines to receive its proportion of the surplus aforesaid, on the terms before named, the same shall be deposited with the other States, agreeing to accept the same on deposite in the proportion aforesaid : *And provided further,* That when said money, or any part thereof, shall be wanted by the said Secretary, to meet appropriations by law, the same shall be called for, in rateable proportions, within one year, as nearly as conveniently may be, from the different States, with which the same is deposited, and shall not be called for, in sums exceeding ten thousand dollars, from any one State, in any one month, without previous notice of thirty days, for every additional sum of twenty thousand dollars, which may at any time be required.

SEC. 14. *And be it further enacted,* That the said deposites shall be made with the said States in the following proportions, and at the following times, to wit: one quarter part on the first day of January, eighteen hundred and thirty-seven, or as soon thereafter as may be; one quarter part on the first day of April, one quarter part on the first day of July, and one quarter part on the first day of October, all in the same year.

[Approved, June 23, 1836. 5 Statutes at Large, 52.]

NOTE. — By the Act of July 5, 1838, the operation of the last clause of section 5, prohibiting the receipt in payments to the United States of the notes of any bank which shall issue notes of less than five dollars after July 4, 1836, is suspended until October 1, 1838; but from said last mentioned date the notes of no bank shall be so received, which shall after that date issue, reissue, or pay out any note of less than five dollars. 5 Statutes at Large, 255.

1835–36, Chap. CXVI. — *An Act authorizing the Secretary of the Treasury to act as the agent of the United States in all matters relating to their stock in the Bank of the United States.*

[Sections 1, 2, and 3 make it the duty of the Secretary of the Treasury to act as agent for the United States "over property in the Bank of the United States, whether the same be standing on the books of the bank in the name of the United States, or of the Treasurer of the United States, for the use of the Secretary of the Navy, for the payment of navy pensions;" and gives the Secretary of the Treasury authority to vote at any meeting of stockholders, and to perform any other act as stockholder on behalf of the United States, and also to receive and deposit in the Treasury any dividends made of the capital or surplus profits of the bank. And the directors of the bank or any trustees thereof are required to furnish the Secretary of the Treasury, as often as he may require, with statements of the capital stock of the corporation undivided, of its debts due beyond the same, of moneys on deposit, of notes outstanding, and of specie on hand; and it is declared that the Secretary shall have the same right as any stockholder to examine all accounts of the bank relating to such statements.]

SEC. 4. *And be it further enacted,* That the Secretary of the Treasury shall be, and he hereby is, authorized and empowered to receive the capital stock belonging to the United States, in the late Bank of the United States, in such instalments, and payable at such times, and with such rates of interest, as he shall see fit to agree to; and also, to settle and adjust the claim for surplus profits, accruing on said capital stock, on such terms as he may think proper, and in like manner to receive the amount thereof in such instalments, and payable at such times, and with such rates of interest, as he may agree to.

[Approved, June 23, 1836.   5 Statutes at Large, 66.]

1835–36, Chap. CCCLIII. — *An Act in addition to the act entitled "An act making appropriations, in part, for the support of Government, for the year eighteen hundred and thirty-six, and for other purposes."*

SEC. 10. *And be it further enacted,* . . . That the duties and powers of the commissioners of the sinking fund are hereby suspended until revived by law, and that the records of the commissioners be transferred to the custody of the Secretary of the Treasury, who is hereby authorized and directed to pay out of any money in the Treasury not otherwise appropriated any outstanding debts of the United States and the interest thereon.

[Approved, July 4, 1836.   5 Statutes at Large, 115.]

1836–37, Resolution No. 5. — *A Resolution authorizing the Secretary of the Treasury to receive from the Bank of the United States, under the Pennsylvania charter, payment for the stock of the United States, in the late Bank of the United States.*

Resolved by the Senate and House of Representatives, . . . That the Secretary of the Treasury be directed to accept the terms of settlement proposed by the President and Directors of the Bank of the United States, under the Pennsylvania charter, in their memorial to Congress, presented at the present session, for the payment to the United States of the capital stock owned by them in the late Bank of the United States, and the final adjustment and settlement of the claims connected with, or arising out of the same ; and to take such obligation for the payment of the several instalments in said proposed terms of settlement mentioned, as he may think proper: *Provided*, That nothing herein contained shall prejudice or affect in any way the question, between the General Government of the United States, and the late Bank of the United States, respecting the claim for damages on account of the protest of the bill of exchange, drawn on the French Government.

[Approved, March 3, 1837.   5 Statutes at Large, 200.]

1837, Chap. I. — *An Act to postpone the fourth instalment of deposites with the State.*

Be it enacted, . . . That the transfer of the fourth instalment of deposites directed to be made with the States, under the thirteenth section of the act of June twenty-third, eighteen hundred and thirty-six, be and the same is hereby postponed till the first day of January, one thousand eight hundred and thirty-nine; *Provided*, That the three first instalments under the said act shall remain on deposite with the States, until otherwise directed by Congress.

[Approved, October 2, 1837.   5 Statutes at Large, 201.]

1837, Chap. II. — *An Act to authorize the issuing of Treasury Notes.*

Be it enacted, . . . That the President of the United States is hereby authorized to cause Treasury notes for such sum or sums as the exigencies of the Government may require, but not exceeding, in the whole amount of notes issued, the sum of ten millions of dollars, and of denominations not less than fifty dollars for any one note, to be prepared, signed, and issued in the manner hereinafter provided.

SEC. 2. *And be it further enacted*, That the said Treasury notes, authorized to be issued by the first section of this act, shall be reimbursed and redeemed by the United States, at the Treasury thereof, after the expiration of one year from the dates of the said notes respectively; from which said dates, for the term of one year, and no longer, they shall bear such interest as shall be expressed upon the face of the said notes; which rate of interest upon each several issue of the said notes shall be fixed by the Secretary of the Treasury, by and with the advice and approbation of the President; but shall in no case exceed the rate of interest of six per centum per annum. The reimbursement herein provided for shall be made at the Treasury of the United States to the holders of the said notes respectively, upon presentment, and shall include the principal of each note, and the interest which may be due thereon at the time of payment. For this reimbursement, at the time and times herein specified, the faith of the United States is hereby solemnly pledged.

[Section 3 provides that the said Treasury notes shall be signed by the Treasurer and countersigned by the Register of the Treasury, and that those officers shall keep separate accounts thereof, as checks upon each other.]

SEC. 4. *And be it further enacted,* That the Secretary of the Treasury is hereby authorized, with the approbation of the President of the United States, to cause to be issued such portion of the said Treasury notes as the President may think expedient, in payment of debts due by the United States to such public creditors or other persons as may choose to receive such notes in payment, as aforesaid, at par. And the Secretary of the Treasury is further authorized, with the approbation of the President of the United States, to borrow, from time to time, not under par, such sums as the President may think expedient, on the credit of such notes.

SEC. 5. *And be it further enacted,* That the said Treasury notes shall be transferable by delivery and assignment endorsed thereon, by the person to whose order the same shall, on the face thereof, have been made payable.

SEC. 6. *And be it further enacted,* That the said Treasury notes shall be received in payment of all duties and taxes laid by the authority of the United States, of all public lands sold by the said authority, and of all debts to the United States, of any character whatsoever, which may be due and payable at the time when said Treasury notes may be so offered in payment. And on every such payment, credit shall be given for the amount of the principal and interest which, on the day of such payment, may be due on the note or notes thus given in payment.

[Section 7 provides for the accounts to be kept by collectors and other receivers of the public moneys, of treasury notes received by them, and for the charging and crediting of accrued interest on such notes when paid out by them.]

SEC. 8. *And be it further enacted*, That the Secretary of the Treasury be, and he is hereby, authorized and directed to cause to be reimbursed and paid the principal and interest of the Treasury notes which may be issued by virtue of this act, at the several time and times when the same, according to the provisions of this act, should be thus reimbursed and paid. And the said Secretary is further authorized to make purchases of the said notes, at par, for the amount of the principal and interest due at the time of purchase on such notes. And so much of any unappropriated money in the Treasury as may be necessary for that purpose, is hereby appropriated, for paying the principal and interest of said notes.

[Sections 9-11 provide for the expenses of the issue and for the punishment of counterfeiting and of the like offences.

Section 12 authorizes the Secretary of the Treasury to make rules as to the safe-keeping, return and cancelling of notes received by any officers for the United States,] —

Provided, That nothing herein contained shall be so construed as to authorize the Secretary of the Treasury to reissue any of said notes, but upon the return of the said notes or any of them to the Treasury, the same shall be cancelled.

SEC. 13. *And be it further enacted*, That it shall be, and hereby is, made the duty of the Secretary of the Treasury to cause a statement to be published monthly, of the amount of all Treasury notes issued or redeemed, in pursuance of the provisions of this act; and that the power to issue Treasury notes conferred on the President of the United States by this act, shall cease and determine on the thirty-first day of December, eighteen hundred and thirty-eight.

[Approved, October 12, 1837. 5 Statutes at Large, 201.]

1837, Chap. IX. — *An Act for adjusting the remaining claims upon the late deposite banks.*

Be it enacted, . . . That the Secretary of the Treasury be, and he is hereby, authorized to continue to withdraw the public moneys now remaining in any of the former deposite banks, in a manner as gradual and convenient to the institutions as shall be consistent with the pecuniary wants of the Government, and the safety of the funds thus to be drawn; and that no further interest than that required by the deposite act of the twenty-third of June, one thousand eight hundred and thirty-six, under which those deposites were made, shall be demanded of any bank which has met, and shall hereafter meet the requisitions of the Department. This provision shall also extend to such public moneys as may remain in any of the said banks, whether standing to the credit of the Treasurer of the United States, or of any disbursing or other public officer of the Government.

Sec. 2. *And be it further enacted,* That in case of neglect or refusal by any of the said banks to comply with the requisitions of the Secretary of the Treasury, as he shall make them, in conformity with the first section of this act, suits shall be instituted, where that has not already been done, to recover the amounts due to the United States, unless the defaulting bank shall forthwith cause to be executed and delivered to the Secretary of the Treasury a bond, with security to be approved by the Solicitor of the Treasury, to pay to the United States the whole moneys due from it, in three instalments: the first to be paid on the first day of July next, the second on the first day of January, eighteen hundred and thirty-nine, and the remaining instalment on the first day of July, eighteen hundred and thirty-nine; and the default mentioned in this act, on which interest is to commence at the rate of six per [centum per annum,] shall be understood to be the neglect or omission of said banks, or any of them, to answer the drafts or requisitions of the Secretary of the Treasury made on them according to the provisions of the first section of this act; and interest thereon at the rate of six per centum per annum, from the time of default, together with any damages which may have accrued to the United States from protests of drafts drawn upon it, or from any other consequence of its failure to fulfil its obligations to the public treasury.

[Approved, October 16, 1837. 5 Statutes at Large, 206.]

1837, Chap. X. — *An Act making further appropriations for the year eighteen hundred and thirty-seven.*

Sec. 3. *And be it further enacted,* That the Secretary of the Treasury be, and he is hereby authorized, to arrange and settle any of the outstanding transfer drafts given to transfer moneys to the States under the act of twenty-third of June, 1836, and which have not been paid by the depositories upon which they were drawn, or otherwise arranged and settled by the United States, by receiving such drafts at par in payment of any debts due to the United States, without any allowance of interest for the time the drafts have been outstanding and unpaid, or any other allowance for interest or damages of any description.

[Approved, October 16, 1837. 5 Statutes at Large, 207.]

1837-38, Chap. LXXXII. — *An Act to authorize the issuing of Treasury notes to meet the current expenses of the Government.*

Be it enacted, . . . That the Secretary of the Treasury, with the approbation of the President of the United States, is hereby authorized to cause Treasury notes to be issued, according to the provisions of, and subject to, all the conditions, limitations, and restrictions contained in an act entitled "An act to authorize the issuing of Treasury notes," approved the Twelfth day of October last, in place of such notes as have been, or may be, issued under the authority of the act aforesaid, and which have been, or may hereafter be, paid into the Treasury and cancelled.

[Approved, May 21, 1838. 5 Statutes at Large, 228.]

1837-8, Resolution No. 4. — *A Resolution relating to the public revenue and dues to the Government.*

Resolved by the Senate and House of Representatives, . . . That it shall not be lawful for the Secretary of the Treasury to make or to continue in force, any general order, which shall create any difference between the different branches of revenue, as to the money or medium of payment, in which debts or dues, accruing to the United States, may be paid.

[Approved, May 31, 1838. 5 Statutes at Large, 810.]

1837-38, Chap. CLXXXIV. — *An Act to authorize the sale of certain bonds belonging to the United States.*

Be it enacted, . . . That the Secretary of the Treasury be, and he is hereby, authorized to sell upon the best terms he can command for money in hand in the markets of this or of any foreign country, as upon inquiry he shall find most for the interest of the United States, the two bonds held by the United States against " the president, directors, and company of the Bank of the United States," chartered by the State of Pennsylvania, which will fall due in the month of September, in the year one thousand eight hundred and thirty-nine, and one thousand eight hundred and forty, being the two last of four several bonds, dated on the tenth day of May, one thousand eight hundred and thirty-seven, given to secure the payment of the sum of one million nine hundred and eighty-six thousand, five hundred and eighty-nine dollars and four cents each, with interest upon each bond, at the rate of six per centum per annum, from the third day of March, one thousand eight hundred and thirty-six until paid, the said four bonds having been received by the United States as security for the final payment of the stock held by the United States, in the late Bank of the United States, chartered by Congress, and to execute under his hand and the seal of his office, to the purchaser or purchasers of the said bonds, suitable and proper assignments to transfer to the said purchaser or purchasers, his, her, or their representatives, or assigns, all the right, title and interest of the United States, of, in, and to the money due and to become due upon the bonds sold and assigned in pursuance of this act: *Provided,* That no sale of either of the said bonds shall be made upon terms less favorable to the United States than the par value of the bond sold, at the time of sale, calculated according to the rules for estimating the par value of securities upon which interest has run for a time, but which securities have not reached maturity.

SEC. 2. *And be it further enacted*, That all money received upon the sale of the said bonds, shall be immediately paid into the Treasury of the United States, or placed to the credit of the Treasurer thereof in some proper depository, in the same manner that other moneys, received for dues to the Government, are by law directed to be paid into the Treasury.

[Approved, July 7, 1838. 5 Statutes at Large, 296.]

1837–38, Chap. CLXXXV. — *An Act to prevent the issuing and circulation of the bills, notes and other securities of corporations created by acts of Congress which have expired.*

[Section 1 makes it a high misdemeanor for any director, agent, or trustee of any corporation created by act of Congress, the charter whereof has expired, to reissue or knowingly put in circulation any bill, note, check, draft, or other security of such expired corporation; and section 2 gives to the circuit courts of the United States jurisdiction, on bill or petition, to restrain the issue or transfer of such bills, notes, and other securities when in the possession or control of any director, agent, or trustee of such expired corporation, and to cause such of said bills, notes, and securities as have been redeemed to be delivered up and cancelled.]

[Approved, July 7, 1838. 5 Statutes at Large, 297.]

1838–39, Chap. XXXVII. — *An Act to revise and extend "An act to authorize the issuing of Treasury notes to meet the current expenses of the Government," approved the twenty-first of May, eighteen hundred and thirty-eight.*

Be it enacted, . . . That the Secretary of the Treasury, with the approbation of the President of the United States, is hereby authorized to cause to be issued the remainder of the Treasury notes authorized to be issued by the "act to authorize the issuing of Treasury notes to meet the current expenses of the Government," approved the twenty-first day of May, eighteen hundred and thirty-eight, according to the provisions of said act, at any time prior to the thirtieth

day of June next, any limitation in the act aforesaid or in
the act " to authorize the issuing of Treasury notes," approved the twelfth day of October, eighteen hundred and
thirty-seven, to the contrary notwithstanding.

[Approved, March 2, 1839. 5 Statutes at Large, 323.]

1839–40, Chap. V. — An Act additional to the act on the subject of Treasury Notes.

Be it enacted, . . . That the regulations and provisions
contained in the act passed the twelfth day of October, in
the year one thousand eight hundred and thirty-seven, entitled " An act to authorize the issuing of Treasury Notes,"
and in the subsequent acts in addition thereto, be, and the
same are hereby, renewed, and made in full force, excepting
the limitations concerning the times within which such notes
may be issued, and restricting the amount thereof as hereafter provided.

SEC. 2. *And be it further enacted*, That under the regulations and provisions contained in said act, Treasury Notes
may be issued in lieu of others hereafter or heretofore redeemed, but not to exceed in the amount of notes outstanding at any one time, the aggregate of five millions of dollars;
and to be redeemed sooner than one year, if the means of the
Treasury will permit, by giving notice sixty days of those
notes which the Department is ready to redeem; no interest to be allowed thereon after the expiration of said sixty
days.

SEC. 3. *And be it further enacted*, That this act shall
continue in force for one year and no longer.

[Approved, March 31, 1840. 5 Statutes at Large, 370.]

1839–40, Chap. XLI. — An Act to provide for the collection, safe-keeping, transfer, and disbursement of the public revenue.

Be it enacted, . . . That there shall be prepared and
provided, within the new Treasury building now erecting at
the seat of Government, suitable and convenient rooms for

the use of the Treasurer of the United States, his assistants
and clerks: and sufficient and secure fire-proof vaults and
safes for the keeping of the public moneys in the possession
and under the immediate control of the said Treasurer;
which said rooms, vaults, and safes, are hereby constituted
and declared to be, the Treasury of the United States. And
the said Treasurer of the United States shall keep all the
public moneys which shall come to his hands in the Treasury
of the United States, as hereby constituted, until the same
are drawn therefrom according to law.

[Section 2 provides that the Mint at Philadelphia and the Branch Mint
at New Orleans, and the vaults and safes thereof, shall be places of deposit, and that the Treasurers of the said Mint and Branch Mint, respectively, shall have custody of all public moneys deposited therein and
perform all the duties prescribed by this act relating to such moneys.

Sections 3 and 4 require that in the custom-houses of New York and
Boston, and at the cities of Charleston and St. Louis, suitable rooms
and sufficient and secure fire-proof vaults and safes shall be prepared,
for the use of the Receivers General of public money, who shall have the
custody of all public moneys deposited therein and shall perform all the
duties prescribed by this act relating to such moneys.]

SEC. 5. *And be it further enacted*, That the President
shall nominate, and by and with the advice and consent of
the Senate, appoint four officers, to be denominated "receivers-general of public money," which said officers shall
hold their respective offices for the term of four years, unless
sooner removed therefrom; one of which shall be located at
the city of New York, in the State of New York; one other
of which shall be located at the city of Boston, in the State
of Massachusetts; one other of which shall be located at the
city of Charleston, in the State of South Carolina; and the
remaining one of which shall be located at the city of St.
Louis, in the State of Missouri; and all of which said officers shall give bonds to the United States, with sureties
according to the provisions hereinafter contained, for the
faithful discharge of the duties of their respective offices.

SEC. 6. *And be it further enacted*, That the Treasurer
of the United States, the treasurer of the Mint of the United
States, the treasurers, and those acting as such, of the various

Branch Mints, all collectors of the customs, all surveyors of the customs acting also as collectors, all receivers-general of public moneys, all receivers of public moneys at the several land offices, and all post-masters, except as is hereinafter particularly provided, be, and they are hereby, required to keep safely, without loaning or using, all the public money collected by them, or otherwise at any time placed in their possession and custody, till the same is ordered by the proper department or officer of the Government to be transferred or paid out; and when such orders for transfer or payment are received, faithfully and promptly to make the same as directed, and to do and perform all other duties as fiscal agents of the Government, which may be imposed by this or any other acts of Congress, or by any regulation of the Treasury Department, made in conformity to law; and also to do and perform all acts and duties required by law, or by direction of any of the Executive Departments of the Government, as agents for paying pensions, or for making any other disbursements which either of the heads of those departments may be required by law to make, and which are of a character to be made by the depositaries hereby constituted, consistently with the other official duties imposed upon them.

[Sections 7 and 8 provide for the official bonds to be given by the Treasurer of the United States, the Treasurer of the Mint, the Treasurer of the Branch Mint at New Orleans, the Receivers General and other depositaries, and for the renewal and increase of their bonds as occasion may require.

By sections 9, 10, and 11, it is required that all collectors and receivers of public moneys shall, as often as may be directed, pay over the moneys collected by them, those in the District of Columbia to the Treasurer of the United States, those in Philadelphia and New Orleans to the Treasurers of the Mints respectively, and those in New York, Boston, Charleston, and St. Louis to the Receivers General in their respective cities, and it is made the duty of the Secretary of the Treasury and Postmaster General to direct such payments to be made as often as once in every week. Provision is made for the transfer of money from one depositary to any other, at the direction of the Secretary of the Treasury, and for the like transfer of moneys belonging to the Post Office Department by the Postmaster General; and every depositary is required to keep his account of money belonging to that Department separate from his account of other public moneys. And all moneys in the hands of any depositary are to be considered as deposited to the credit of the Treasurer of the United States and to be, at all times, subject to his draft.

By sections 12 and 13, provision is made for the examination of the accounts and money on hand of the several depositaries by special agents appointed for that purpose, and further for a like examination, at least once in every quarter, by public officers who are required to act as a check upon all receivers, collectors, treasurers, and persons acting as such.]

SEC. 15. *And be it further enacted*, That the Secretary of the Treasury shall, with as much promptitude as the convenience of the public business, and the safety of the public funds will permit, withdraw the balances remaining with the present depositaries of the public moneys, and confine the safe-keeping, transfer, and disbursement of those moneys to the depositaries established by this act.

[By sections 17 all officers entrusted with public moneys, except those connected with the Post Office Department, are required to keep an accurate account of all receipts and payments, showing the kind of currency received or paid; and it is declared to be embezzlement and felony for any such officer or for any officer of the Post Office Department to convert to his own use, or to use by investment, or to loan any portion of the public moneys entrusted to him.]

SEC. 19. *And be it further enacted*, That from and after the thirtieth day of June, which will be in the year one thousand eight hundred and forty, the resolution of Congress of the thirtieth day of April, in the year one thousand eight hundred and sixteen, so far as it authorizes the receipt in payment of duties, taxes, sales of public lands, debts and sums of money, accruing or becoming payable to the United States, to be collected and paid in the notes of specie-paying banks, shall be so modified as that one fourth part of all such duties, taxes, sales of public lands, debts, and sums of money accruing or becoming due to the United States, shall be collected in the legal currency of the United States; and from and after the thirtieth day of June, which will be in the year one thousand eight hundred and forty-one, one other fourth part of all such duties, taxes, sales of public lands, debts, and sums of money, shall be so collected; and that from and after the thirtieth day of June, which will be in the year one thousand eight hundred and forty-two, one other fourth part of all such duties, taxes, sales of public lands, debts and sums of money, shall be so collected; and from and after the thirtieth day of June, which will be in the year one thousand eight hundred and forty-three, the remaining fourth part of the said duties, taxes, sales of public lands, debts, and sums of money, shall be also collected in the legal currency of the United States; and from and after the last mentioned day, all sums accruing, or becoming payable to the United States, for duties, taxes, sales of public lands, or other debts, and also all sums due for postages, or otherwise, to the General Post Office Department, shall be paid in gold and silver only.

Sec. 20. *And be it further enacted*, That from and after the thirtieth day of June, which will be in the year one thousand eight hundred and forty-three, every officer or agent engaged in making disbursements on account of the United States, or of the General Post Office, shall make all payments in gold and silver coin only; and any receiving or disbursing officer, or agent, who shall neglect, evade, or violate, the provisions of this and the last preceding section of this act, shall, by the Secretary of the Treasury, be immediately reported to the President of the United States, with the facts of such neglect, evasion, or violation, and also to Congress, if in session, and, if not in session, at the commencement of its session next after the violation takes place.

[Section 21 forbids any disbursing officer to make any exchange of funds other than an exchange for gold and silver, and requires every such officer to make his payments in the currency furnished him when legally receivable under the provisions of this act, "unless . . . he can exchange the means in his hands for gold and silver at par, and so as to facilitate his payments, or otherwise accommodate the public service and promote the circulation of a metallic currency."]

Sec. 22. *And be it further enacted*, That it shall not be lawful for the Secretary of the Treasury to make or continue in force, any general order, which shall create any difference

9

between the different branches of revenue, as to the funds or
medium of payment, in which debts or dues accruing to the
United States may be paid.

[Sections 23 and 25 make it the duty of the Secretary of the Treasury
to make regulations prescribing the time within which drafts on the depositaries shall be presented for payment, but require him "to guard,
as far as may be, against those drafts being used or thrown into circulation, as a paper currency, or medium of exchange." The Treasurer of
the United States, however, is authorized to receive payments for public
lands in advance, and to give therefor his receipts, which shall be receivable for public lands in the same manner as the currency authorized by
law, *provided*, that such receipts shall not be negotiable or transferable
by delivery or assignment, but shall be in all cases presented in payment
by or for the person named therein.]

[Approved, July 4, 1840. 5 Statutes at Large, 385.]

1840–41, Chap. V. — *An Act to authorize the issuing of
Treasury Notes.*

Be it enacted, . . . That the President of the United.
States is hereby authorized to cause Treasury notes to be
issued for such sum or sums as the exigencies of the Government may require ; but not exceeding the sum of five
millions of dollars of this emission, outstanding at any one
time, to be reimbursed in the last quarters of the year, if the
condition of the Treasury will permit it, and to be issued
under the limitations and other provisions, contained in the
act, entitled "An act to authorize the issuing of Treasury
notes," approved the twelfth day of October, one thousand
eight hundred and thirty-seven, and as modified by an act,
entitled "An act additional to the act on the subject of
Treasury notes," approved the thirty-first day of March,
one thousand eight hundred and forty, except that this law
shall expire in one year from and after its passage : *Provided*, That in case the Treasury notes outstanding and unredeemed, issued under former laws of Congress, added to
the amount of such notes issued under this act, and actually
expended or issued to meet payments due and payable before the fourth day of March next, shall, on the fourth day
of March, next, exceed the sum of five millions of dollars,

then the President of the United States shall be, and he is hereby, authorized to issue, by virtue of the provisions of this act, such further amount of the said notes as will make the whole amount issued under this act, and applicable to payments falling due after the third day of March next, the full sum of five millions of dollars.

[Approved, February 15, 1841.   5 Statutes at Large, 411.]

1841, Chap. III. — *An Act authorizing a loan not exceeding the sum of twelve millions of dollars.*

Be it enacted, . . . That the President of the United States is hereby authorized, at any time within one year from the passage of this act, to borrow, on the credit of the United States, a sum not exceeding twelve millions of dollars, or so much thereof as in his opinion the exigencies of the Government may require, at a rate of interest, payable quarterly or semi-annually, not exceeding six per centum per annum, which loan shall be made reimbursable either at the will of the Secretary of the Treasury, after six months' notice, or at any time after three years from the first day of January next; and said money so borrowed shall be applied, in addition to the money now in the Treasury, or which may be received therein from other sources, to the payment and redemption of the Treasury notes heretofore authorized, which are or may be outstanding and unpaid, and to defray any of the public expenses which have been heretofore or which may be authorized by law, which stock shall be transferable only on the books of the Treasury.

[Sections 2 and 3 authorize the preparation and sale of certificates of the stock, "*provided,* That no stock be sold below par," and the employment of agents for the negotiation of the same, with a commission not exceeding one-tenth of one per cent. on the amount so negotiated.]

SEC. 4. *And be it further enacted,* That the Secretary of the Treasury is hereby authorized to purchase, at any time before the period herein limited for the redemption of stock hereby authorized, such portion thereof as the funds of the Government may admit of, after meeting all the demands on the Treasury, and any surplus in the Treasury is hereby appropriated to that object.

SEC. 5. *And be it further enacted*, That the faith of the United States be, and is hereby, pledged for the punctual payment of the interest and redemption of said stock.

[Approved, July 21, 1841. 5 Statutes at Large, 438.]

1841, Chap. VII. — *An Act to repeal the act entitled "An act to provide for the collection, safe-keeping, transfer and disbursement of the public revenue," and to provide for the punishment of embezzlers of public money, and for other purposes.*

Be it enacted, . . . That the act entitled "An act to provide for the collection, safe-keeping, transfer and disbursement of the public revenue," approved on the fourth day of July, A. D., one thousand eight hundred and forty, be, and the same is hereby, repealed : *Provided, always,*

[That offenders against section 17 of the repealed act may be prosecuted, and that all liabilities arising upon bonds or otherwise under the said act shall remain unimpaired.

Section 2 makes it felony for any officer entrusted with public moneys, or connected with the Post Office Department, to convert to his own use, or to use by investment, or to loan any portion of the public moneys entrusted to him, and the neglect to pay over or transfer such moneys on legal requirement is declared to be prima facie evidence of conversion.]

SEC. 3. *And be it further enacted*, That the act entitled "An act to regulate the deposits of the public money," approved on the twenty-third day of June, eighteen hundred and thirty-six, excepting the thirteenth and fourteenth sections thereof, be and the same hereby is repealed.

[Section 4 repeals so much of the act of April 14, 1836, as forbids the offer of bank notes of less denomination than ten dollars, and after March 3, 1837, of less than twenty dollars, in payments by the United States or the Post Office Department. See page 11Q.]

[Approved, August 13, 1841. 5 Statutes at Large, 439.]

1841–42, Chap. II. — *An Act to authorize an issue of Treasury notes.*

Be it enacted, . . . That the President of the United States is hereby authorized to cause Treasury notes to be issued for

such sum or sums as the exigencies of the Government may
require, and in place of such of the same as may be redeemed
to cause others to be issued, but not exceeding the sum of
five millions of dollars of this emission outstanding at any one
time, and to be issued under the limitations and other provisions contained in the act entitled "An act to authorize the
issuing of Treasury notes," approved the twelfth of October,
one thousand eight hundred and thirty-seven, except that the
authority hereby given to issue Treasury notes shall expire at
the end of one year from the passage of this act.

[Approved, January 31, 1842. 5 Statutes at Large, 469.]

1841-42, Chap. XXVI. — *An Act for the extension of the
loan of eighteen hundred and forty-one, and for an addition of five millions of dollars thereto; and for allowing interest on Treasury notes due.*

Be it enacted, . . . That the time limited by the first section of the act of Congress, entitled "An act authorizing a
loan not exceeding the sum of twelve millions of dollars," approved July twenty-first, eighteen hundred and forty-one, for
obtaining said loan, shall be, and the same is hereby, extended
for one year from the passage of this act.

SEC. 2. *And be it further enacted,* That so much of said
loan as may be obtained after the passage of this act shall be
made reimbursable, as shall be agreed upon and determined
at the time of issuing said stock, either at the will of the Secretary of the Treasury, after six months' notice, or at any
time not exceeding twenty years from the first day of January
next.

SEC. 3. *And be it further enacted,* That the certificates
hereafter to be issued for said loan may, when required, be in
such form as shall be prescribed by the Secretary of the
Treasury, so that the stock may be transferable by delivery
of the certificate, instead of being assignable on the books of
the Treasury.

SEC. 4. *And be it further enacted,* That the Secretary of
the Treasury be, and he hereby is, authorized to dispose of

the stock hereafter to be issued, or any part thereof, at its par value, but no part thereof shall be disposed of under par until the same has been advertised a reasonable time, and proposals for subscription to said loan invited.   And the said Secretary is hereby authorized to accept such proposals, if he deem it for the interest of the United States so to do, as shall offer the highest price for said stock or any part thereof; or to appoint an agent or agents as provided in the third section of the act, approved July twenty-first, eighteen hundred and forty-one, before recited, to negotiate the same: *Provided*, That no stocks shall be disposed of at a lower rate than the highest price offered in said proposals.

SEC. 5. *And be it further enacted*, That the moneys arising from duties on goods, wares, and merchandise, which may be imported into the United States, or so much thereof as shall be equal to the payment, from time to time, of the interest, and to the ultimate redemption of the principal of the said stock, be, and the same are hereby, pledged for the payment and redemption of the stock hereafter to be issued under and by virtue of this act and the said act of July twenty-first, eighteen hundred and forty-one, hereby amended; and so much thereof as may be necessary to pay the interest on said stock, and redeem the same when due, is hereby appropriated to that object, to be first applied by the Secretary of the Treasury to such payments and redemption.

SEC. 6. *And be it further enacted*, That it shall be the duty of the Secretary of the Treasury to report to Congress, at the commencement of the next session, the amount of money borrowed under this act and the act hereby amended, and of whom and upon what terms it shall have been obtained, with an abstract or brief statement of all the proposals submitted for the same, distinguishing between those accepted and those rejected; and a detailed statement of the expense of making such loans.

. SEC. 7. *And be it further enacted*, That all the provisions of the said act, not hereby modified or changed, shall be and remain in force, and apply to this act.

SEC. 8. *And be it further enacted*, That the President of

the United States is hereby authorized to borrow an additional sum, not exceeding the sum of five millions of dollars, if, in his opinion, the exigencies of the Government may require the same; which additional loan shall be made within the time and according to the provisions of said act, as modified by this.

SEC. 9. *And be it further enacted,* That all Treasury notes heretofore issued under the act entitled "An act to authorize the issuing of Treasury notes," approved the twelfth day of October, eighteen hundred and thirty-seven, and the acts subsequent thereto, and now outstanding and unredeemed, or which may hereafter be issued under and by virtue of the same, shall, if due and unpaid before the fifth day of March, eighteen hundred and forty-two, bear interest at the rate of six per cent. per annum from that day; and when they may become due hereafter, or may have become due since the said fifth day of March, eighteen hundred and forty-two, shall bear interest from the day of their so becoming due, at the rate of six per cent. per annum, until they shall be respectively redeemed: *Provided,* That such interest shall cease at the expiration of sixty days' notice, to be given at any time, by the Secretary of the Treasury in one or more of the principal papers published at the seat of Government, of a readiness to redeem the same. And the said interest shall be payable semi-annually at the Treasury of the United States, on the first days of January and July in every year.

[Approved, April 15, 1842. 5 Statutes at Large, 473.]

1841-42, Chap. CCLXXXVII. — *An Act to limit the sale of the public stock to par, and to authorize the issue of Treasury notes, in lieu thereof, to a certain amount.*

[Section 1 provides that no stock authorized under the Act of July 21, 1841, and the amendatory Act of April 15, 1842, shall hereafter be sold below par; and the Secretary of the Treasury is authorized to issue treasury notes in lieu of so much thereof as cannot be negotiated at or above par, to an amount not exceeding six millions of dollars.]

SEC. 2. *And be it further enacted,* That the Treasury notes authorized to be issued by virtue of this act shall not be issued after the time limited by said last mentioned act, being the fifteenth day of April, eighteen hundred and forty-three, for making said loan, and they shall be issued under the provisions and limitations contained in the act entitled "An act to authorize the issuing of Treasury notes," approved the twelfth day of October, eighteen hundred and thirty-seven, and as modified by the act entitled "An act additional to the act on the subject of Treasury notes," approved March thirty-first, eighteen hundred and forty : *Provided*, That the notes authorized to be issued by virtue of this act may, when redeemed, be reissued, or new notes issued in lieu of such as may be redeemed within the time above prescribed for issuing the same, provided that not more than six millions in amount shall be outstanding at any one time under the authority of this act.

SEC. 3. *And be it further enacted*, That nothing in the act contained, entitled an act authorizing the loan, above referred to, and an act amendatory of the same, shall be so construed as to authorize the issue of certificates of stock, for debts now due or to become due by the United States, for any other purpose than a bona fide loan to the Government according to the original intention of that law, and that no certificate for any loan shall be issued for a less sum than one hundred dollars.

[Approved, August 31, 1842.   5 Statutes at Large, 581.]

1842–43, Chap. LXXXI. — *An Act authorizing the reissue of treasury notes and for other purposes.*

Be it enacted, . . . That when any outstanding treasury notes, issued in pursuance of the act of thirty-first August, one thousand eight hundred and forty-two, entitled "An act to limit the sale of public stock to par, and to authorize the issue of treasury notes, in lieu thereof, to a certain amount," or any previous act of Congress, shall, after the passage of this act, be redeemed at any time before the first day of July, one thousand eight hundred and forty-four, the Secretary of the Treasury, should the wants of the public service require, may cause other notes, to the same amount, to be issued in place of such as may be redeemed, under the limitations and other provisions of the respective acts by which said notes were originally authorized and issued.

SEC. 2. *And be it further enacted,* That, after maturity of the treasury notes issued under the said act of thirty-first August, or of this act, interest may be paid thereon, in the same manner as on treasury notes authorized previous to the fifteenth April last, under the ninth section of the act approved on that day, entitled "An act for the extension of the loan of one thousand eight hundred and forty-one, and for an addition of five millions of dollars thereto, and for allowing interest on treasury notes due."

SEC. 3. *And be it further enacted,* That, in lieu of issuing the treasury notes in the manner authorized by the first section of this act, the President, if in his opinion it shall be for the interest of the United States so to do, may cause any of said notes now outstanding, to be redeemed and cancelled as they become due, if the Secretary of the Treasury cannot redeem them out of the funds in the treasury, by an issue of stock of the United States, for the amount thus redeemed, in the same form, for the same time, and under the same restrictions, limitations, and provisions, as are contained in an act approved April fifteen, eighteen hundred and forty-two, entitled "An act for the extension of the loan of eighteen hundred and forty-one, and for an addition of five millions of dollars thereto, and for allowing interest on treasury notes due," except that no commissions shall be allowed or paid for the negotiation of such business ; and except also that said stock so to be issued, shall be redeemable at a period not longer than ten years from the issue thereof.

[Approved, March 8, 1843. 5 Statutes at Large, 614.]

1845-46, Chap. LXIV. — *An Act to authorize an Issue of Treasury Notes and a Loan.*

Be it enacted, . . . That the President of the United States is hereby authorized to cause treasury notes to be issued for such sum or sums as the exigencies of the govern-

ment may require ; and, in place of such of the same as may
be redeemed, to cause others to be issued ; but not exceeding the sum of ten millions of dollars of this emission outstanding at any one time, and to be issued under the limitations
and other provisions contained in the act entitled " An Act
to authorize the Issue of Treasury Notes," approved the
twelfth of October, one thousand eight hundred and thirty-
seven, except that the authority hereby given to issue treasury
notes shall expire at the end of one year from the passage
of this act.

[Section 2 provides that the President, instead of issuing the whole
amount of treasury notes thus authorized, may borrow by the issue of
stock of the United States, in the form and under the provisions prescribed by the Act of April 15, 1842, on page 133. *Provided*, That the
sum thus borrowed, together with the treasury notes issued, shall not
exceed ten millions of dollars, that the stock created shall be redeemable
at a period not longer than ten years from its issue, and that no commission shall be paid for the negotiation of this loan]

SEC. 3. *And be it further enacted*, That the treasury notes
and the stock issued under the provisions of this act shall
not bear a higher rate of interest than six per centum per
annum, and no part thereof shall be disposed of at less
than par.

[Approved, July 22, 1846. 9 Statutes at Large, 39.]

1845–46, Chap. XC. — *An Act to provide for the better Organization of the Treasury, and for the Collection,
Safe-keeping, Transfer, and Disbursement of the
public Revenue.*

WHEREAS, by the fourth section of the act entitled "An Act to
establish the Treasury Department," approved September two,
seventeen hundred and eighty-nine, it was provided that it should
be the duty of the treasurer to receive and keep the moneys of
the United States, and to disburse the same upon warrants drawn
by the Secretary of the Treasury, countersigned by the comptroller, and recorded by the register, and not otherwise; and
whereas it is found necessary to make further provisions to enable the treasurer the better to carry into effect the intent of the
said section in relation to the receiving and disbursing the
moneys of the United States: Therefore —

Be it enacted, . . . That the rooms prepared and provided in the new treasury building at the seat of government for the use of the treasurer of the United States, his assistants and clerks, and occupied by them, and also the fireproof vaults and safes erected in said rooms for the keeping of the public moneys in the possession and under the immediate control of said treasurer, and such other apartments as are provided for in this act as places of deposit of the public money, are hereby constituted and declared to be the treasury of the United States. And all moneys paid into the same shall be subject to the draft of the treasurer, drawn agreeably to appropriations made by law.

[Sections 2, 3, and 4 establish as "places of deposit" the Mint at Philadelphia and the Branch Mint at New Orleans, and the vaults and safes thereof; and the Treasurers of said Mint and Branch Mint, respectively, are made Assistant Treasurers under the provisions of this act, and are to have custody of all public moneys deposited therein, and to perform all the duties required as to the receipt, safe-keeping, transfer, and disbursement of the same. The rooms, safes, and vaults, prepared in the custom-houses of New York and Boston and in the cities of Charleston and St. Louis, for the use of Receivers General under the act of July 4, 1840, are declared to be for the use of the Assistant Treasurers now to be appointed at those places respectively; and the said Assistant Treasurers are to have custody of said rooms, vaults, and safes, and of public moneys therein deposited, and to perform all duties required in relation to such moneys. By subsequent acts the Mints at San Francisco, Carson City, and Denver, and the Assay Office at Boisé City are declared to be places of deposit, and the superintendents thereof are made Assistant Treasurers. See Revised Statutes, sections 3592, 3594.]

SEC. 5. *And be it further enacted,* That the President shall nominate, and by and with the advice and consent of the Senate appoint, four officers to be denominated "assistant-treasurers of the United States," which said officers shall hold their respective offices for the term of four years, unless sooner removed therefrom ; one of which shall be located at the city of New York, in the State of New York ; one other of which shall be located at the city of Boston, in the State of Massachusetts ; one other of which shall be located at the city of Charleston, in the State of South Carolina ; and one other at St. Louis, in the State of Missouri. And all of which said officers shall give bonds to the United States, with sureties, according to the provisions hereinafter contained, for the faithful discharge of the duties of their respective offices.

[Assistant Treasurers are provided for, by subsequent acts, at Baltimore, Cincinnati, and Chicago. Revised Statutes, section 3595. By the Coinage act of February 12, 1873, section 65, the Assistant Treasurers in Philadelphia, New Orleans, and San Francisco ceased to be Treasurers of the Mints in those cities respectively. 17 Statutes at Large, 424. By the act of August 15, 1876, the office of Assistant Treasurer at Charleston is discontinued. 19 Statutes at Large, 155.]

SEC. 6. *And be it further enacted,* That the treasurer of the United States, the treasurer of the mint of the United States, the treasurers, and those acting as such, of the various branch mints, all collectors of the customs, all surveyors of the customs acting also as collectors, all assistant treasurers, all receivers of public moneys at the several land offices, all postmasters, and all public officers of whatsoever character, be, and they are hereby, required to keep safely, without loaning, using, depositing in banks, or exchanging for other funds than as allowed by this act, all the public money collected by them, or otherwise at any time placed in their possession and custody, till the same is ordered, by the proper department or officer of the government, to be transferred or paid out; and when such orders for transfer or payment are received, faithfully and promptly to make the same as directed. . . .

[The same officers are also required to perform all duties imposed upon them by law as fiscal agents of the Government, and as agents for paying pensions, or for making any other disbursements which can be made by them consistently with their other duties. But by the Act of February 5, 1867, the payment of pensions was transferred to pension agents in the several States. 14 Statutes at Large, 391.

Sections 7 and 8 provide for the official bonds to be given by the Treasurer of the United States, the Treasurer of the Mint, the Treasurer of the Branch Mint at New Orleans, the Assistant Treasurers and other depositaries, and for the renewal and increase of their bonds as occasion may require.

Sections 9–12 repeat without material change the provisions of sections 9–13 of the Act of July 4, 1840, substituting, however, the Assistant Treasurers for the Receivers General provided for by that act.

By section 14 the Secretary of the Treasury is authorized to transfer, at his discretion, balances remaining with any of the present depositaries to any other of them, and also to draw upon such balances in making payments as he may find advisable, but is not to transfer such balances to the depositaries constituted by this act before January 1, 1847.

Section 16 requires all officers entrusted with public moneys, except those connected with the Post Office Department, to keep an accurate account of all receipts and payments; and if any such officer or any officer of the Post Office Department shall convert to his own use, or use by investment, or loan, or deposit in any bank, or exchange except as herein allowed any portion of the public moneys entrusted to him, the act is to be deemed an embezzlement, and is declared to be felony; and any failure to pay over or produce such moneys is to be taken as *prima facie* evidence of such embezzlement.]

And whereas, by the thirtieth section of the act entitled " An Act to regulate the Collection of Duties imposed by Law on the Tonnage of Ships or Vessels, and on Goods, Wares, and Merchandises, imported into the United States," approved July thirty-one, seventeen hundred and eighty-nine, it was provided that all fees and duties collected by virtue of that act should be received in gold and silver coin only; and whereas, also, by the fifth section of the act approved May ten, eighteen hundred, entitled " An Act to amend the Act entitled 'An Act providing for the Sale of the Lands of the United States in the Territory North-west of the Ohio, and above the Mouth of Kentucky River,' " it was provided that payment for the said lands shall be made by all purchasers in specie, or in evidences of the public debt; and whereas, experience has proved that said provisions ought to be revived and enforced, according to the true and wise intent of the constitution of the United States. —

SEC. 18. *Be it further enacted.* That on the first day of January, in the year one thousand eight hundred and forty-seven, and thereafter, all duties, taxes, sales of public lands, debts, and sums of money accruing or becoming due to the United States, and also all sums due for postages or otherwise, to the general post-office department, shall be paid in gold and silver coin only, or in treasury notes issued under the authority of the United States: *Provided,* That the Secretary of the Treasury shall publish, monthly, in two newspapers at the city of Washington, the amount of specie at the several places of deposit, the amount of treasury notes or drafts issued, and the amount outstanding on the last day of each month.

SEC. 19. *And be it further enacted*, That on the first day of April, one thousand eight hundred and forty-seven, and thereafter, every officer or agent engaged in making disbursements on account of the United States, or of the general post-office, shall make all payments in gold and silver coin, or in treasury notes, if the creditor agree to receive said notes in payment; and any receiving or disbursing officer or agent who shall neglect, evade, or violate, the provisions of this and the last preceding section of this act, shall, by the Secretary of the Treasury, be immediately reported to the President of the United States, with the facts of such neglect, evasion, or violation; and also to Congress, if in session; and if not in session, at the commencement of its session next after the violation takes place.

[Section 20 forbids any disbursing officer to make any exchange of funds other than an exchange for gold and silver, and requires every such officer, when the means of disbursement are furnished to him in gold and silver, to make his payments in the same; and when the means are furnished in drafts to make his payments in the money received therefor, unless he can exchange the means in his hands for gold and silver at par. But disbursing officers having credits in the banks may be allowed until January 1, 1847, to check on the same, allowing the public creditors to receive their pay from the banks either in specie or in bank notes.

Section 21 makes it the duty of the Secretary of the Treasury to make regulations prescribing the time within which drafts on the depositaries shall be presented for payment, but requires him "to guard, as far as may be, against those drafts being used or thrown into circulation as a paper currency or medium of exchange." And no officer shall sell, for a premium, any treasury note, draft, warrant, or other public security, not his private property, or sell the proceeds of any such note or security in his hands for disbursement, without charging such premium in his accounts to the credit of the United States, under penalty of dismissal.]

[Approved, August 6, 1846. 9 Statutes at Large, 59.]

1846–47, Chap. V. — *An Act authorizing the Issue of Treasury Notes, a Loan, and for other purposes.*

Be it enacted, . . . That the President of the United States is hereby authorized to cause treasury notes, for such sum or sums as the exigencies of the government may require, but not exceeding, in the whole amount of notes issued, the sum of twenty-three millions of dollars, and of denominations not less than fifty dollars for any one note, to be prepared, signed, and issued, in the manner hereinafter provided.

SEC. 2. *And be it further enacted*, That the said treasury notes authorized to be issued by the first section of this act, shall be reimbursed and redeemed by the United States, at the treasury thereof, after the expiration of one year or two years from the dates of the said notes respectively; from which said dates they shall bear such interest, until they shall be respectively redeemed, as shall be expressed upon the face of the said notes; which rate of interest upon each several issue of the said notes shall be fixed by the Secretary of the Treasury, by and with the advice and approbation of the President; but shall in no case exceed the rate of interest of six per centum per annum: *Provided*, That after the maturity of any of the said notes, such interest shall cease at the expiration of sixty days' notice, to be given at any time by the Secretary of the Treasury, in one or more of the principal papers published at the seat of government, of a readiness to redeem the same. The reimbursement herein provided for shall be made at the treasury of the United States to the holders of the said notes respectively, upon presentment, and shall include the principal of each note, and the interest which may be due thereon at the time of payment. For this reimbursement, at the time and times herein specified, the faith of the United States is hereby solemnly pledged.

[Section 3, providing for the signing of notes, follows closely the language of section 3, of the Act of October 12, 1837.]

SEC. 4. *And be it further enacted*, That the Secretary of the Treasury is hereby authorized, with the approbation of the President of the United States, to cause to be issued such portion of the said treasury notes as the President may think expedient in payment of debts due by the United

States, to such public creditors, or other persons, as may choose to receive such notes in payment, as aforesaid, at par. And the Secretary of the Treasury is further authorized, with the approbation of the President of the United States, to borrow from time to time such sums as the President may think expedient on the credit of such notes : *Provided, however,* That no treasury notes shall be pledged, hypothecated, sold, or disposed of in any wise for any purpose whatever, directly or indirectly, for any sum less than the amount of such notes, including the principal and interest thereon when disposed of.

Sec. 5. *And be it further enacted,* That the said treasury notes shall be transferable, by delivery and assignment endorsed thereon, by the person to whose order the same shall on the face thereof have been made payable.

Sec. 6. *And be it further enacted,* That the said treasury notes shall be received in payment of all duties and taxes laid by the authority of the United States, of all public lands sold by the said authority, and of all debts to the United States of any character whatsoever, which may be due and payable at the time when said treasury notes may be so offered in payment; and on every such payment credit shall be given for the amount of the principal and interest which, on the day of such payment, may be due on the note or notes thus given in payment.

Sec. 7. *And be it further enacted,* That every collector, receiver of public moneys, or other officer or agent of the United States, shall, on the receipt of any treasury notes in payment for the government, take from the holder thereof a receipt on the back of each of said notes, stating distinctly the date, and the amount received ; and shall keep, according to such forms as shall be prescribed by the Secretary of the Treasury, entries of whom received, the number, date, and respective amounts of principal and interest of each and every treasury note thus received ; and on delivering the same to the treasury shall receive credit for the amount paid as prescribed by the last section : *Provided,* no error shall appear.

[Sections 8–10, providing for the reimbursement or purchase of the notes, and for the punishment of counterfeiting and the like offences, follow the language of sections 9–11 of the Act of October 12, 1837.

Section 11, authorizing the Secretary of the Treasury to make rules for the safe-keeping, return, and cancelling of notes received by any officers for the United States, is nearly identical with section 12 of the same act, but omits the provision forbidding the reissue of notes.]

SEC. 12. *And be it further enacted,* That, in lieu of the notes authorized by this act which may be redeemed, other notes may be issued: *Provided, however,* The amount of such notes outstanding, together with the stock issued by virtue of the thirteenth and sixteenth sections of this act, shall not exceed the sum of twenty-three millions of dollars.

SEC. 13. *And be it further enacted,* That it shall be lawful for the holders of the aforesaid treasury notes to present them, at any time, to the treasury of the United States, or to any assistant treasurer, or to such collectors of the customs and receivers of public moneys as may be designated by the Secretary of the Treasury; and the holders of the said treasury notes shall be entitled to receive therefor the amount of the principal of the said notes in a certificate or certificates of funded stock, bearing interest at six per centum per annum, from the date of such presentment of said treasury notes, and for the interest, shall be paid in money; and the stock thus to be issued shall be transferable on the books of the treasury: *Provided, however, and be it further enacted,* That it shall be lawful for the United States to reimburse the stock thus created, at any time after the last day of December, one thousand eight hundred and sixty-seven.

SEC. 14. *And be it further enacted,* That it shall and may be lawful for the holder of any treasury notes issued, or authorized to be issued, under this act or any laws heretofore passed, to convert the same into certificates of funded stock, upon the same terms and in the same manner hereinbefore provided in relation to the treasury notes authorized by the first section of this act.

SEC. 15. *And be it further enacted,* That the authority to issue treasury notes authorized by the " Act authorizing an

10

Issue of Treasury Notes and a Loan," approved July twenty-second, one thousand eight hundred and forty-six, be, and the same is hereby, extended to the same period fixed for the treasury notes authorized by this act, and upon the same terms and conditions herein specified : *Provided*, That the treasury notes authorized by this section shall not exceed five million of dollars.

[Sections 16–18 authorize the President, in lieu of treasury notes, to issue stock of the United States, bearing interest at a rate not exceeding six per cent., and redeemable after December 31, 1867: *provided*, that the whole amount of treasury notes and of stock together shall not exceed twenty-three millions of dollars, and *"provided further*, That no stock shall be issued at a less rate than par."]

SEC. 19. *And be it further enacted*, That, for the payment of the stock which may be created under the provisions of this act the sales of the public lands are hereby pledged, and it is hereby made the duty of the Secretary of the Treasury to use and apply all moneys which may be received into the treasury for the sales of the public lands after the first day of January, eighteen hundred and forty-eight, first, to pay the interest on all stocks issued by virtue of this act ; and, secondly, to use the balance of said receipts, after paying the interest aforesaid, in the purchase of said stocks at their market value : *Provided*, No more than par shall be paid for said stocks.

[The proviso to the above section was repealed by section 3 of the civil and diplomatic appropriation act of March 3, 1849. 9 Statutes at Large, 369.]

SEC. 21. *And be it further enacted*, That it shall be, and hereby is, made the duty of the Secretary of the Treasury to cause a statement to be published monthly of the amount of all treasury notes issued or redeemed in pursuance of the provisions of this act ; and that the power to issue treasury notes conferred on the President of the United States by this act shall cease and determine six months after the exchange and ratification of a treaty of peace with the Republic of Mexico.

[Section 22 makes it the duty of the Secretary of the Treasury to report to Congress at the beginning of every session the amount of treasury notes issued, redeemed, purchased, or reissued, during the preceding year.]

[Approved, January 28, 1847.   9 Statutes at Large, 118.]

1847–48. Chap. XXVI. — *An Act to authorize a Loan not to exceed the Sum of Sixteen Millions of Dollars.*

[Section 1 authorizes the President to borrow on the credit of the United States, within one year from the passage of this act, a sum not exceeding sixteen millions of dollars, at a rate of interest not exceeding six per cent., and reimbursable at any time after twenty years from July 1, 1848.]

SEC. 2. *And be it further enacted*, That the Secretary of the Treasury be, and he is hereby authorized, with the consent of the President of the United States, to cause to be prepared certificates of stock, which shall be signed by the Register of the Treasury and sealed with the seal of the Treasury Department, for the sum to be borrowed as aforesaid, or any part thereof, bearing an interest not to exceed six per centum per annum, and transferable and reimbursable as aforesaid, and to cause said certificates of stock to be sold : *Provided*, That no part of said stock be sold below par : *And provided, also*, That, whenever required so to do, the Secretary of the Treasury shall cause to be attached to any certificate or certificates to be issued under this act, coupons of interest ; and any certificate having such coupons of interest attached to it, may be transferable by delivery of the certificate, instead of being assignable on the books of the treasury ; but no certificate of stock shall be issued for a less amount than fifty dollars.

[By section 3 the Secretary of the Treasury is directed, before disposing of this stock, to advertise for sealed proposals, to be handed in after not less than twenty nor more than sixty days, and in the advertisement to state the amount required and the conditions fixed for its payment into the Treasury.

Section 4 pledges the faith of the United States for the provision of sufficient revenues to secure the payment of the interest and redemption of the principal.]

SEC. 5. *And be it further enacted*, That the Secretary of the Treasury be, and he is hereby, authorized to purchase, at any time before the period herein limited for the redemption of the stock hereby created, such portion thereof at the market price, not below par, as the funds of the government may admit of, after meeting all the demands on the treasury ; and any surplus that hereafter may be in the treasury is hereby appropriated to that object.

[Section 6 provides for a report to be made to Congress of all transactions under this act, in language identical with that of section 6 of the Act of April 15, 1842, on page 134.]

[Approved, March 31, 1848.   9 Statutes at Large, 217.]

1849-50, Chap. XLIX. — *An Act proposing to the State of Texas the Establishment of her Northern and Western Boundaries, the Relinquishment by the said State of all Territory claimed by her exterior to said Boundaries, and of all her Claims upon the United States, and to establish a territorial Government for New Mexico.*

[SEC. 1.]   FOURTH. The United States, in consideration of said establishment of boundaries, cession of claim to territory, and relinquishment of claims, will pay to the State of Texas the sum of ten millions of dollars in a stock bearing five per cent. interest, and redeemable at the end of fourteen years, the interest payable half-yearly at the treasury of the United States.

FIFTH. Immediately after the President of the United States shall have been furnished with an authentic copy of the act of the general assembly of Texas accepting these propositions, he shall cause the stock to be issued in favor of the State of Texas, as provided for in the fourth article of this agreement : *Provided, also*, That no more than five millions of said stock shall be issued until the creditors of the State holding bonds and other certificates of stock of Texas for which duties on imports were specially pledged, shall first file at the treasury of the United States releases of all claim against the United States for or on account of said bonds or certificates in such form as shall be prescribed by the Secretary of the Treasury and approved by the President of the United States : . . .

[Approved, September 9, 1850.   9 Statutes at Large, 446.]

1852-53, Chap. XCVII. — *An Act making appropriations for the Civil and Diplomatic Expenses of Government for the year ending the thirtieth of June, eighteen hundred and fifty-four.*

Sec. 9. *And be it further enacted*, That the Secretary of the Treasury be and he is hereby authorized to purchase at the current market price any of the outstanding stocks of the United States as he may think most advisable, from any surplus funds in the Treasury: *Provided*, That the balance in the Treasury shall not at any time be reduced below six millions of dollars.

[Approved, March 3, 1853. 10 Statutes at Large, 212.]

1857-58, Chap. I. — *An Act to authorize the Issue of Treasury Notes.*

Be it enacted, . . . That the President of the United States is hereby authorized to cause treasury notes for such sum or sums as the exigencies of the public service may require, but not to exceed, at any time, the amount of twenty millions of dollars, and of denominations not less than one hundred dollars for any such note, to be prepared, signed, and issued in the manner hereinafter provided.

Sec. 2. *And be it further enacted*, That such treasury notes shall be paid and redeemed by the United States at the treasury thereof after the expiration of one year from the dates of said notes, from which dates, until they shall be respectively paid and redeemed, they shall bear such rate of interest as shall be expressed in said notes, which rate of interest upon the first issue, which shall not exceed six millions of dollars of such notes shall be fixed by the Secretary of the Treasury, with the approbation of the President, but shall in no case exceed the rate of six per centum per annum. The residue shall be issued in whole or in part, after public advertisement of not less than thirty days, as the Secretary of the Treasury may direct, by exchanging them at their par value for specie to the bidder or bidders who shall agree to make such exchange at the lowest rate of interest, not exceeding six per centum, upon the said notes : *Provided*, That after the maturity of any of said notes, interest thereon shall cease at the expiration of sixty days' notice of readiness to pay and redeem the same, which may at any time or times be given by the Secretary of the Treasury in one or more newspapers published at the seat of government. The payment or redemption of said notes herein provided shall be made to the lawful holders thereof, respectively, upon presentment at the treasury, and shall include the principal of each note and the interest which shall be due thereon. And for such payment and redemption, at the time or times herein specified, the faith of the United States is hereby solemnly pledged.

[Section 3 provides for the signing of the notes, and the accounts to be kept of their preparation, redemption, and cancellation.

Sections 4–7, providing for the issue, transfer, receipt, and payment of the notes, follow the language of sections 4–7 of the Act of January 28, 1847, on page 143.

Section 8 authorizes the establishment of rules for the custody and disposal of notes received ; and section 9 makes the same provision for the redemption of the notes at maturity and their purchase at any time, as section 8 of the Act of October 12, 1837, on page 120.]

SEC. 10. *And be it further enacted*, That, in place of such treasury notes as may have been paid and redeemed, other treasury notes to the same amount may be issued : *Provided*, That the aggregate sum outstanding, under the authority of this act, shall at no time exceed twenty millions of dollars : *And provided further*, That the power to issue and reissue treasury notes, conferred on the President of the United States by this act, shall cease and determine on the first day of January, eighteen hundred and fifty-nine.

[Sections 12 and 13 provide for the punishment of counterfeiting and of the like offences ; and section 14 requires the publication of a monthly statement of the amount of Treasury notes issued, paid, redeemed, and outstanding under this act.]

[Approved, December 23, 1857.   11 Statutes at Large, 257.]

1857-58, Chap. CLXV. — *An Act to authorize a Loan not exceeding the Sum of Twenty Millions of Dollars.*

[Section 1 empowers the President to borrow on the credit of the United States, within one year from the passage of this act, a sum not exceeding twenty millions of dollars, *provided,* that the loan thus made shall be reimbursable at any time after fifteen years from January 1, 1859.]

SEC. 2. *And be it further enacted,* That stock shall be issued for the amount so borrowed, bearing interest not exceeding five per centum per annum, payable semi-annually, with coupons for the semi-annual interest attached to the certificates of stock thus created, and the Secretary of the Treasury be, and hereby is, authorized, with the consent of the President, to cause certificates of stock to be prepared, which shall be signed by the Register, and sealed with the seal of the Treasury Department, for the amount so borrowed in favor of the parties lending the same, or their assigns ; *Provided,* That no certificate shall be issued for a less sum than one thousand dollars.

[By section 3 the Secretary of the Treasury is required, before awarding the loan, to advertise that sealed proposals for the stock will be received until a date not less than thirty days distant, and to " accept the most favorable proposals offered by responsible bidders ; " and he is also required to report to Congress, at its next session, all transactions under this act, " *provided,* that no stock shall be disposed of at less than its par value."]

SEC. 4. *And be it further enacted,* That the faith of the United States is hereby pledged for the due payment of the interest and the redemption of the principal of said stock.

[Approved, June 14, 1858. 11 Statutes at Large, 365.]

1858-59, Chap. LXXXII. — *An Act making Appropriations for sundry Civil Expenses of the Government for the Year ending the thirtieth of June, eighteen hundred and sixty.*

SEC. 5. *And be it further enacted,* That the power to issue and reissue treasury notes, conferred on the President of the

United States, by the act entitled "An act to authorize the issue of treasury notes," approved the twenty-third December, eighteen hundred and fifty-seven, be, and the same hereby is, revived and continued in force from the passage of this act until the first day of July eighteen hundred and sixty; and to defray the expenses thereof the sum of five thousand dollars is hereby appropriated: *Provided,* That the said notes may be issued bearing an interest not exceeding six per centum per annum; and that it shall not be necessary, as directed by the original act aforesaid, after advertisement to exchange them for specie to the bidder or bidders who shall agree to make such exchange at the lowest rate of interest upon said notes; and that in all other respects the reissue of said treasury notes shall be subject to the terms and conditions of the act aforesaid.

SEC. 6. *And be it further enacted,* That the Secretary of the Treasury is hereby authorized, under the act of June fourteenth, eighteen hundred and fifty-eight, to issue coupon or registered stock, as the purchaser may elect.

[Approved, March 3, 1859. 11 Statutes at Large, 430.]

1859–60, Chap. CLXXX. — *An Act authorizing a Loan and providing for the Redemption of Treasury Notes.*

Be it enacted, . . . That the President of the United States be, and hereby is, authorized, at any time within twelve months from the passage of this act, to borrow, on the credit of the United States, a sum not exceeding twenty-one millions of dollars, or so much thereof as, in his opinion, the exigencies of the public service may require, to be used in the redemption of Treasury notes now outstanding and to replace in the Treasury any amount of said notes which shall have been paid and received for public dues, and for no other purposes.

SEC. 2. *And be it further enacted,* That stock shall be issued for the amount so borrowed, bearing interest, not exceeding six per centum per annum, and to be reimbursed within a period not beyond twenty years and not less than ten years; and the Secretary of the Treasury be, and is hereby authorized, with the consent of the President, to cause certificates of stock to be prepared, which shall be signed by the Register, and sealed with the seal of the Treasury Department, for the amount so borrowed, in favor of the parties lending the same, or their assigns, which certificates may be transferred on the books of the Treasury, under such regulations as may be established by the Secretary of the Treasury ; *Provided*, That no certificate shall be issued for a less sum than one thousand dollars ; *And provided also,* That, whenever required, the Secretary of the Treasury may cause coupons of semi-annual interest payable thereon to be attached to certificates issued under this act ; and any certificate with such coupons of interest attached may be assigned and transferred by delivery of the same, instead of being transferred on the books of the Treasury.

[Section 3 provides for sealed proposals, and the acceptance of the most favorable, and for a report of all transactions to Congress, as in section 3 of the Act of June 14, 1858, on page 151; "*Provided,* That no stock shall be disposed of at less than its par value."]

SEC. 4. *And be it further enacted,* That the faith of the United States is hereby pledged for the due payment of the interest and the redemption of the principal of said stock.

[Approved, June 22, 1860. 12 Statutes at Large, 79.]

PART II.

CURRENCY, FINANCE, AND BANKING.

1860–1890.

1860–61, Chap. I. — *An Act to authorize the Issue of Treasury Notes, and for other Purposes.*

Be it enacted, ... That the President of [the] United [States] be hereby authorized to cause treasury notes, for such sum or sums as the exigencies of the public service may require, but not to exceed at any time the amount of ten millions of dollars, and of denominations not less than fifty dollars for any such note, to be prepared, signed, and issued in the manner hereinafter provided.

Sec. 2. *And be it further enacted,* That such treasury notes shall be paid and redeemed by the United States at the Treasury thereof after the expiration of one year from the date of issue of such notes; from which dates, until they shall be respectively paid and redeemed, they shall bear such rate of interest as shall be expressed in such notes, which rate of interest shall be six per centum per annum: *Provided,* That, after the maturity of any of said notes, interest thereon shall cease at the expiration of sixty days' notice of readiness to redeem and pay the same, which may at any time or times be given by the Secretary of the Treasury in one or more newspapers at the seat of government. The redemption and payment of said notes, herein provided, shall be made to the lawful holders thereof respectively upon presentment at the Treasury, and shall include the principal of each note and the interest which shall be due thereon. And for the payment and redemption of such notes at the time and times therein specified, the faith of the United States is hereby solemnly pledged.

[Section 3 provides for the signing of the treasury notes and the accounts to be kept thereof.]

SEC. 4. *And be it further enacted*, That the Secretary of the Treasury is hereby authorized, with the approbation of the President, to cause such portion of said treasury notes as may be deemed expedient, to be issued by the Treasurer in payment of warrants in favor of public creditors, or other persons lawfully entitled to payment, who may choose to receive such notes in payment at par ; and the Secretary of the Treasury is hereby authorized, with the approbation of the President, to issue the notes hereby authorized to be issued, at such rate of interest as may be offered by the lowest responsible bidder or bidders who may agree to take the said notes at par after public advertisement of not less than ten days in such papers as the President may direct, the said advertisement to propose to issue such notes at par to those who may offer to take the same at the lowest rate of interest. But in deciding upon those bids no fraction shall be considered which may be less than one-fourth per centum per annum.

[Sections 5–9, providing for the transfer, receipt. custody, redemption, and cancellation of the notes, are identical with sections 5–9 of the Act of December 23, 1857, on page 150.]

SEC. 10. *And be it further enacted*, That, in place of such treasury notes as may have been paid and redeemed, other treasury notes to the same amount may be issued : *Provided*, That the aggregate sum outstanding under the authority of this act shall at no time exceed the sum of ten millions of dollars : *And provided further*, That the power to issue and reissue treasury notes conferred by this act shall cease and determine on the first day of January, in the year eighteen hundred and sixty-three.

[Section 14 requires the publication of a monthly statement of the amount of notes issued, paid, redeemed, and outstanding under this act, as in section 14 of the act last mentioned.]

Section 15 requires that all money hereafter contracted for under the act of June 22, 1860, on page 152, shall be used for the redemption of treasury notes now outstanding or to be issued.]

[Approved, December 17, 1860. 12 Statutes at Large, 121.]

1860-61, Chap. XXIX. — *An Act authorizing a Loan.*

SECTION 1. *Be it enacted,* . . . That the President of the United States be and hereby is authorized, at any time before the first day of July next, to borrow, on the credit of the United States, a sum not exceeding twenty-five millions of dollars, or so much thereof as, in his opinion, the exigencies of the public service may require to be used in the payment of the current demands upon the Treasury and for the redemption of treasury notes now outstanding, and to replace in the Treasury any amount of said notes which shall have been paid and received for public dues.

[Section 2 provides that stock shall be issued, bearing interest not exceeding six per cent., and "to be reimbursed within a period not beyond twenty years and not less than ten years," the stock being transferable on the books of the Treasury, and no certificate being issued for less than one thousand dollars;] —

And provided, also, That, whenever required, the Secretary of the Treasury may cause coupons of semi-annual interest payable thereon to be attached to certificates issued under this act; and any certificate with such coupons of interest attached may be assigned and transferred by delivery of the same, instead of being transferred on the books of the Treasury.

[Section 3 provides for sealed proposals, to be received for a period of not less than ten days, for the acceptance of the most favorable offers made by responsible bidders, and for a report of all transactions to Congress.]

SEC. 4. *And be it further enacted,* That the faith of the United States is hereby pledged for the due payment of the interest and the redemption of the principal of said stock.

[By section 5 the residue of the loan authorized by the act of June 22, 1860, on page 152, is to be applied to the redemption of treasury notes issued under the act of December 17, 1860, on page 155; and bonds au-

thorized by said first mentioned act may be exchanged at par for said
treasury notes and their accrued interest.]

SEC. 7. *And be it further enacted,* That the Secretary of
the Treasury shall not be obliged to accept the most favorable
bids as hereinbefore provided, unless he shall consider it advantageous to the United States to do so, but for any portion
of such loan, not taken under the first advertisement, he may
advertise again at his discretion.

[Approved, February 8, 1861.   12 Statutes at Large, 129.]

1860–61, Chap. LXVIII. — *An Act to provide for the Payment of outstanding Treasury Notes, to authorize a
Loan, to regulate and fix the Duties on Imports, and
for other Purposes.*

Be it enacted, . . . That the President of the United States
be, and hereby is, authorized, at any time within twelve months
from the passage of this act, to borrow, on the credit of the
United States, a sum not exceeding ten millions of dollars, or
so much thereof as, in his opinion, the exigencies of the public
service may require, to be applied to the payment of appropriations made by law, and the balance of treasury notes now
outstanding, and no other purposes, in addition to the money
received or which may be received, into the treasury from
other sources : *Provided,* That no stipulation or contract shall
be made to prevent the United States from reimbursing any
sum borrowed under the authority of this act at any time after
the expiration of ten years from the first day of July next, by
the United States giving three months' notice, to be published
in some newspaper published at the seat of government, of
their readiness to do so ; and no contract shall be made to
prevent the redemption of the same at any time after the expiration of twenty years from the said first day of July next,
without notice.

[Section 2 provides for the issue of either registered or coupon certificates as may be required, bearing interest not exceeding six per cent., in
language identical with that of section 2 of the Act of February 8, 1861,
omitting, however, any provision as to the time of reimbursement.
Section 3 provides for sealed proposals, to be received within a period

of not less than thirty days, for the acceptance of the most favorable offers made by responsible bidders, and for a report of all transactions to Congress : *"provided,* That no stock shall be disposed of at less than its par value : *And provided further,* That no part of the loan hereby authorized shall be applied to the service of the present fiscal year."]

SEC. 4. *And be it further enacted,* That in case the proposals made for said loan, or for so much thereof as the exigencies of the public service shall require, shall not be satisfactory, the President of the United States shall be, and hereby is, authorized to decline to accept such offer if for less than the par value of the bonds constituting the said stock, and in lieu thereof, and to the extent and the amount of the loan authorized to be made by this act, to issue treasury notes for sums not less than fifty dollars, bearing interest at the rate of six per centum per annum, payable semi-annually on the first days of January and July in each year, at proper places of payment to be prescribed by the Secretary, with the approval of the President ; and under the like circumstances and conditions, the President of the United States is hereby authorized to substitute treasury notes of equal amount for the whole or any part of the loans for which he is now by law authorized to contract and issue bonds. And the treasury notes so issued under the authority herein given, shall be received in payment for all debts due to the United States when offered, and in like manner shall be given in payment for any sum due from the United States, when payment in that mode is requested by the person to whom payment is to be made, or for their par value in coin. And the faith of the United States is hereby pledged for the due payment of the interest and the redemption of the principal of the stock or treasury notes which may be issued under the authority of this act ; and the sum of twenty thousand dollars is hereby appropriated, out of any money in the treasury not otherwise appropriated, to pay the expenses of preparing the certificates of stock or treasury notes herein authorized, to be done in the usual mode and under the restrictions as to employment and payment of officers contained in the laws authorizing former loans and issues of treasury notes ; and it shall be at the option of holders of

the treasury notes hereby authorized by this act, to exchange
the same for the stock herein authorized, at par, or for bonds,
in lieu of which said treasury notes were issued : *Provided*,
That no certificate shall be exchanged for treasury notes, or
bonds, in sums less than five hundred dollars : *And provided,
further*, That the authority to issue the said treasury notes,
or give the same in payment for debts due from the United
States, shall be limited to the thirtieth day of June, eighteen
hundred and sixty-two ; and that the same may be redeemable
at the pleasure of the United States at any time within two
years after the passage of this act; and that said notes shall
cease to bear interest after they shall have been called in
by the Secretary of the Treasury under the provisions of
this act.

[The remaining sections of this act contain what is known as the
Morrill tariff.]
[Approved, March 2, 1861.   12 Statutes at Large, 178.]

1861, Chap. V. — *An Act to authorize a National Loan,
and for other Purposes.*

Be it enacted, . . . That the Secretary of the Treasury be
and he is hereby, authorized to borrow on the credit of the
United States, within twelve months from the passage of this
act, a sum not exceeding two hundred and fifty millions of
dollars, or so much thereof as he may deem necessary for the
public service, for which he is authorized to issue coupon
bonds, or registered bonds, or treasury notes, in such proportions of each as he may deem advisable ; the bonds to bear
interest not exceeding seven per centum per annum, payable
semi-annually, irredeemable for twenty years, and after that
period redeemable at the pleasure of the United States ; and
the treasury notes to be of any denomination fixed by the
Secretary of the Treasury, not less than fifty dollars, and
to be payable three years after date, with interest at the
rate of seven and three tenths per centum per annum, payable
semi-annually.   And the Secretary of the Treasury may also
issue in exchange for coin, and as part of the above loan, or may
pay for salaries or other dues from the United States, treasury

notes of a less denomination than fifty dollars, not bearing interest, but payable on demand by the Assistant Treasurers of the United States at Philadelphia, New York, or Boston, or treasury notes bearing interest at the rate of three and sixty-five hundredths per centum, payable in one year from date, and exchangeable at any time for treasury notes for fifty dollars, and upwards, issuable under the authority of this act, and bearing interest as specified above : *Provided*, That no exchange of such notes in any less amount than one hundred dollars shall be made at any one time : *And provided further*, That no treasury notes shall be issued of a less denomination than ten dollars, and that the whole amount of treasury notes, not bearing interest, issued under the authority of this act, shall not exceed fifty millions of dollars.

[Section 3 authorizes the Secretary of the Treasury to open books for subscriptions for the treasury notes, at such places as he may select; and, if he thinks expedient, before opening such books, to pay out for public dues, or for coin, or for the public debt, any amount of said treasury notes not exceeding one hundred millions of dollars.

Section 4 provides for the issue of proposals in the United States for such portion of the loan in bonds as the Secretary may determine, " *Provided*, That no offer shall be accepted at less than par."

Section 5 authorizes the Secretary of the Treasury to negotiate any part of the loan, not exceeding one hundred millions of dollars, in any foreign country; to make the principal and interest payable either in the United States or in Europe; and to fix the rate of exchange at which the principal shall be received, which rate shall also be the rate of exchange for the payment of the principal and interest in Europe.]

SEC. 6. *And be it further enacted*, That whenever any treasury notes of a denomination less than fifty dollars, authorized to be issued by this act, shall have been redeemed, the Secretary of the Treasury may reissue the same, or may cancel them and issue new notes to an equal amount: *Provided*, That the aggregate amounts of bonds and treasury notes issued under the foregoing provisions of this act shall never exceed the full amount authorized by the first section of this act; and the power to issue or reissue such notes shall cease and determine after the thirty-first of December, eighteen hundred and sixty-two.

SEC. 7. *And be it further enacted*, That the Secretary of the Treasury is hereby authorized, whenever he shall deem it expedient, to issue in exchange for coin, or in payment for public dues, treasury notes of any of the denominations hereinbefore specified, bearing interest not exceeding six per centum per annum, and payable at any time not exceeding twelve months from date, provided that the amount of notes so issued, or paid, shall at no time exceed twenty millions of dollars.

SEC. 9. *And be it further enacted*, That the faith of the United States is hereby solemnly pledged for the payment of the interest and redemption of the principal of the loan authorized by this act.

[Approved, July 17, 1861. 12 Statutes at Large, 259.]

1861, Chap. XLVI. — *An Act supplementary to an Act entitled "An Act to authorize a National Loan, and for other Purposes."*

[Section 1 authorizes the Secretary of the Treasury to issue bonds bearing interest at six per cent. per annum, and payable at the pleasure of the United States after twenty years from date, to be given in exchange for such treasury notes, bearing interest at seven and three tenths per cent., issued under the act of July 17, 1861, as the holders may present for exchange before or at the maturity thereof. Any part of the treasury notes payable on demand, authorized by said act, may be made payable by the Assistant Treasurer at St. Louis, or the depositary at Cincinnati.

Section 3 provides that the demand notes issued under the previous act may be of denominations not less than five dollars.]

SEC. 5. *And be it further enacted*, That the treasury notes authorized by the act to which this is supplementary, of a less denomination than fifty dollars, payable on demand without interest, and not exceeding in amount the sum of fifty millions of dollars, shall be receivable in payment of public dues.

SEC. 6. *And be it further enacted*, That the provisions of the act entitled " An act to provide for the better organization of the Treasury, and for the collection, safe-keeping, transfer, and disbursements of the public revenue," passed August six, eighteen hundred and forty-six, be and the same are hereby suspended, so far as to allow the Secretary of the Treasury to deposit any of the moneys obtained on any of the loans now authorized by law, to the credit of the Treasurer of the United States, in such solvent specie-paying banks as he may select;

and the said moneys, so deposited, may be withdrawn from such deposit for deposit with the regular authorized depositaries, or for the payment of public dues, or paid in redemption of the notes authorized to be issued under this act, or the act to which this is supplementary, payable on demand, as may seem expedient to, or be directed by, the Secretary of the Treasury.

SEC. 7. *And be it further enacted,* That the Secretary of the Treasury may sell or negotiate, for any portion of the loan provided for in the act to which this is supplementary, bonds payable not more than twenty years from date, and bearing interest not exceeding six per centum per annum, payable semi-annually, at any rate not less than the equivalent of par, for the bonds bearing seven per centum interest, authorized by said act.

[Approved, August 5, 1861. 12 Statutes at Large, 313.]

1861-62, Chap. XX. — *An Act to authorize an additional Issue of United States Notes.*

Be it enacted, . . . That the Secretary of the Treasury, in addition to the fifty millions of notes payable on demand of denominations not less than five dollars, heretofore authorized by the acts of July seventeenth and August fifth, eighteen hundred and sixty-one, be, and he is hereby, authorized to issue like notes, and for like purposes, to the amount of ten millions of dollars, and said notes shall be deemed part of the loan of two hundred and fifty millions of dollars authorized by said acts.

[Approved, February 12, 1862. 12 Statutes at Large, 338.]

1861-62, Chap. XXXIII. — *An Act to authorize the Issue of United States Notes, and for the Redemption or Funding thereof, and for Funding the Floating Debt of the United States.*

Be it enacted, . . . That the Secretary of the Treasury is hereby authorized to issue, on the credit of the United States, one hundred and fifty millions of dollars of United States notes, not bearing interest, payable to bearer, at the Treasury of the United States, and of such denominations as he may deem expedient, not less than five dollars each: *Provided, however,* That fifty millions of said notes shall be in lieu of the demand treasury notes authorized to be issued by the act of July seventeen, eighteen hundred and sixty-one; which said demand notes shall be taken up as rapidly as practicable, and the notes herein provided for substituted for them: *And provided further,* That the amount of the two kinds of notes together shall at no time exceed the sum of one hundred and fifty millions of dollars, and such notes herein authorized shall be receivable in payment of all taxes, internal duties, excises, debts, and demands of every kind due to the United States, except duties on imports, and of all claims and demands against the United States of every kind whatsoever, except for interest upon bonds and notes, which shall be paid in coin, and shall also be lawful money and a legal tender in payment of all debts, public and private, within the United States, except duties on imports and interest as aforesaid. And any holders of said United States notes depositing any sum not less than fifty dollars, or some multiple of fifty dollars, with the Treasurer of the United States, or either of the Assistant Treasurers, shall receive in exchange therefor duplicate certificates of deposit, one of which may be transmitted to the Secretary of the Treasury, who shall thereupon issue to the holder an equal amount of bonds of the United States, coupon or registered, as may by said holder be desired, bearing interest at the rate of six per centum per annum, payable semi-annually, and redeemable at the pleasure of the United States after five years, and payable twenty years from the date thereof. And such United States notes shall be received the same as coin, at their par value, in payment for any loans that may be hereafter sold or negotiated by the Secretary of the Treasury, and may be re-issued from time to time as the exigencies of the public interests shall require.

SEC. 2. *And be it further enacted,* That to enable the Secretary of the Treasury to fund the treasury notes and floating debt of the United States, he is hereby authorized to issue, on the credit of the United States, coupon bonds, or registered bonds, to an amount not exceeding five hundred millions of dollars, redeemable at the pleasure of the United States after five years, and payable twenty years from date, and bearing interest at the rate of six per centum per annum, payable semi-annually. And the bonds herein authorized shall be of such denominations, not less than fifty dollars, as may be determined upon by the Secretary of the Treasury. And the Secretary of the Treasury may dispose of such bonds at any time, at the market value thereof, for the coin of the United States, or for any of the treasury notes that have been or may hereafter be issued under any former act of Congress, or for United States notes that may be issued under the provisions of this act; and all stocks, bonds, and other securities of the United States held by individuals, corporations, or associations, within the United States, shall be exempt from taxation by or under State authority.

SEC. 4. *And be it further enacted,* That the Secretary of the Treasury may receive from any person or persons, or any corporation, United States notes on deposit for not less than thirty days, in sums of not less than one hundred dollars, with any of the Assistant Treasurers or designated depositaries of the United States authorized by the Secretary of the Treasury to receive them, who shall issue therefor certificates of deposit, made in such form as the Secretary of the Treasury shall prescribe, and said certificates of deposit shall bear interest at the rate of five per centum per annum; and any amount of United States notes so deposited may be withdrawn from deposit at any time after ten days' notice on the return of said certificates: *Provided,* That the interest on all such deposits shall cease and determine at the pleasure of the Secretary of the Treasury : *And provided further,* That the aggregate of such deposit shall at no time exceed the amount of twenty-five millions of dollars.

SEC. 5. *And be it further enacted,* That all duties on imported goods shall be paid in coin, or in notes payable on demand heretofore authorized to be issued and by law receivable in payment of public dues, and the coin so paid shall be set apart as a special fund, and shall be applied as follows:

First. To the payment in coin of the interest on the bonds and notes of the United States.

Second. To the purchase or payment of one per centum of the entire debt of the United States, to be made within each fiscal year after the first day of July, eighteen hundred and sixty-two, which is to be set apart as a sinking fund, and the interest of which shall in like manner be applied to the purchase or pay ment of the public debt as the Secretary of the Treasury shall from time to time direct.

Third. The residue thereof to be paid into the Treasury of the United States.

[Approved, February 25, 1862. 12 Statutes at Large, 345.]

1861–62, Chap. XXXV.— *An Act to authorize the Secretary of the Treasury to Issue Certificates of Indebtedness to Public Creditors.*

Be it enacted, . . . That the Secretary of the Treasury be, and he is hereby authorized, to cause to be issued to any public creditor who may be desirous to receive the same, upon requisition of the head of the proper department in satisfaction of audited and settled demands against the United States, certificates for the whole amount due or parts thereof not less than one thousand dollars, signed by the Treasurer of the United States, and countersigned as may be directed by the Secretary of the Treasury ; which certificates shall be payable in one year from date or earlier, at the option of the Government, and shall bear interest at the rate of six per centum per annum.

[Approved, March 1, 1862. 12 Statutes at Large, 352.]

1861–62, Chap. XLV.— *An Act to authorize the Purchase of Coin, and for other Purposes.*

Be it enacted, . . . That the Secretary of the Treasury may purchase coin with any of the bonds or notes of the United States, authorized by law, at such rates and upon such terms as he may deem most advantageous to the public interest; and may issue, under such rules and regulations as he may prescribe, certificates of indebtedness, such as are authorized by an act entitled " An act to authorize the Secretary of the Treasury to issue certificates of indebtedness to public creditors," approved March first, eighteen hundred and sixty-two, to such creditors as may desire to receive the same, in discharge of checks drawn by disbursing officers upon sums placed to their credit on the books of the Treasurer, upon requisitions of the proper departments, as well as in discharge of audited and settled accounts, as provided by said act.

SEC. 2. *And be it further enacted,* That the demand-notes authorized by the act of July seventeenth, eighteen hundred and sixty-one, and by the act of February twelfth, eighteen hundred and sixty-two, shall, in addition to being receivable in payment of duties on imports, be receivable, and shall be lawful money and a legal tender, in like manner, and for the same purposes, and to the same extent, as the notes authorized by an act entitled "An act to authorize the issue of United States notes, and for the redemption or funding thereof, and for funding the floating debt of the United States," approved February twenty-fifth, eighteen hundred and sixty-two.

SEC. 3. *And be it further enacted,* That the limitation upon, temporary deposits of United States notes with any Assistant Treasurers or designated depositaries, authorized by the Secretary of the Treasury to receive such deposits, at five per cent. interest, to twenty-five millions of dollars, shall be so far modified as to authorize the Secretary of the Treasury to receive such deposits to an amount not exceeding fifty millions of dollars, and that the rates of interest shall be prescribed by the Secretary of the Treasury not exceeding the annual rate of five per centum.

[Approved, March 17, 1862.   12 Statutes at Large, 370.]

1861–62, Chap. CXLII. — *An Act to authorize an additional Issue of United States Notes, and for other Purposes.*

Be it enacted, . . . That the Secretary of the Treasury is hereby authorized to issue, in addition to the amounts heretofore authorized, on the credit of the United States, one hundred and fifty millions of dollars of United States notes, not bearing interest, payable to bearer at the Treasury of the United States, and of such denominations as he may deem expedient: *Provided,* That no note shall be issued for the fractional part of a dollar, and not more than thirty-five millions shall be of lower denominations than five dollars; and such notes shall be receivable in payment of all loans made to the United States, and of all taxes, internal duties, excises, debts, and demands of every kind due to the United States, except duties on imports and interest, and of all claims and demands against the United States, except for interest upon bonds, notes, and certificates of debt or deposit; and shall also be lawful money and a legal tender in payment of all debts, public and private, within the United States, except duties on imports and interest, as aforesaid. And any holder of said United States notes depositing any sum not less than fifty dollars, or some multiple of fifty dollars, with the Treasurer of the United States, or either of the assistant treasurers, shall receive in exchange therefor duplicate certificates of deposit, one of which may be transmitted to the Secretary of the Treasury, who shall thereupon issue to the holder an equal amount of bonds of the United States, coupon or registered, as may by said holder be desired, bearing interest at the rate of six per centum per annum, payable semi-annually, and redeemable at the pleasure of the United States after five years, and payable twenty years from the date thereof: *Provided, however,* That any notes issued under this act may be paid in coin, instead of being received in exchange for certificates of deposit as above specified, at the direction of the Secretary of the Treasury. And the Secretary of the Treasury may exchange for such notes, on such terms as he shall think most beneficial to the public interest, any bonds of the United States bearing six per centum interest, and redeemable after five and payable in twenty years, which have been or may be lawfully issued under the provisions of any existing act; may reissue the notes so received in exchange; may receive and cancel any notes heretofore lawfully issued under any act of Congress, and in lieu thereof issue an equal amount in notes such as are authorized by this act; and may purchase, at rates not exceeding that of the current market, and cost of purchase not exceeding one-eighth of one per centum, any bonds or certificates of debt of the United States as he may deem advisable.

Sec. 3. *And be it further enacted,* That the limitation upon temporary deposits of United States notes with any Assistant Treasurer or designated depositary authorized by the Secretary of the Treasury to receive such deposits, to fifty millions of dollars be, and is hereby, repealed; and the Secretary of the Treasury is authorized to receive such deposits, under such regulations as he may prescribe, to such amount as he may deem expedient, not exceeding one hundred millions of dollars, for not less than thirty days, in sums not less than one hundred dollars, at a rate of interest not exceeding five per centum per annum; and any amount so deposited may be withdrawn from deposit, at any time after ten days' notice, on the return of the certificate of deposit. And of the amount of United States notes authorized by this act, not less than fifty millions of dollars shall be reserved for the purpose of securing prompt payment of such deposits when demanded, and shall be issued and used only when, in the judgment of the Secretary of the Treasury, the same or any part thereof may be needed for that purpose. And certificates of deposit and of indebtedness issued under this or former acts may be received on the same terms as United States notes in payment for bonds redeemable after five and payable in twenty years.

Sec. 4. *And be it further enacted*, That the Secretary of the Treasury may, at any time until otherwise ordered by Congress, and under the restrictions imposed by the "Act to authorize a national loan, and for other purposes," borrow, on the credit of the United States, such part of the sum of two hundred and fifty millions mentioned in said act as may not have been borrowed, under the provisions of the same, within twelve months from the passage thereof.

Sec. 6. *And be it further enacted,* That all the provisions of the act entitled "An act to authorize the issue of United States notes, and for the redemption or funding thereof, and for funding the floating debt of the United States," approved February twenty-five, eighteen hundred and sixty-two, so far as the same can or may be applied to the provisions of this act, and not inconsistent therewith, shall apply to the notes hereby authorized to be issued.

[Approved, July 11, 1862. 12 Statutes at Large, p. 532.]

1861–62, Chap. CXCVI. — *An Act to authorize Payments in Stamps, and to prohibit Circulation of Notes of less Denomination than One Dollar.*

Be it enacted, . . . That the Secretary of the Treasury be, and he is hereby directed to furnish to the Assistant Treasurers, and such designated depositaries of the United States as may be by him selected, in such sums as he may deem expedient, the postage and other stamps of the United States, to be exchanged by them, on application, for United States notes; and from and after the first day of August next such stamps shall be receivable in payment of all dues to the United States less than five dollars, and shall be received in exchange for United States notes when presented to any Assistant Treasurer or any designated depository selected as aforesaid in sums not less than five dollars.

Sec. 2. *And be it further enacted,* That from and after the first day of August, eighteen hundred and sixty-two, no private corporation, banking association, firm, or individual shall make, issue, circulate, or pay any note, check, memorandum, token, or other obligation, for a less sum than one dollar, intended to circulate as money or to be received or used in lieu of lawful money of the United States. . . .

[Approved, July 17, 1862.   12 Statutes at Large, 592.]

1862–63, Resolution No. IX. — *Joint Resolution to provide for the immediate Payment of the Army and Navy of the United States.*

Whereas it is deemed expedient to make immediate provision for the payment of the army and navy : therefore,

Be it resolved, . . . That the Secretary of the Treasury be, and he is hereby, authorized, if required by the exigencies of the public service, to issue on the credit of the United States the sum of one hundred millions of dollars of United States notes, in such form as he may deem expedient, not bearing interest, payable to bearer on demand, and of such denominations not less than one dollar, as he may prescribe, which notes so issued shall be lawful money and a legal tender, like the similar notes heretofore authorized in payment of all debts, public and private, within the United States, except for duties on imports and interest on the public debt ; and the notes so issued shall be part of the amount provided for in any bill now pending for the issue of treasury notes, or that may be passed hereafter by this Congress.

[Approved, January 17, 1863.   12 Statutes at Large, p. 822.]

1862–63, Chap. LVIII. — *An Act to provide a National Currency, secured by a Pledge of United States Stocks, and to provide for the Circulation and Redemption thereof.*

[This act was repealed and superseded by the act of similar title approved June 3, 1864, but with so little change in its leading features as to make it sufficient in this place to refer to the note appended to the act of 1864, where the principal points of difference are recited, and to extract here only the sections providing for the apportionment of the bank circulation and for the issue of secured notes by State banks.]

Sec. 17. *And be it further enacted,* That the entire amount of circulating notes to be issued under this act shall not exceed three hundred millions of dollars. One hundred and fifty millions of which sum shall be apportioned to associations in the States, in the District of Columbia, and in the Territories, according to representative population, and the remainder shall be apportioned by the Secretary of the Treasury among associations formed in the several States, in the District of Columbia, and in the Territories, having due regard to the existing banking capital, resources, and business, of such States, District, and Territories.

Sec. 61. *And be it further enacted,* That any banking association or corporation lawfully in existence as a bank of circulation on the first day of January, Anno Domini eighteen hundred and sixty-three, organized in any state, either under a special act of incorporation or a general banking law, may, at any time within —— years after the passage of this act become an association under the provisions of this act; that in such case the certificate of association provided for by this act shall be signed by the directors of such banking association or corporation, and in addition to the specifications required by this act, shall specify that such directors are authorized by the owners of two-thirds of the capital stock of such banking association or corporation, to make such certificate of association, and such certificate of association shall thereafter have the same effect, and the same proceedings shall be had thereon, as is provided for as to other associations organized under this act. And such association or corporation thereafter shall

have the same powers and privileges, and shall be subject to
the same duties, responsibilities, and rules, in all respects, as
is [are] prescribed in this act for other associations organized
under it, and shall be held and regarded as an association
under this act.

SEC. 62. *And be it further enacted,* That any bank or banking association, authorized by any State law to engage in the
business of banking, and duly organized under such State law
at the time of the passage of this act, and which shall be the
holder and owner of United States bonds to the amount of
fifty per centum of its capital stock, may transfer and deliver
to the treasurer of the United States such bonds, or any part
thereof, in the manner provided by this act ; and upon making
such transfer and delivery, such bank or banking association
shall be entitled to receive from the comptroller of the currency, circulating notes, as herein provided, equal in amount
to eighty per centum of the amount of the bonds so transferred
and delivered.

SEC. 63. *And be it further enacted,* That upon the failure
of any such State bank or banking association, to redeem any
of its circulating notes issued under the provisions of the preceding section, the comptroller of the currency shall, when
satisfied that such default has been made, and within thirty
days after notice of such default, proceed to declare the bonds
transferred and delivered to the treasurer, forfeited to the
United States, and the same shall thereupon be forfeited accordingly. And thereupon the circulating notes which have
been issued by such bank or banking association shall be redeemed and paid at the treasury of the United States, in the
same manner as other circulating notes issued under the provisions of this act are redeemed and paid.

SEC. 64. *And be it further enacted,* That the bonds forfeited, as provided in the last preceding section, may be cancelled to an amount equal to the circulating notes redeemed
and paid, or such bonds may be sold, under the direction of
the Secretary of the Treasury, and after retaining out of the
proceeds a sum sufficient to pay the whole amount of circulating notes, for the redemption of which such bonds are held,

the surplus, if any remains, shall be paid to the bank, or banking association from which such bonds were received.

SEC. 65. *And be it further enacted*, That Congress reserves the right, at any time, to amend, alter, or repeal this act.

[Approved, February 25, 1863.   12 Statutes at Large, 665.]

1862-63, Chap. LXXIII. — *An Act to provide Ways and Means for the Support of the Government.*

Be it enacted, ... That the Secretary of the Treasury be, and he is hereby, authorized to borrow, from time to time, on the credit of the United States, a sum not exceeding three hundred millions of dollars for the current fiscal year, and six hundred millions for the next fiscal year, and to issue therefor coupon or registered bonds, payable at the pleasure of the government after such periods as may be fixed by the Secretary, not less than ten nor more than forty years from date, in coin, and of such denominations not less than fifty dollars, as he may deem expedient, bearing interest at a rate not exceeding six per centum per annum, payable on bonds not exceeding one hundred dollars, annually, and on all other bonds semi-annually, in coin; and he may in his discretion dispose of such bonds at any time, upon such terms as he may deem most advisable, for lawful money of the United States, or for any of the certificates of indebtedness or deposit that may at any time be unpaid, or for any of the treasury notes heretofore issued or which may be issued under the provisions of this act. And all the bonds and treasury notes or United States notes issued under the provisions of this act shall be exempt from taxation by or under State or municipal authority: *Provided*, That there shall be outstanding of bonds, treasury notes, and United States notes, at any time, issued under the provisions of this act, no greater amount altogether than the sum of nine hundred millions of dollars.

SEC. 2. *And be it further enacted*, That the Secretary of the Treasury be, and he is hereby, authorized to issue, on the credit of the United States, four hundred millions of dollars in treasury notes, payable at the pleasure of the United States, or at such time or times not exceeding three years from date, as may be found most beneficial to the public interest, and bearing interest at a rate not exceeding six per centum per annum, payable at periods expressed on the face of said treasury notes; and the interest on the said treasury notes and on certificates of indebtedness and deposit hereafter issued, shall be paid in lawful money. The treasury notes thus issued shall be of such denomination as the Secretary may direct, not less than ten dollars, and may be disposed of on the best terms that can be obtained, or may be paid to any creditor of the United States willing to receive the same at par. And said treasury notes may be made a legal tender to the same extent as United States notes, for their face value excluding interest; or they may·be made exchangeable under regulations prescribed by the Secretary of the Treasury, by the holder thereof, at the Treasury in the city of Washington, or at the office of any Assistant Treasurer or depositary designated for that purpose, for United States notes equal in amount to the treasury notes offered for exchange, together with the interest accrued and due thereon at the date of interest payment next preceding such exchange. And in lieu of any amount of said treasury notes thus exchanged, or redeemed or paid at maturity, the Secretary may issue an equal amount of other treasury notes; and the treasury notes so exchanged, redeemed, or paid, shall be cancelled and destroyed as the Secretary may direct. In order to secure certain and prompt exchanges of United States notes for treasury notes, when required as above provided, the Secretary shall have power to issue United States notes to the amount of one hundred and fifty millions of dollars, which may be used if necessary for such exchanges; but no part of the United States notes authorized by this section shall be issued for or applied to any other purposes than said exchanges; and whenever any amount shall have been so issued and applied, the same shall be replaced as soon as practicable from the sales of treasury notes for United States notes.

SEC. 3. *And be it further enacted,* That the Secretary of the Treasury be, and he is hereby, authorized, if required by the exigencies of the public service, for the payment of the army and navy, and other creditors of the government, to issue on the credit of the United States the sum of one hundred and fifty millions of dollars of United States notes, including the amount of such notes heretofore authorized by the joint resolution approved January seventeen, eighteen hundred and sixty-three, in such form as he may deem expedient, not bearing interest, payable to bearer, and of such denominations, not less than one dollar, as he may prescribe, which notes so issued shall be lawful money and a legal tender in payment of all debts, public and private, within the United States, except for duties on imports and interest on the public debt; and any of the said notes, when returned to the Treasury, may be re-issued from time to time as the exigencies of the public service may require. And in lieu of any of said notes, or any other United States notes, returned to the Treasury, and cancelled or destroyed, there may be issued equal amounts of United States notes, such as are authorized by this act. And so much of the act to authorize the issue of United States notes, and for other purposes, approved February twenty-five, eighteen hundred and sixty-two, and of the act to authorize an additional issue of United States notes, and for other purposes, approved July eleven, eighteen hundred and sixty-two, as restricts the negotiation of bonds to market value, is hereby repealed. And the holders of United States notes, issued under and by virtue of said acts, shall present the same for the purpose of exchanging the same for bonds, as therein provided, on or before the first day of July, eighteen hundred and sixty-three, and thereafter the right so to exchange the same shall cease and determine.

SEC. 4. *And be it further enacted,* That in lieu of postage and revenue stamps for fractional currency, and of fractional notes, commonly called postage currency, issued or to be issued, the Secretary of the Treasury may issue fractional notes of like amounts in such form as he may deem expedient, and may provide for the engraving, preparation and issue thereof, in the Treasury Department building. And all such notes issued shall be exchangeable by the Assistant Treasurers and designated depositaries for United States notes, in sums not less than three dollars, and shall be receivable for postage and revenue stamps, and also in payment of any dues to the United States less than five dollars, except duties on imports, and shall be redeemed on presentation at the Treasury of the United States in such sums and under such regulations as the Secretary of the Treasury shall prescribe: *Provided,* That the whole amount of fractional currency issued, including postage and revenue stamps issued as currency, shall not exceed fifty millions of dollars.

SEC. 5. *And be it further enacted,* That the Secretary of the Treasury is hereby authorized to receive deposits of gold coin and bullion with the Treasurer or any Assistant Treasurer of the United States, in sums not less than twenty dollars, and to issue certificates therefor, in denominations of not less than twenty dollars each, corresponding with the denominations of the United States notes. The coin and bullion deposited for or representing the certificates of deposit shall be retained in the Treasury for the payment of the same on demand. And certificates representing coin in the Treasury may be issued in payment of interest on the public debt, which certificates, together with those issued for coin and bullion deposited, shall not at any time exceed twenty per centum beyond the amount of coin and bullion in the Treasury; and the certificates for coin or bullion in the Treasury shall be received at par in payment for duties on imports.

[Section 7, after providing for taxes to be laid upon the circulation of all banks and corporations, whether established under state laws or under the act of February 25, 1863, directs that all banks, corporations, or individuals issuing notes for any fractional part of a dollar after April 1, 1863, shall be taxed ten per cent. per annum upon the amount of such fractional notes.]

[Approved, March 3, 1863. 12 Statutes at Large, 709.]

1862–63, Chap. LXXIV. — *An Act to amend an Act entitled " An Act to provide Internal Revenue to support the Government and pay Interest on the Public Debt," approved July first, eighteen hundred and sixty-two, and for other Purposes.*

[Section 4, after prescribing that all contracts for the purchase or sale of coin or bullion, and all contracts for loans upon the pledge thereof, if to be performed after a period exceeding three days, shall be in writing and shall be taxed, provides as follows:]

And no loan of currency or money on the security of gold or silver coin of the United States, as aforesaid, or of any certificate or other evidence of deposit payable in gold or silver coin, shall be made exceeding in amount the par value of the coin pledged or deposited as security; and any such loan so made, or attempted to be made, shall be utterly void: *Provided*, That if gold or silver coin be loaned at its par value it shall be subject only to the duty imposed on other loans: *Provided, however*, That nothing herein contained shall apply to any transaction by or with the government of the United States.

[Approved, March 3, 1863. 12 Statutes at Large, 719.]

1863–64, Chap. XVII. — *An Act supplementary to an Act entitled "An Act to provide Ways and Means for the Support of the Government," approved March third, eighteen hundred and sixty-three.*

Be it enacted, . . . That, in lieu of so much of the loan authorized by the act of March third, eighteen hundred and sixty-three, to which this is supplementary, the Secretary of the Treasury is authorized to borrow, from time to time, on the credit of the United States, not exceeding two hundred millions of dollars during the current fiscal year, and to prepare and issue therefor coupon or registered bonds of the United States, bearing date March first, eighteen hundred and sixty-four, or any subsequent period, redeemable at the pleasure of the Government after any period not less than five years, and payable at any period not more than forty years from date, in coin, and of such denominations as may be found expedient, not less than fifty dollars, bearing interest not exceeding six per centum a year, payable on bonds not over one hundred dollars, annually, and on all other bonds semi-annually, in coin; and he may dispose of such bonds at any time, on such terms as he may deem most advisable, for lawful money of the United States, or, at his discretion, for Treasury notes, certificates of indebtedness, or certificates of deposit, issued under any act of Congress; and all bonds issued under this act shall be exempt from taxation by or under State or municipal authority.

[Section 2 authorizes the Secretary of the Treasury to issue bonds under the Act of February 25, 1862, in excess of five hundred millions of dollars, to the amount of eleven millions, to such persons as subscribed for them on or before January 21, 1864, and have paid for them.]

[Approved, March 3, 1864. 13 Statutes at Large, 13.]

1863–64, Resolution No. XX. — *Joint Resolution to authorize the Secretary of the Treasury to anticipate the Payment of Interest on the Public Debt, and for other Purposes.*

Be it resolved, . . . That the Secretary of the Treasury be authorized to anticipate the payment of interest on the publi debt, by a period not exceeding one year, from time to time, either with or without a rebate of interest upon the coupons, as to him may seem expedient; and he is hereby authorized to dispose of any gold in the Treasury of the United States not necessary for the payment of interest of the public debt: *Provided,* That the obligation to create the sinking fund according to the Act of February twenty-fifth, eighteen hundred and sixty-two, shall not be impaired thereby.

[Approved, March 17, 1864. 13 Statutes at Large, 404.]

1863–64, Chap. CVI. — *An Act to provide a National Currency, secured by a Pledge of United States Bonds, and to provide for the Circulation and Redemption thereof.*

Be it enacted, . . . That there shall be established in the Treasury Department a separate bureau, which shall be charged with the execution of this and all other laws that may be passed by Congress respecting the issue and regulation of a national currency secured by United States bonds. The chief officer of the said bureau shall be denominated the Comptroller of the Currency, and shall be under the general direction of the Secretary of the Treasury. He shall be appointed by the President, on the recommendation of the Secretary of the Treasury, by and with the advice and consent of the Senate, and shall hold his office for the term of five years unless sooner removed by the President, upon reasons to be communicated by him to the Senate; he shall receive an annual salary of five thousand dollars. . . .

[He shall give a bond in the penalty of $100,000 for the faithful discharge of his duties; shall have a competent deputy, who shall give a like bond for $50,000; and neither the Comptroller nor the Deputy-Comptroller shall "be interested" in any association issuing currency under the provisions of this act.

Section 5 provides that an association for carrying on the business of banking may be formed by any number of persons not less than five, who shall enter into articles stating the object of the association and containing provisions for regulating its business not inconsistent with this act. A copy of these articles must be forwarded to the Comptroller, together with a certificate of organization, specifying the name of the association, which shall be subject to the approval of the Comptroller, the place where it is located, the amount of its capital, and the names and residences of its stockholders. But the association shall not begin the business of banking until it is authorized by the Comptroller. It shall be a body-corporate from the date of its organization-certificate, and shall continue for twenty years unless sooner dissolved under the provisions of this act, and shall have all such incidental powers as are necessary to carry on the business of banking, by discounting, receiving deposits, lending money on personal security, buying and selling exchange, coin and bullion, and issuing and circulating notes under the provisions of this act.]

SEC. 7. *And be it further enacted*, That no association shall be organized under this act, with a less capital than one hundred thousand dollars, nor in a city whose population exceeds fifty thousand persons, with a less capital than two hundred thousand dollars: *Provided*, That banks with a capital of not less than fifty thousand dollars may, with the approval of the Secretary of the Treasury, be organized in any place the population of which does not exceed six thousand inhabitants.

[Every association is to be managed by not less than five directors, one of whom shall be its president; every director must own at least ten shares of the capital stock in his own right and in no way pledged for any debt; all elections of directors, after the first, are to be held annually in the month of January; every shareholder is to have one vote for every share of the stock owned by him; but no shareholder whose liability is past due and unpaid is to be allowed to vote.]

SEC. 12. *And be it further enacted*, That the capital stock of any association formed under this act shall be divided into shares of one hundred dollars each, and be deemed personal property and transferable on the books of the association in such manner as may be prescribed in the by-laws or articles of association. . . . The shareholders of each association formed under the provisions of this act, and of each existing bank or banking asso-

ciation that may accept the provisions of this act, shall be held
individually responsible, equally and ratably, and not one for
another, for all contracts, debts, and engagements of such association to the extent of the amount of their stock therein at the
par value thereof, in addition to the amount invested in such
shares. . . .

[But shareholders of any banking association now existing under
State laws, having not less than five millions of capital and a surplus of
twenty per cent. on hand, shall be liable only to the amount invested in
their shares ; but said surplus shall be in addition to that elsewhere required by this act, and shall be kept undiminished.

Section 13 provides that any association may increase its capital or
may diminish the same, subject to the approval of the Comptroller.]

SEC. 14. *And be it further enacted,* That at least fifty per
centum of the capital stock of every association shall be paid in
before it shall be authorized to commence business ; and the remainder of the capital stock of such association shall be paid in
instalments of at least ten per centum each on the whole amount
of the capital as frequently as one instalment at the end of each
succeeding month from the time it shall be authorized by the
Comptroller to commence business ; and the payment of each
instalment shall be certified to the Comptroller, under oath, by
the president or cashier of the association.

SEC. 16. *And be it further enacted,* That every association,
after having complied with the provisions of this act, preliminary
to the commencement of banking business under its provisions,
and before it shall be authorized to commence business, shall transfer and deliver to the Treasurer of the United States any United
States registered bonds bearing interest to an amount not less
than thirty thousand dollars nor less than one third of the capital
stock paid in, which bonds shall be deposited with the Treasurer
of the United States and by him safely kept in his office until the
same shall be otherwise disposed of, in pursuance of the provisions of this act. . . . And the deposit of bonds shall be, by every
association, increased as its capital may be paid up or increased, so
that every association shall at all times have on deposit with the
Treasurer registered United States bonds to the amount of at
least one third of its capital stock actually paid in : *Provided,*

That nothing in this section shall prevent an association that may desire to reduce its capital or to close up its business and dissolve its organization from taking up its bonds upon returning to the Comptroller its circulating notes in the proportion hereinafter named in this act, nor from taking up any excess of bonds beyond one third of its capital stock and upon which no circulating notes have been delivered.

SEC. 21. *And be it further enacted,* That·upon the transfer and delivery of bonds to the Treasurer, as provided in the foregoing section, the association making the same shall be entitled to receive from the Comptroller of the Currency circulating notes of different denominations, in blank, registered and countersigned as hereinafter provided, equal in amount to ninety per centum of the current market value of the United States bonds so transferred and delivered, but not exceeding ninety per centum of the amount of said bonds at the par value thereof, if bearing interest at a rate not less than five per centum per annum ; and at no time shall the total amount of such notes, issued to any such association, exceed the amount at such time actually paid in of its capital stock.

SEC. 22. *And be it further enacted,* That the entire amount of notes for circulation to be issued under this act shall not exceed three hundred millions of dollars. In order to furnish suitable notes for circulation, the Comptroller of the Currency is hereby authorized and required, under the direction of the Secretary of the Treasury, to cause plates and dies to be engraved, in the best manner to guard against counterfeiting and fraudulent alterations, and to have printed therefrom, and numbered, such quantity of circulating notes, in blank, of the denominations of one dollar, two dollars, three dollars, five dollars, ten dollars, twenty dollars, fifty dollars, one hundred dollars, five hundred dollars, and one thousand dollars, as may be required to supply, under this act, the associations entitled to receive the same ; which notes shall express upon their face that they are secured by United States bonds, deposited with the Treasurer of the United States by the written or engraved signatures of the Treasurer and Register, and by the imprint of the seal of the Treasury ; and shall also express upon their face the promise of the association receiving the same to pay on demand, attested by the signatures of the president or vice-president and cashier. And the said notes shall bear such devices and such other statements, and shall be in such form, as the Secretary of the Treasury shall, by regulation, direct: *Provided*, That not more than one-sixth part of the notes furnished to an association shall be of a less denomination than five dollars, and that after specie 'payments shall be resumed no association shall be furnished with notes of a less denomination than five dollars.

Sec. 23. *And be it further enacted*, That after any such association shall have caused its promise to pay such notes on demand to be signed by the president or vice-president and cashier thereof, in such manner as to make them obligatory promissory notes, payable on demand, at its place of business, such association is hereby authorized to issue and circulate the same as money ; and the same shall be received at par in all parts of the United States in payment of taxes, excises, public lands, and all other dues to the United States, except for duties on imports; and also for all salaries and other debts and demands owing by the United States to individuals, corporations, and associations within the United States, except interest on the public debt, and in redemption of the national currency. And no such association shall issue post notes or any other notes to circulate as money than such as are authorized by the foregoing provisions of this act.

[Section 24 provides that the Comptroller shall receive the worn-out or mutilated notes of any association, and shall deliver to it fresh notes in place thereof, and that the worn-out or mutilated notes shall be burned in presence of four persons, appointed by the Secretary of the Treasury, the Comptroller, the Treasurer of the United States and the association, respectively.]

Sec. 26. *And be it further enacted*, That the bonds transferred to and deposited with the Treasurer of the United States, as hereinbefore provided, by any banking association for the security of its circulating notes, shall be held exclusively for that purpose, until such notes shall be redeemed, except as provided in this act ; but the Comptroller of the Currency shall give to any such banking association powers of attorney to receive and appropriate to its own use the interest on the bonds which it shall have so transferred to the Treasurer; but such powers shall become inoperative whenever such banking association shall fail to redeem its circulating notes as aforesaid. Whenever the market or cash value of any bonds deposited with the Treasurer of the United States, as aforesaid, shall be reduced below the amount of the circulation issued for the same, the Comptroller of the Currency is hereby authorized to demand and receive the amount of such depreciation in other United States bonds at cash value, or in money, from the association receiving said bills, to be deposited with the Treasurer of the United States as long as such depreciation continues.

[And the Comptroller may permit the exchange of any of the bonds so deposited for other bonds of the United States, or the return of any of them upon the surrender and cancellation of a proportionate amount of the circulating notes; *provided*, the remaining bonds are sufficient for the requirements of this act, and the association has not failed to redeem its circulating notes.

Section 28 forbids any association to hold real estate, except such as may be necessary for its accommodation in its business, or may be mortgaged to it as security for debts previously contracted, or conveyed to it in satisfaction thereof, or may be purchased by it in order to secure debts due to it; or to hold possession under a mortgage, or to retain real estate purchased to secure debts, for more than five years.]

SEC. 29. *And be it further enacted,* That the total liabilities to any association, of any person, or of any company, corporation, or firm for money borrowed, including in the liabilities of a company or firm the liabilities of the several members thereof, shall at no time exceed one tenth part of the amount of the capital stock of such association actually paid in: *Provided,* that the discount of *bonâ fide* bills of exchange drawn against actually existing values, and the discount of commercial or business paper actually owned by the person or persons, corporation, or firm negotiating the same shall not be considered as money borrowed.

[Section 30 authorizes every association to charge upon loans or discounts made by it the rate of interest which the law of the State where it is established allows banks, organized under State laws, to charge; and, where no rate is fixed by the law of the State, to charge a rate not exceeding seven per cent. But the purchase or sale of a *bonâ fide* bill of exchange, payable at another place, at not more than the current rate of exchange in addition to the interest, shall not be considered as taking a greater rate of interest.]

SEC. 31. *And be it further enacted,* That every association in the cities hereinafter named shall, at all times, have on hand, in lawful money of the United States, an amount equal to at least twenty-five per centum of the aggregate amount of its notes in circulation and its deposits; and every other association shall, at all times, have on hand, in lawful money of the United States, an amount equal to at least fifteen per centum of the aggregate amount of its notes in circulation, and of its deposits. And whenever the lawful money of any association in any of the cities hereinafter named shall be below the amount of twenty-five per centum of its circulation and deposits, and whenever the lawful money of any other association shall be below fifteen per centum of its circulation and deposits, such association shall not increase its liabilities by making any new loans or discounts otherwise than by discounting or purchasing bills of exchange payable at sight, nor make any dividend of its profits until the required proportion between the aggregate amount of its outstanding notes of circulation and deposits and its lawful money of the United States shall be restored: *Provided,* That three fifths of said fifteen per centum may consist of balances due to an association available for the redemption of its circulating notes from associations approved by the Comptroller of the Currency, organized under this act, in the cities of Saint Louis, Louisville, Chicago, Detroit, Milwaukie, New Orleans, Cincinnati, Cleveland, Pittsburg, Baltimore, Philadelphia, Boston, New York, Albany, Leavenworth, San Francisco, and Washington City: *Provided, also,* That clearing-house certificates, representing specie or lawful money specially deposited for the purpose of any clearing-house association, shall be deemed to be lawful money in the possession of any association belonging to such clearing-house holding and owning such certificate, and shall be considered to be a part of the lawful money which such association is required to have under the foregoing provisions of this section: *Provided,* That the cities of Charleston and Richmond may be added to the list of cities in the national associations of which other associations may keep three fifths of their lawful money, whenever, in the opinion of the Comptroller of the Currency, the condition of the Southern States will warrant it. And it shall be competent for the Comptroller of the Currency to notify any association, whose lawful money reserve as aforesaid shall be below the amount to be kept on hand as aforesaid, to make good such reserve; and if such association shall fail for thirty days thereafter so to make good its reserve of lawful money of the United States, the Comptroller may, with the concurrence of the Secretary of the Treasury, appoint a receiver to wind up the business of such association, as provided in this act.

SEC. 32. *And be it further enacted,* That each association organized in any of the cities named in the foregoing section shall select, subject to the approval of the Comptroller of the Currency, an association in the city of New York, at which it will redeem its circulating notes at par. And each of such associations may keep one half of its lawful money reserve in cash deposits in the city of New York. And each association not organized within the cities named in the preceding section shall select, subject to the approval of the Comptroller of the Currency, an association in either of the cities named in the preceding section at which it will redeem its circulating notes at par, and the Comptroller shall give public notice of the names of the associations so selected at which redemptions are to be made by the respective associations, and of any change that may be made of the association at which the notes of any association are redeemed. If any association shall fail either to make the selection or to redeem its notes as aforesaid, the Comptroller of the Currency may, upon receiving satisfactory evidence thereof, appoint a receiver, in the manner provided for in this act, to wind up its affairs: *Provided,* That nothing in this section shall relieve any association from its liability to redeem its circulating notes at its own counter, at par, in lawful money, on demand: *And provided, further,* That every association formed or existing under the provisions of this act shall take and receive at par, for any debt or liability to said association, any and all notes or bills issued by any association existing under and by virtue of this act.

SEC. 33. *And be it further enacted*, That the directors of any association may, semi-annually, each year, declare a dividend of so much of the net profits of the association as they shall judge expedient; but each association shall, before the declaration of a dividend, carry one tenth part of its net profits of the preceding half year to its surplus fund until the same shall amount to twenty per centum of its capital stock.

[Section 34 provides for quarterly reports of the condition of every association, to be made by its officers to the Comptroller and published by him, and also for monthly reports to be made to him. This section was superseded by the Act of March 3, 1869, which directs that every association shall make at least five reports annually of its resources and liabilities on any past day specified by the Comptroller, and shall publish the same in a newspaper in the place where the association is established; and that every association shall also report to the Comptroller the amount of its net earnings and dividends, and make such further special reports as he may call for. 15 Statutes at Large, 326.]

SEC. 35. *And be it further enacted*, That no association shall make any loan or discount on the security of the shares of its own capital stock, nor be the purchaser or holder of any such shares, unless such security or purchase shall be necessary to prevent loss upon a debt previously contracted in good faith; and stock so purchased or acquired shall, within six months from the time of its purchase, be sold or disposed of at public or private sale, in default of which a receiver may be appointed to close up the business of the association, according to the provisions of this act.

SEC. 36. *And be it further enacted*, That no association shall at any time be indebted, or in any way liable, to an amount exceeding the amount of its capital stock at such time actually paid in and remaining undiminished by losses or otherwise, except on the following accounts, that is to say: —

First. On account of its notes of circulation.

Second. On account of moneys deposited with, or collected by, such association.

Third. On account of bills of exchange or drafts drawn

against money actually on deposit to the credit of such association, or due thereto.

Fourth. On account of liabilities to its stockholders for dividends and reserved profits.

SEC. 37. *And be it further enacted,* That no association shall, either directly or indirectly, pledge or hypothecate any of its notes of circulation, for the purpose of procuring money to be paid in on its capital stock, or to be used in its banking operations, or otherwise; nor shall any association use its circulating notes, or any part thereof, in any manner or form, to create or increase its capital stock.

[Section 38 forbids any association, while continuing its business, to withdraw or permit to be withdrawn any of its capital, except as provided in section 13, or to make any dividend to an amount exceeding its net profits then on hand, deducting therefrom its losses and bad debts; and for this purpose all debts on which interest is past due and unpaid for six months, unless they are well secured and in process of collection, are to be held bad.

Section 39 forbids any association to pay out or put in circulation the notes of any bank or association which are not at the time receivable at par by the association paying them out; or to pay out or put in circulation the notes of any bank or association which is not redeeming its notes in lawful money.]

SEC. 41. *And be it further enacted,* That the plates and special dies to be procured by the Comptroller of the Currency for the printing of such circulating notes shall remain under his control and direction, and the expenses necessarily incurred in executing the provisions of this act respecting the procuring of such notes, and all other expenses of the bureau, shall be paid out of the proceeds of the taxes or duties now or hereafter to be assessed on the circulation, and collected from associations organized under this act.

[It is then provided that every association shall pay to the United States a tax of one per cent. per annum on the average amount of its notes in circulation, one half of one per cent. on the average amount of its deposits, and one half of one per cent. on its capital stock beyond the amount invested in United States bonds. But the shares of any association may be taxed as personal property by the State in which it is located, and not elsewhere, at a rate not greater than is imposed upon other moneyed capital in the hands of the citizens of the State, or upon the shares of banks organized under the authority of the State; and the real estate of associations shall be subject to State, county, and municipal taxes to the same extent as other real estate.

Section 42 provides for the closing of any association upon the vote of shareholders owning two thirds of its capital, and for calling in its notes. Under this section, as modified by the Act of July 14, 1870, any association thus voting to close its affairs must within six months pay to the Treasurer of the United States the amount of its outstanding notes in lawful money; whereupon the bonds pledged as security for its circulation shall be returned to it, and its notes shall from that time be redeemed at the Treasury and destroyed, and the association discharged from all liability therefor. 16 Statutes at Large, 274.

Section 44 provides that any bank established under the laws of any State may by vote of the owners of two thirds of its capital stock be reorganized as an association under this act, without change of stockholders or directors or in the amount of its shares, provided that its capital shall not be less than is prescribed for associations under this act.]

SEC. 45. *And be it further enacted*, That all associations under this act, when designated for that purpose by the Secretary of the Treasury, shall be depositaries of public money, except receipts from customs, under such regulations as may be prescribed by the Secretary; and they may also be employed as financial agents of the government; and they shall perform all such reasonable duties, as depositaries of public moneys and financial agents of the government, as may be required of them. And the Secretary of the Treasury shall require of the associations thus designated satisfactory security, by the deposit of United States bonds and otherwise, for the safe-keeping and prompt payment of the public money deposited with them, and for the faithful performance of their duties as financial agents of the government: *Provided*, that every association which shall be selected and designated as receiver or depositary of the public money shall take and receive at par all of the national currency bills, by whatever association issued, which have been paid in to the government for internal revenue, or for loans or stocks.

[Section 46 *et seq.* provides that if any association shall fail to redeem in lawful money any of its circulating notes, when payment thereof is demanded at the proper place during the usual hours of business, the holder of such notes may cause them to be protested and notify the

Comptroller of the failure. The Comptroller, if satisfied that the association has refused to pay its notes and is in default, shall declare the bonds pledged by the association to be forfeited to the United States and shall notify the holders of its notes to present them for payment at the Treasury. And for the notes thus paid at the Treasury, the Comptroller may either cancel an amount of the bonds equal at the market rate, not exceeding par, to the notes so paid, or may cause the necessary amount of the bonds to be sold by public auction in the city of New York, or may sell the necessary amount by private sale, provided that they shall not be sold by private sale for less than the market rate nor less than par. And if the proceeds of the bonds pledged by the association are insufficient to reimburse the amount expended in payment of its notes, the United States shall have a first and paramount lien for the deficiency upon all the assets of the association, to be made good in preference to all other claims.

Section 50 authorizes the Comptroller, when satisfied that any association has refused to pay its circulating notes and is in default, to appoint a receiver, who shall take charge of all the books and assets of the association and collect all debts and property belonging to it, and, if necessary, enforce the individual liability of the shareholders under section 12 of this act. And the Comptroller, after reimbursing to the United States, from the fund thus collected, any deficiency due from the association for the redemption of its notes, shall make a ratable payment of the debts of the association, and the remainder of the fund, if any, after payment of these debts, he shall pay over to the shareholders, in proportion to the stock held by each.]

SEC. 54. *And be it further enacted*, That the Comptroller of the Currency, with the approbation of the Secretary of the Treasury, as often as shall be deemed necessary or proper, shall appoint a suitable person or persons to make an examination of the affairs of every banking association, which person shall not be a director or other officer in any association whose affairs he shall be appointed to examine, and who shall have power to make a thorough examination into all the affairs of the association, and, in doing so, to examine any of the officers and agents thereof on oath; and shall make a full and detailed report of the condition of the association to the Comptroller.

[Succeeding sections provide penalties for embezzlement by the officers of any association, for the mutilation or disfigurement of notes with the intent to make them unfit for reissue, and for counterfeiting, passing counterfeit notes, or having in possession such notes or the engraved plates or paper for making such notes, with intent to use.]

Section 61 requires the Comptroller to report annually to Congress the condition of every association as shown by its reports, with abstract statements of the total amount of liabilities, resources, and reserves, the amount of circulation redeemed and outstanding for associations which have closed their business during the year, and finally such changes in the laws relative to banking as may improve the system and increase its security.

Section 62 repeals the Act of February 25, 1863, but provides that the repeal shall not affect organizations or proceedings begun or had under said act, and that circulation issued by any association organized under it shall be deemed a part of the circulation authorized by the present act. And it is further provided that any association established or organizing under the former act may change its name, with the approval of the Comptroller.]

SEC. 63. *And be it further enacted,* That persons holding stock as executors, administrators, guardians, and trustees, shall not be personally subject to any liabilities as stockholders ; but the estates and funds in their hands shall be liable in like manner and to the same extent as the testator, intestate, ward, or person interested in said trust-funds would be if they were respectively living and competent to act and hold the stock in their names.

SEC. 64. *And be it further enacted,* That Congress may at any time amend, alter, or repeal this act.

[By the Act of March 1, 1872, Leavenworth is struck out from the list of redemption cities in section 31 above. 17 Statutes at Large, 32.

The use of the word "national," as a part of the name of any bank not organized under the national currency act above, is forbidden by the Act of March 3, 1873. 17 Statutes at Large, 603.]

[Approved, June 3, 1864. 13 Statutes at Large, 99.]

NOTE. — The above act is in substance a revision of that of February 25, 1863, with only such changes as experience had shown to be necessary for the trial of the system. Some of the principal points of difference between the two acts are the following : —

The Act of 1863 made no provision for the redemption of the circulation by the banks of the principal cities, such as is contained in sections 31 and 32 of the Act of 1864; but simply required that every bank should redeem its circulation at its own counter, and that it should have for that and other purposes a reserve equal to twenty-five per cent. of its circulation and deposits, of which reserve three-fifths might be deposited with associations in nine principal cities named in the act.

The prohibition of the issue of circulating notes of a less denomination than five dollars, took effect at once in the Act of 1863.

Under the Act of 1863, coupon bonds might be deposited to secure the circulation, but by the Act of 1864 only registered bonds.

The Act of 1863 required a smaller minimum of capital for a new bank than the Act of 1864, required a smaller proportion to be paid in before beginning business, and allowed a longer time for the payment of the remainder.

The Act of 1864 makes more complete provision than that of 1863 for the conversion of State banks into national associations, permitting the retention of the former name of a bank after conversion, and in section 12 exempting the stockholders of such banks from personal liability under certain conditions, which were intended to meet the case of the Bank of Commerce in the city of New York.

The Act of 1863 failed to provide as to the taxation of shares by State authority.

The Act of 1863 required the apportionment of the total circulation among the States and Territories, one half according to representative population and one half having due regard to the existing banking capital and resources.

For changes in the provision made in section 22, as to the total amount of bank notes and for the apportionment thereof, see *below*, pages 199, 202, 204, 212, 213, 214.

For changes in the limit of circulation allowed to any bank in section 21, and in the amount of bonds to be held, see *below*, pages 199, 203, 204, 211, 216, 221, 222.

1863–64, Chap. CXXVII. — *An Act to prohibit certain Sales of Gold and Foreign Exchange.*

Be it enacted, . . . That it shall be unlawful to make any contract for the purchase or sale and delivery of any gold coin or bullion to be delivered on any day subsequent to the day of making such contract, or for the payment of any sum, either fixed or contingent, in default of the delivery of any gold coin or bullion, or to make such contract upon any other terms than the actual delivery of such gold coin or bullion, and the payment in full of the agreed price thereof, on the day on which such contract is made, in United States notes or national currency, and not otherwise ; or to make any contract for the purchase or sale and delivery of any foreign exchange to be delivered at any time beyond ten days subsequent to the making of such contract ; or for the payment of any sum, either fixed or contingent, in default of the delivery of any foreign exchange, or upon any other terms than the actual delivery of such foreign exchange within ten days from the making of such contract, and the immediate payment in full of the agreed price thereof on the day of de livery in United States notes or national currency ; or to make any contract whatever for the sale and delivery of any gold coin or bullion of which the person making such contract shall not, at the time of making the same, be in actual possession. And it shall be unlawful to make any loan of money or currency not being in coin to be repaid in coin or bullion, or to make any loan of coin or bullion to be repaid in money or currency other than coin.

SEC. 2. *And be it further enacted*, That it shall be further unlawful for any banker, broker, or other person, to make any purchase or sale of any gold coin or bullion, or of any foreign exchange, or any contract for any such purchase or sale, at any other place than the ordinary place of business of either the seller or purchaser, owned or hired, and occupied by him individ- ually, or by a partnership of which he is a member.

SEC. 3. *And be it further enacted*, That all contracts made in violation of this act shall be absolutely void.

SEC. 4. *And be it further enacted*, That any person who shall violate any provisions of this act shall be held guilty of a mis- demeanor, and, on conviction thereof, be fined in any sum not less than one thousand dollars, nor more than ten thousand dol- lars, or be imprisoned for a period not less than three months, nor longer than one year, or both, at the discretion of the court, and shall likewise be subject to a penalty of one thousand dollars for each offence.

SEC. 5. *And be it further enacted*, That the penalties imposed by the fourth section of this act may be recovered in an action at law in any court of record of the United States, or any court of competent jurisdiction, which action may be brought in the name of the United States by any person who will sue for said penalty, one half for the use of the United States, and the other half for the use of the person bringing such action. And the recovery and satisfaction of a judgment in any such action shall be a bar to the imposition of any fine for the same offence in any prosecution instituted subsequent to the recovery of such judgment, but shall not be a bar to the infliction of punishment by imprisonment, as provided by said fourth section.

SEC. 6. *And be it further enacted,* That all acts and parts of acts inconsistent with the provisions of this act are hereby repealed.   [Approved, June 17, 1864.   13 Statutes at Large, 132.]

NOTE. — The above Act was repealed by the Act approved July 2, 1864. See 13 Statutes at Large, 344.

1863–64, Chap. CLXXII. — *An Act to provide Ways and Means for the Support of the Government, and for other Purposes.*

Be it enacted, . . . That the Secretary of the Treasury be, and he is hereby, authorized to borrow, from time to time, on the credit of the United States, four hundred millions of dollars, and to issue therefor coupon or registered bonds of the United States, redeemable at the pleasure of the government, after any period not less than five, nor more than thirty, years, or, if deemed expedient, made payable at any period not more than forty years from date. And said bonds shall be of such denominations as the Secretary of the Treasury shall direct, not less than fifty dollars, and bear an annual interest not exceeding six per centum, payable semi-annually in coin. And the Secretary of the Treasury may dispose of such bonds, or any part thereof, and of any bonds commonly known as five-twenties remaining unsold, in the United States, or, if he shall find it expedient, in Europe, at any time, on such terms as he may deem most advisable, for lawful money of the United States, or, at his discretion, for treasury notes, certificates of indebtedness, or certificates of deposit issued under any act of Congress. And all bonds, treasury notes, and other obligations of the United States shall be exempt from taxation by or under State or municipal authority.

SEC. 2. *And be it further enacted,* That the Secretary of the Treasury may issue on the credit of the United States, and in lieu of an equal amount of bonds authorized by the preceding section, and as a part of said loan, not exceeding two hundred millions of dollars, in treasury notes of any denomination not less than ten dollars, payable at any time not exceeding three years from date, or, if thought more expedient, redeemable at any time after three years from date, and bearing interest not exceeding the rate of seven and three-tenths per centum, payable in lawful money at maturity, or, at the discretion of the Secretary, semi-annually. And the said treasury notes may be disposed of by the Secretary of the Treasury, on the best terms that can be obtained, for lawful money; and such of them as shall be made payable, principal and interest, at maturity, shall be a legal tender to the same extent as United States notes for their face value, excluding interest, and may be paid to any creditor of the United States at their face value, excluding interest, or to any creditor willing to receive them at par, including interest; and any treasury notes issued under the authority of this act may be made convertible, at the discretion of the Secretary of the Treasury, into any bonds issued under the authority of this act. And the Secretary of the Treasury may redeem, and cause to be cancelled and destroyed, any treasury notes or United States notes heretofore issued under authority of previous acts of Congress, and substitute, in lieu thereof, an equal amount of treasury notes such as are authorized by this act, or of other United States notes: *Provided*, That the total amount of bonds and treasury notes authorized by the first and second sections of this act shall not exceed four hundred millions of dollars, in addition to the amounts heretofore issued; nor shall the total amount of United States notes, issued or to be issued, ever exceed four hundred millions of dollars, and such additional sum, not exceeding fifty millions of dollars, as may be temporarily required for the redemption of temporary loan; nor shall any treasury note bearing interest, issued under this act, be a legal tender in payment or redemption of any notes issued by any bank, banking association, or banker, calculated or intended to circulate as money.

[Section 3 authorizes the Secretary of the Treasury to exchange bonds heretofore issued on which the interest is payable annually, for others bearing interest payable semi-annually. The treasury notes heretofore issued, bearing seven and three-tenths per cent. interest, may be exchanged for the six per cent. bonds heretofore authorized, at any time within three months after notice of redemption given by the Secretary, after which interest on such notes shall cease; and the interest on such notes after maturity shall be paid in lawful money. So much of the Act of March 8, 1864, as limits the loan therein authorized to the current fiscal year, is repealed. The authority to issue bonds or notes, conferred by section 1 of the Act of March 3, 1863, is to cease on the passage of this act, except so far as it may affect seventy-five millions of bonds already advertised.]

SEC. 4. *And be it further enacted,* That the Secretary of the Treasury may authorize the receipt, as a temporary loan, of United States notes, or the notes of national banking associations, on deposit for not less than thirty days, in sums of not less than fifty dollars, by any of the Assistant Treasurers of the United States, or depositaries designated for that purpose, other than national banking associations, . . .

[Certificates of deposit shall be given, bearing interest not exceeding six per cent. per annum, and payable upon ten days' notice; and the Secretary may increase the rate of interest, if below six per cent., or may lower the same on ten days' notice, at his discretion.]

but the aggregate of such deposits shall not exceed one hundred and fifty millions of dollars ; and the Secretary of the Treasury may issue, and shall hold in reserve for payment of such deposits, United States notes not exceeding fifty millions of dollars, including the amount already applied in such payment; and the United States notes, so held in reserve, shall be used only when needed, in his judgment, for the prompt payment of such deposits on demand, and shall be withdrawn and placed again in reserve as the amount of deposits shall again increase.

[Section 5 authorizes the Secretary of the Treasury to issue "notes of the fractions of a dollar as now used for currency," and to provide for their redemption when mutilated or defaced, and for their receipt in payment of debts to the United States, except for customs, in sums not over five dollars; but the whole amount of all notes or stamps less than one dollar issued as currency shall not exceed fifty millions of dollars.

Section 7 authorizes the issue of registered bonds in lieu of coupon bonds, already or hereafter to be issued.]

[Approved, June 30, 1864. 13 Statutes at Large, 218.]

1864–65, Chap. XXII.—*An Act to amend an Act entitled "An Act to provide Ways and Means for the Support of the Government, and for other Purposes," approved June thirtieth, eighteen hundred and sixty-four.*

Be it enacted, ... That in lieu of any bonds authorized to be issued by the first section of the act entitled "An act to provide ways and means for the support of the government," approved June thirtieth, eighteen hundred and sixty-four, that may remain unsold at the date of this act, the Secretary of the Treasury may issue, under the authority of said act, treasury notes of the description and character authorized by the second section of said act: *Provided,* That the whole amount of bonds authorized as aforesaid, and treasury notes issued and to be issued in lieu thereof, shall not exceed the sum of four hundred millions of dollars; and such treasury notes may be disposed of for lawful money, or for any other treasury notes or certificates of indebtedness or certificates of deposit issued under any previous act of Congress; and such notes shall be exempt from taxation by or under State or municipal authority.

Sec. 2. *And be it further enacted,* That any bonds known as five-twenties, issued under the act of twenty-fifth February, eighteen hundred and sixty-two, remaining unsold to an amount not exceeding four millions of dollars, may be disposed of by the Secretary of the Treasury in the United States, or, if he shall find it expedient, in Europe, at any time, on such terms as he may deem most advisable: *Provided,* That this act shall not be so construed as to give any authority for the issue of any legal tender notes, in any form, beyond the balance unissued of the amount authorized by the second section of the act to which this is an amendment.

[Approved, January 28, 1865. 13 Statutes at Large, 425.]

1864–65, Chap. LXXVII. — *An Act to provide Ways and Means for the Support of the Government.*

Be it enacted, ... That the Secretary of the Treasury be, and ne is hereby, authorized to borrow, from time to time, on the credit of the United States, in addition to the amounts heretofore authorized, any sums not exceeding in the aggregate six hundred millions of dollars, and to issue therefor bonds or treasury notes of the United States, in such form as he may prescribe ; and so much thereof as may be issued in bonds shall be of denominations not less than fifty dollars, and may be made payable at any period not more than forty years from date of issue, or may be made redeemable at the pleasure of the government, at or after any period not less than five years nor more than forty years from date, or may be made redeemable and payable as aforesaid, as may be expressed upon their face; and so much thereof as may be issued in treasury notes may be made convertible into any bonds authorized by this act, and may be of such denominations — not less than fifty dollars — and bear such dates, and be made redeemable or payable at such periods as in the opinion of the Secretary of the Treasury may be deemed expedient.   And the interest on such bonds shall be payable semi-annually; and on treasury notes authorized by this act the interest may be made payable semi-annually, or annually, or at maturity thereof; and the principal, or interest, or both, may be made payable in coin or in other lawful money: *Provided,* That the rate of interest on any such bonds or treasury notes, when payable in coin, shall not exceed six per centum per annum ; and when not payable in coin shall not exceed seven and three-tenths per centum per annum ; and the rate and character of interest shall be expressed on all such bonds or treasury notes : *And provided, further,* That the act entitled " An act to provide ways and means for the support of the government, and for other purposes," approved June thirtieth, eighteen hundred and sixty-four, shall be so construed as to authorize the issue of bonds of any description authorized by this act.   And any treasury notes or other obligations bearing interest, issued under any act of Congress, may, at the discretion of the Secretary of the Treasury, and with the consent of the holder, be converted into any description of bonds authorized by this act; and no bonds so authorized shall be considered a part of the amount of six hundred millions hereinbefore authorized.

[Section 2 authorizes the Secretary of the Treasury to dispose of any of the obligations issued under this act, where and under such condition, and at such rates as he thinks best, for coin or other lawful money, treasury notes, or certificates of indebtedness or of deposit, and the like; and to issue bonds or treasury notes authorized by this act in payment of requisitions for materials or supplies, on receiving notice that the owner of the claim for which any requisition is made desires to subscribe for a portion of the loan; "and all bonds or other obligations issued under this act shall be exempt from taxation by or under state or municipal authority."

Section 3 contains a proviso, "That nothing herein contained shall be construed as authorizing the issue of legal-tender notes in any form."]

[Approved, March 3, 1865. 13 Statutes at Large, 468.]

1864-65, Chap. LXXVIII. — *An Act to amend an Act entitled " An Act to provide Internal Revenue to support the Government, to pay Interest on the Public Debt, and for other Purposes," approved June thirtieth, eighteen hundred and sixty-four.*

SEC. 6. *And be it further enacted*, That every national banking association, State bank, or State banking association, shall pay a tax of ten per centum on the amount of notes of any State bank or State banking association, paid out by them after the first day of July, eighteen hundred and sixty-six.

[By subsequent legislation this provision is made to include also the notes of any person, firm, association, corporation, town, city, or municipal corporation, and the tax is imposed both on the issuer of the notes and on any person, bank, or corporation paying them out. See 13 Statutes at Large, 146; 15 *ibid.*, 6; 18 *ibid.*, 311.]

SEC. 7. *And be it further enacted*, That any existing bank organized under the laws of any State, having a paid-up capital of not less than seventy-five thousand dollars, which shall apply before the first day of July next for authority to become a national bank under the act entitled " An act to provide a national currency secured by a pledge of United States bonds, and to provide for the circulation and redemption thereof," approved June third, eighteen hundred and sixty-four, and shall comply with all the requirements of said act, shall, if such bank be found by the Comptroller of the Currency to be in good standing and credit, receive such authority in preference to new associations applying for the same. . . .

[Approved, March 3, 1865. 13 Statutes at Large, 469.]

1864-65, Chap. LXXXII. — *An Act to amend an Act entitled "An Act to provide a National Currency, secured by a Pledge of United States Bonds, and to provide for the Circulation and Redemption thereof."*

Be it enacted, . . . That section twenty-one of said act be so amended that said section shall read as follows :

[In lieu of the concluding sentence of said section "and at no time shall the total amount of such notes . . . exceed the amount . . . of its capital stock " the following is substituted :]

. . . and the amount of said circulating notes to be furnished to each association shall be in proportion to its paid-up capital as follows, and no more : To each association whose capital shall not exceed five hundred thousand dollars, ninety per centum of such capital ; to each association whose capital exceeds five hundred thousand dollars, but does not exceed one million dollars, eighty per centum of such capital ; to each association whose capital exceeds one million dollars, but does not exceed three millions of dollars, seventy-five per centum of such capital ; to each association whose capital exceeds three millions of dollars, sixty per centum of such capital. And that one hundred and fifty millions of dollars of the entire amount of circulating notes authorized to be issued shall be apportioned to associations in the States, in the District of Columbia, and in the Territories, according to representative population, and the remainder shall be apportioned by the Secretary of the Treasury among associations formed in the several States, in the District of Columbia, and in the Territories, having due regard to the existing banking capital, resources, and business of such States, District, and Territories.

[Approved, March 3, 1865.   13 Statutes at Large, 498.]

1865-66, Chap. XXVIII. — *An Act to amend an Act entitled "An Act to provide Ways and Means to support the Government," approved March third, eighteen hundred and sixty-five.*

Be it enacted, . . . That the act entitled " An act to provide ways and means to support the Government," approved March third, eighteen hundred and sixty-five, shall be extended and construed to authorize the Secretary of the Treasury, at his discretion, to receive any treasury notes or other obligations issued under any act of Congress, whether bearing interest or not, in exchange for any description of bonds authorized by the act to which this is an amendment; and also to dispose of any description of bonds authorized by said act, either in the United States or elsewhere, to such an amount, in such manner, and at such rates as he may think advisable, for lawful money of the United States, or for any treasury notes, certificates of indebtedness, or certificates of deposit, or other representatives of value, which have been or which may be issued under any act of Congress, the proceeds thereof to be used only for retiring treasury notes or other obligations issued under any act of Congress; but nothing herein contained shall be construed to authorize any increase of the public debt: *Provided,* That of United States notes not more than ten millions of dollars may be retired and cancelled within six months from the passage of this act, and thereafter not more than four millions of dollars in any one month: *And provided further,* That the act to which this is an amendment shall continue in full force in all its provisions, except as modified by this act.

[Section 2 requires the Secretary of the Treasury to report to Congress at its next session all transactions under this act and the act to which this is an amendment.]

[Approved, April 12, 1866.   14 Statutes at Large, 31.]

1856-67, Chap. CXCIV. — *An Act to provide Ways and Means for the Payment of Compound Interest Notes.*

[This act directs the Secretary of the Treasury, for the purpose of redeeming any outstanding compound interest notes, to issue temporary loan certificates as prescribed by section 4 of the act of February 25, 1862, bearing interest not exceeding three per cent. per annum, and principal and interest payable in lawful money on demand; the amount of certificates at any time outstanding not to exceed fifty millions of dollars.

And said certificates may be held by any national bank as part of the reserve required by sections 31 and 32 of the National Currency Act of June 3, 1864; but not less than two-fifths of the entire reserve of such bank shall consist of lawful money.]

[Approved, March 2, 1867.   14 Statutes at Large, 558.]

1867–68, Chap. VI. — *An Act to suspend further Reduction of the Currency.*

Be it enacted, . . . That from and after the passage of this act, the authority of the Secretary of the Treasury to make any reduction of the currency, by retiring or cancelling United States notes, shall be, and is hereby, suspended; but nothing herein contained shall prevent the cancellation and destruction of mutilated United States notes, and the replacing of the same with notes of the same character and amount.

NOTE. — The above act having been presented to the President of the United States for his approval, and not having been returned by him to the House of Congress in which it originated within the time prescribed by the Constitution, became a law without his approval, February 4, 1868.

[15 Statutes at Large, 34.]

1867–68, Chap. CCXXXVII. — *An Act to provide for a further Issue of temporary Loan Certificates, for the Purpose of redeeming and retiring the Remainder of the outstanding Compound Interest Notes.*

[For the sole purpose of redeeming the remainder of the compound interest notes, this act adds twenty-five millions of dollars to the amount of three per cent. temporary loan certificates authorized by the act of March 2, 1867.]

[Approved, July 25, 1868.   15 Statutes at Large, 183.]

1868–69, Chap. XXXII. — *An Act to prevent loaning Money upon United States Notes.*

Be it enacted, . . . That no national banking association shall hereafter offer or receive United States notes or national bank notes as security or as collateral security for any loan of money, or for a consideration shall agree to withhold the same from use, or shall offer or receive the custody or promise of custody

of such notes as security, or as collateral security, or consideration for any loan of money. . . .

[Approved, February 19, 1869. 15 Statutes at Large, 270.]

1869, Chap. I. — *An Act to strengthen the Public Credit.*

Be it enacted, . . . That in order to remove any doubt as to
the purpose of the government to discharge all just obligations
to the public creditors, and to settle conflicting questions and in-
terpretations of the laws by virtue of which such obligations
have been contracted, it is hereby provided and declared that
the faith of the United States is solemnly pledged to the payment in coin or its equivalent of all the obligations of the United
States not bearing interest, known as United States notes, and
of all the interest-bearing obligations of the United States, except in cases where the law authorizing the issue of any such
obligation has expressly provided that the same may be paid in
lawful money or other currency than gold or silver. But none
of said interest-bearing obligations not already due shall be redeemed or paid before maturity unless at such time United
States notes shall be convertible into coin at the option of the
holder, or unless at such time bonds of the United States bearing a lower rate of interest than the bonds to be redeemed can
be sold at par in coin. And the United States also solemnly
pledges its faith to make provision at the earliest practicable
period for the redemption of the United States notes in coin.

[Approved, March 18, 1869. 16 Statutes at Large, 1.]

1869-70, Chap. CCLII. — *An Act to provide for the Redemption of the three per cent. temporary Loan Certificates,
and for an Increase of National Bank Notes.*

Be it enacted, . . . That fifty-four millions of dollars in notes
for circulation may be issued to national banking associations,
in addition to the three hundred millions of dollars authorized
by the twenty-second section of the " Act to provide a national
currency, secured by a pledge of United States bonds, and to
provide for the circulation and redemption thereof," approved

June three, eighteen hundred and sixty-four; and the amount
of notes so provided shall be furnished to banking associations
organized or to be organized in those States and Territories
having less than their proportion under the apportionment contemplated by the provisions of the "Act to amend an act to
provide a national currency, secured by a pledge of United
States bonds, and to provide for the circulation and redemption
thereof," approved March three, eighteen hundred and sixty-
five, and the bonds deposited with the Treasurer of the United
States, to secure the additional circulating notes herein authorized, shall be of any description of bonds of the United States
bearing interest in coin, but a new apportionment of the increased circulation herein provided for shall be made as soon as
practicable, based upon the census of eighteen hundred and seventy: *Provided*, That if applications for the circulation herein
authorized shall not be made within one year after the passage
of this act by banking associations organized or to be organized
in States having less than their proportion, it shall be lawful for
the Comptroller of the Currency to issue such circulation to
banking associations applying for the same in other States or
Territories having less than their proportion, giving the preference to such as have the greatest deficiency: *And providea
further*, That no banking association hereafter organized shall
have a circulation in excess of five hundred thousand dollars.

[Section 2 provides that at the end of every month the Secretary of
the Treasury shall call in and redeem an amount of the three per cent.
temporary loan certificates issued under the Acts of March 2, 1867, and
July 25, 1868, not less than the amount of circulating notes issued to national banking associations under the preceding section during the previous month.]

SEC. 3. *And be it further enacted*, That upon the deposit of
any United States bonds, bearing interest payable in gold, with
the Treasurer of the United States, in the manner prescribed in
the nineteenth and twentieth sections of the national currency
act, it shall be lawful for the Comptroller of the Currency to
issue to the association making the same, circulating notes of
different denominations, not less than five dollars, not exceeding
in amount eighty per centum of the par value of the bonds de-

posited, which notes shall bear upon their face the promise of the association to which they are issued to pay them, upon presentation at the office of the association, in gold coin of the United States, and shall be redeemable upon such presentation in such coin: *Provided*, That no banking association organized under this section shall have a circulation in excess of one million of dollars.

SEC. 4. *And be it further enacted*, That every national banking association formed under the provisions of the preceding section of this act shall at all times keep on hand not less than twenty-five per centum of its outstanding circulation in gold or silver coin of the United States, and shall receive at par in the payment of debts the gold notes of every other such banking association which at the time of such payments shall be redeeming its circulating notes in gold coin of the United States.

SEC. 5. *And be it further enacted*, That every association organized for the purpose of issuing gold notes as provided in this act shall be subject to all the requirements and provisions of the national currency act, except the first clause of section twenty-two, which limits the circulation of national banking associations to three hundred millions of dollars; the first clause of section thirty-two, which, taken in connection with the preceding section, would require national banking associations organized in the city of San Francisco to redeem their circulating notes at par in the city of New York; and the last clause of section thirty-two, which requires every national banking association to receive in payment of debts the notes of every other national banking association at par: *Provided*, That in applying the provisions and requirements of said act to the banking associations herein provided for, the terms "lawful money," and "lawful money of the United States," shall be held and construed to mean gold or silver coin of the United States.

SEC. 6. *And be it further enacted*, That to secure a more equitable distribution of the national banking currency there may be issued circulating notes to banking associations organized in States and Territories having less than their proportion as herein set forth. And the amounts of circulation in this section authorized shall, under the direction of the Secretary of the

Treasury, as it may be required for this purpose, be withdrawn, as herein provided, from banking associations organized in States having a circulation exceeding that provided for by the act entitled "An act to amend an act entitled 'An act to provide for a national banking currency, secured by pledge of United States bonds, and to provide for the circulation and redemption thereof,'" approved March three, eighteen hundred and sixty-five, but the amount so withdrawn shall not exceed twenty-five million dollars.

[It is then provided that the redistribution shall be made, when required, by withdrawing from banks having a circulation exceeding one million dollars such excess, in States having more than their proportion; and then from banks having a circulation exceeding three hundred thousand dollars their excess over that amount, beginning with States having the largest proportion in excess, and proceeding, if necessary, to those having a smaller proportion. Upon the failure of any association to retire the amount of its circulation required as above, the Comptroller of the Currency is authorized to sell the necessary amount of its bonds and to redeem its notes to the amount required. But no circulation is to be withdrawn under this section until the fifty-four millions granted in section 1 shall have been taken up.

Section 7 provides that after six months from the passage of this act any association may be removed from any State having more than its proportion of circulation to any State having less than its proportion; but the amount of the issue of said association shall not be deducted from the new issue herein provided for.]

[Approved, July 12, 1870. 16 Statutes at Large, 251.]

1869–70, Chap. CCLVI. — *An Act to authorize the Refunding of the National Debt.*

Be it enacted, . . . That the Secretary of the Treasury is hereby authorized to issue, in a sum or sums not exceeding in the aggregate two hundred million dollars, coupon or registered bonds of the United States, in such form as he may prescribe, and of denominations of fifty dollars, or some multiple of that sum, redeemable in coin of the present standard value, at the pleasure of the United States, after ten years from the date of their issue, and bearing interest, payable semi-annually in such coin, at the rate of five per cent. per annum; also a sum or sums not exceeding in the aggregate three hundred million dollars of like bonds, the same in all respects, but payable at the pleasure of the United States, after fifteen years from the date of their issue, and bearing interest at the rate of four and a half per cent. per annum; also a sum or sums not exceeding in the aggregate one thousand million dollars of like bonds, the same in all respects, but payable at the pleasure of the United States, after thirty years from the date of their issue, and bearing interest at the rate of four per cent. per annum; all of which said several classes of bonds and the interest thereon shall be exempt from the payment of all taxes or duties of the United States, as well as from taxation in any form by or under State, municipal, or local authority; and the said bonds shall have set forth and expressed upon their face the above-specified conditions, and shall, with their coupons, be made payable at the Treasury of the United States. But nothing in this act, or in any other law now in force, shall be construed to authorize any increase whatever of the bonded debt of the United States.

[By the amendatory Act of January 20, 1871, the amount of bonds to be issued bearing interest at five per cent. is increased to five hundred millions of dollars, but without any increase of the total amount of bonds provided for above; and the Secretary of the Treasury is authorized to make the interest of any of the bonds so provided for payable quarter-yearly. 16 Statutes at Large, 399. By an act of December 17, 1873, it is provided that the holders of bonds of the loan of 1858 may, if they so elect, exchange the same, on or before February 1, 1874, for bonds of the funded loan of 1870. 18 Statutes at Large, 1.] *

SEC. 2. *And be it further enacted,* That the Secretary of the Treasury is hereby authorized to sell and dispose of any of the bonds issued under this act, at not less than their par value for coin, and to apply the proceeds thereof to the redemption of any of the bonds of the United States outstanding, and known as five-twenty bonds, at their par value, or he may exchange the same for such five-twenty bonds, par for par; but the bonds hereby authorized shall be used for no other purpose whatsoever. And a sum not exceeding one-half of one per cent. of the bonds herein authorized is hereby appropriated to pay the expense of preparing, issuing, advertising, and disposing of the same.

[Section 3 provides that, after the maturity of any of the bonds herein authorized, payment thereof shall be made at the discretion of the Secretary of the Treasury, the bonds to be called for by public notice specifying their dates and numbers, beginning with the bonds last dated and numbered, and the interest on bonds thus selected ceasing three months after the date of such notice. Section 4 authorizes the Secretary, with any coin that is lawfully applicable, to pay at par and cancel any of the five-twenty bonds that may become redeemable by the terms of their issue; the bonds to be called for by public notice as above, interest ceasing in like manner, and the bonds to be called in numerical order, beginning with the bonds first numbered and issued.]

Sec. 5. *And be it further enacted*, That the Secretary of the Treasury is hereby authorized, at any time within two years from the passage of this act, to receive gold coin of the United States on deposit for not less than thirty days, in sums of not less than one hundred dollars, with the Treasurer, or any Assistant Treasurer of the United States authorized by the Secretary of the Treasury to receive the same, who shall issue therefor certificates of deposit, made in such form as the Secretary of the Treasury shall prescribe, and said certificates of deposit shall bear interest at a rate not exceeding two and a half per cent. per annum; and any amount of gold coin so deposited may be withdrawn from deposit at any time after thirty days from the date of deposit, and after ten days' notice and on the return of said certificates : *Provided*, That the interest on all such deposits shall cease and determine at the pleasure of the Secretary of the Treasury. And not less than twenty-five per cent. of the coin deposited for or represented by said certificates of deposits shall be retained in the treasury for the payment of said certificates ; and the excess beyond twenty-five per cent. may be applied at the discretion of the Secretary of the Treasury to the payment or redemption of such outstanding bonds of the United States heretofore issued and known as the five-twenty bonds, as he may designate under the provisions of the fourth section of this act; and any certificates of deposit issued as aforesaid, may be received at par with the interest accrued thereon in payment for any bonds authorized to be issued by this act.

Sec. 6. *And be it further enacted*, That the United States bonds purchased and now held in the treasury in accordance

with the provisions relating to a sinking fund, of section five of
the act entitled "An act to authorize the issue of United States
notes, and for the redemption or funding thereof, and for funding
the floating debt of the United States," approved February
twenty-fifth, eighteen hundred and sixty-two, and all other
United States bonds which have been purchased by the Secretary of the Treasury with surplus funds in the treasury, and now
held in the Treasury of the United States, shall be cancelled
and destroyed, a detailed record of such bonds so cancelled and
destroyed to be first made in the books of the Treasury Department.   Any bonds hereafter applied to said sinking fund, and
all other United States bonds redeemed or paid hereafter by the
United States, shall also in like manner be recorded, cancelled
and destroyed, and the amount of the bonds of each class that
have been cancelled and destroyed shall be deducted respectively
from the amount of each class of the outstanding debt of the
United States.   In addition to other amounts that may be applied
to the redemption or payment of the public debt, an amount equal
to the interest on all bonds belonging to the aforesaid sinking
fund shall be applied, as the Secretary of the Treasury shall from
time to time direct, to the payment of the public debt as provided for in section five of the act aforesaid.   And the amount
so to be applied is hereby appropriated annually for that purpose, out of the receipts for duties on imported goods.

[Approved, July 14, 1870.   16 Statutes at Large, 272.]

1869-70, Chap. CCLVII. — *An Act to require national Banks
going into Liquidation to retire their circulating Notes.*

Be it enacted, . . . That every bank that has heretofore
gone into liquidation under the provisions of section forty-
two of the national currency act, shall be required to deposit
lawful money of the United States for its outstanding circulation within sixty days from the date of the passage of this
act.   And every bank that may hereafter go into liquidation
shall be required to deposit lawful money of the United States
for its outstanding circulation within six months from the
date of the vote to go into liquidation ; whereupon the bonds

pledged as security for such circulation shall be surrendered to the association making such deposit. And if any bank shall fail to make the deposit and take up its bonds for thirty days after the expiration of the time specified, the comptroller of the currency shall have power to sell the bonds pledged for the circulation of said bank at public auction in New York city, and after providing for the redemption and cancellation of said circulation, and the necessary expenses of the sale, to pay over any balance remaining from the proceeds to the bank, or its legal representative: *Provided,* That banks which are winding up in good faith for the purpose of consolidating with other banks shall be exempt from the provisions of this act: *And provided further,* That the assets and liabilities of banks so in liquidation shall be reported by the banks with which they are in process of consolidation.

[Approved, July 14, 1870.   16 Statutes at Large, 274.]

1871–72, Chap. CCCXLVI. — *An Act for the better Security of Bank Reserves, and to facilitate Bank Clearing-house Exchanges.*

Be it enacted, . . . That the Secretary of the Treasury is hereby authorized to receive United States notes on deposit, without interest, from national banking associations, in sums not less than ten thousand dollars, and to issue certificates therefor in such form as the secretary may prescribe, in denominations of not less than five thousand dollars;· which certificate shall be payable on demand in United States notes, at the place where the deposits were made.

SEC. 2. That the United States notes so deposited in the Treasury of the United States shall not be counted as part of the legal reserve; but the certificates issued therefor may be held and counted by national banks as part of their legal reserve, and may be accepted in the settlement of clearing-house balances at the places where the deposits therefor were made.

SEC. 3. That nothing contained in this act shall be construed to authorize any expansion or contraction of the currency ; and the United States notes for which such certificates are issued, or other United States notes of like amount, shall be held as spe-

14

cial deposits in the treasury, and used only for the redemption
of such certificates.

[Approved, June 8, 1872.   17 Statutes at Large, 336.]

1873–74, Chap. CCCXLIII. — *An Act fixing the Amount of
United States Notes, providing for a Redistribution of
the National Bank Currency, and for other Purposes.*

Be it enacted, . . . That the act entitled "An act to provide .
a national currency secured by a pledge of United States bonds,
and to provide for the circulation and redemption thereof," ap- .
proved June third, eighteen hundred and sixty-four, shall be
hereafter known as "the national bank act."

SEC. 2. That section thirty-one of the "national bank act" be
so amended that the several associations therein provided for shall
not hereafter be required to keep on hand any amount of money
whatever, by reason of the amount of their respective circula-
tions; but the moneys required by said section to be kept at all
times on hand shall be determined by the amount of deposits in
all respects, as provided for in the said section.

SEC. 3. That every association organized, or to be organized,
under the provisions of the said act, and of the several acts
amendatory thereof, shall at all times keep and have on deposit
in the Treasury of the United States, in lawful money of the
United States, a sum equal to five per centum of its circulation,
to be held and used for the redemption of such circulation;
which sum shall be counted as a part of its lawful reserve, as
provided in section two of this act; and when the circulating
notes of any such associations, assorted or unassorted, shall be
presented for redemption, in sums of one thousand dollars, or
any multiple thereof, to the Treasurer of the United States, the
same shall be redeemed in United States notes. All notes so
redeemed shall be charged by the Treasurer of the United States
to the respective associations issuing the same, and he shall notify
them severally, on the first day of each month, or oftener, at
his discretion, of the amount of such redemptions; and whenever such redemptions for any association shall amount to the
sum of five hundred dollars, such association so notified shall

forthwith deposit with the Treasurer of the United States a sum in United States notes equal to the amount of its circulating notes so redeemed. And all notes of national banks worn, defaced, mutilated, or otherwise unfit for circulation shall, when received by any Assistant Treasurer or at any designated depository of the United States, be forwarded to the Treasurer of the United States for redemption as provided herein. And when such redemptions have been so reimbursed, the circulating notes so redeemed shall be forwarded to the respective associations by which they were issued; but if any of such notes are worn, mutilated, defaced, or rendered otherwise unfit for use, they shall be forwarded to the Comptroller of the Currency and destroyed and replaced as now provided by law: *Provided*, That each of said associations shall reimburse to the treasury the charges for transportation, and the costs for assorting such notes; and the associations hereafter organized shall also severally reimburse to the treasury the cost of engraving such plates as shall be ordered by each association respectively; and the amount assessed upon each association shall be in proportion to the circulation redeemed, and be charged to the fund on deposit with the Treasurer: *And provided further*, That so much of section thirty-two of said national bank act requiring or permitting the redemption of its circulating notes elsewhere than at its own counter, except as provided for in this section, is hereby repealed.

SEC. 4. That any association organized under this act, or any of the acts of which this is an amendment, desiring to withdraw its circulating notes, in whole or in part, may, upon the deposit of lawful money with the Treasurer of the United States in sums of not less than nine thousand dollars, take up the bonds which said association has on deposit with the Treasurer for the security of such circulating notes; which bonds shall be assigned to the bank in the manner specified in the nineteenth section of the national bank act; and the outstanding notes of said association, to an amount equal to the legal tender notes deposited, shall be redeemed at the Treasury of the United States, and destroyed as now provided by law: *Provided*, That the amount of the bonds on deposit for circulation shall not be reduced below fifty thousand dollars.

SEC. 5. That the Comptroller of the Currency shall, under such rules and regulations as the Secretary of the Treasury may prescribe, cause the charter numbers of the association to be printed upon all national bank notes which may be hereafter issued by him.

SEC. 6. That the amount of United States notes outstanding and to be used as a part of the circulating medium, shall not exceed the sum of three hundred and eighty-two million dollars, which said sum shall appear in each monthly statement of the public debt, and no part thereof shall be held or used as a reserve.

SEC. 7. That so much of the act entitled "An act to provide for the redemption of the three per centum temporary loan certificates, and for an increase of national bank notes," as provides that no circulation shall be withdrawn under the provisions of section six of said act, until after the fifty-four millions granted in section one of said act shall have been taken up, is hereby repealed; and it shall be the duty of the Comptroller of the Currency, under the direction of the Secretary of the Treasury, to proceed forthwith, and he is hereby authorized and required, from time to time, as applications shall be duly made therefor, and until the full amount of fifty-five million dollars shall be withdrawn, to make requisitions upon each of the national banks described in said section, and in the manner therein provided, organized in States having an excess of circulation, to withdraw and return so much of their circulation as by said act may be apportioned to be withdrawn from them, or, in lieu thereof, to deposit in the Treasury of the United States lawful money sufficient to redeem such circulation, and upon the return of the circulation required, or the deposit of lawful money, as herein provided, a proportionate amount of the bonds held to secure the circulation of such association as shall make such return or deposit shall be surrendered to it.

SEC. 8. That upon the failure of the national banks upon which requisition for circulation shall be made, or of any of them, to return the amount required, or to deposit in the Treasury lawful money to redeem the circulation required, within thirty days, the Comptroller of the Currency shall at once sell as provided in section forty-nine of the national currency act, approved June third, eighteen hundred and sixty-four, bonds held to secure the redemption of the circulation of the association or associations which shall so fail, to an amount sufficient to redeem the circulation required of such association or associations, and with the proceeds, which shall be deposited in the Treasury of the United States, so much of the circulation of such association or associations shall be redeemed as will equal the amount required and not returned, and if there be any excess of proceeds over the amount required for such redemption, it shall be returned to the association or associations whose bonds shall have been sold. And it shall be the duty of the Treasurer, Assistant Treasurers, designated depositaries, and national bank depositaries of the United States, who shall be kept informed by the Comptroller of the Currency of such associations as shall fail to return circulation as required, to assort and return to the Treasury for redemption the notes of such associations as shall come into their hands until the amount required shall be redeemed, and in like manner to assort and return to the Treasury, for redemption, the notes of such national banks as have failed, or gone into voluntary liquidation for the purpose of winding up their affairs, and of such as shall hereafter so fail or go into liquidation.

SEC. 9. That from and after the passage of this act it shall be lawful for the Comptroller of the Currency, and he is hereby required, to issue circulating notes, without delay, as applications therefor are made, not to exceed the sum of fifty-five million dollars, to associations organized, or to be organized, in those States and Territories having less than their proportion of circulation, under an apportionment made on the basis of population and of wealth, as shown by the returns of the census of eighteen hundred and seventy ; and every association hereafter organized shall be subject to, and be governed by the rules, restrictions, and limitations, and possess the rights, privileges, and franchises, now or hereafter to be prescribed by law as to national banking associations, with the same power to amend, alter, and repeal provided by "the national bank act:" *Provided*, That the whole amount of circulation withdrawn and redeemed from banks transacting business shall not exceed fifty-five million dollars, and

that such circulation shall be withdrawn and redeemed as it shall
be necessary to supply the circulation previously issued to the
banks in those States having less than their apportionment : *And
provided further*, That not more than thirty million dollars shall
be withdrawn and redeemed as herein contemplated during the
fiscal year ending June thirtieth, eighteen hundred and seventy-
five.

[Approved, June 20, 1874. 18 Statutes at Large, 123.]

1874–75, Chap. XV. — *An Act to provide for the Resumption of Specie Payments.*

Be it enacted, . . . That the Secretary of the Treasury is
hereby authorized and required, as rapidly as practicable, to
cause to be coined at the mints of the United States, silver coins
of the denominations of ten, twenty-five, and fifty cents, of
standard value, and to issue them in redemption of an equal
number and amount of fractional currency of similar denominations, or, at his discretion, he may issue such silver coins through
the mints, the subtreasuries, public depositaries, and post-offices
of the United States ; and, upon such issue, he is hereby authorized and required to redeem an equal amount of such fractional
currency, until the whole amount of such fractional currency
outstanding shall be redeemed.

[An act approved April 17, 1876, makes further provision for the
issue of silver coin in redemption of fractional currency, and also provides that the fractional currency so redeemed shall be held to be a part
of the sinking-fund, and that interest shall be computed thereon, as in
the case of bonds belonging to the sinking-fund. See 19 Statutes at
Large, 33, and also *ibid.*, 215.]

SEC. 2. That so much of section three thousand five hundred and twenty-four of the Revised Statutes of the United
States as provides for a charge of one-fifth of one per centum
for converting standard gold bullion into coin is hereby repealed,
and hereafter no charge shall be made for that service.

SEC. 3. That section five thousand one hundred and seventy-
seven of the Revised Statutes of the United States, limiting the
aggregate amount of circulating notes of national banking associations, be, and is hereby, repealed; and each existing banking
association may increase its circulating notes in accordance with

existing law without respect to said aggregate limit; and new banking associations may be organized in accordance with existing law without respect to said aggregate limit; and the provisions of law for the withdrawal and redistribution of national bank currency among the several States and Territories are hereby repealed. And whenever, and so often, as circulating notes shall be issued to any such banking association, so increasing its capital or circulating notes, or so newly organized as aforesaid, it shall be the duty of the Secretary of the Treasury to redeem the legal tender United States notes in excess only of three hundred millions of dollars, to the amount of eighty per centum of the sum of national bank notes so issued to any such banking association as aforesaid, and to continue such redemption as such circulating notes are issued until there shall be outstanding the sum of three hundred million dollars of such legal tender United States notes, and no more. And on and after the first day of January, anno Domini eighteen hundred and seventy-nine, the Secretary of the Treasury shall redeem, in coin, the United States legal tender notes then outstanding on their presentation for redemption, at the office of the Assistant Treasurer of the United States in the city of New York, in sums of not less than fifty dollars. And to enable the Secretary of the Treasury to prepare and provide for the redemption in this act authorized or required, he is authorized to use any surplus revenues, from time to time, in the Treasury not otherwise appropriated, and to issue, sell, and dispose of, at not less than par, in coin, either of the descriptions of bonds of the United States described in the Act of Congress approved July fourteenth, eighteen hundred and seventy, entitled, " An Act to authorize the refunding of the national debt," with like qualities, privileges, and exemptions, to the extent necessary to carry this act into full effect, and to use the proceeds thereof for the purposes aforesaid. And all provisions of law inconsistent with the provisions of this act are hereby repealed.

[The limit of circulation fixed by section 5177 of the Revised Statutes is that prescribed on page 202 by section 1 of the Act of July 12, 1870.]

[Approved, January 14, 1875. 18 Statutes at Large, 296.]

1874–75, Chap. XIX. — *An Act to remove the Limitation restricting the Circulation of Banking Associations issuing Notes payable in Gold.*

Be it enacted, . . . That so much of section five thousand one hundred and eighty-five of the Revised Statutes of the United States as limits the circulation of banking associations, organized for the purpose of issuing notes payable in gold, severally to one million dollars, be, and the same is hereby, repealed; and each of such existing banking associations may increase its circulating notes, and new banking associations may be organized, in accordance with existing law, without respect to such limitation.

[Approved, January 19, 1875. 13 Statutes at Large, 302.]

[The limit of circulation fixed by section 5185 of the Revised Statutes is that prescribed on page 204, by section 3 of the Act of July 12, 1870.]

1874–75, Chap. CXXX. — *An Act making Appropriations for sundry Civil Expenses of the Government for the fiscal year ending June thirtieth, eighteen hundred and seventy-six, and for other purposes.*

SEC. 11. That the Secretary of the Treasury is hereby authorized, at such times as may be necessary, for the purpose of obtaining bonds for the sinking-fund, in compliance with sections three thousand six hundred and ninety-four to three thousand six hundred and ninety-seven, inclusive, of the Revised Statutes of the United States, to give public notice that he will redeem, in coin, at par, any bonds of the United States, bearing interest at the rate of six per centum, of the kind known as five-twenties; and in three months after the date of such public notice, the interest on the bonds so selected and called for payment shall cease.

[Approved, March 3, 1875. 13 Statutes at Large, 401.]

[The provisions of sections 3694-97 of the Revised Statutes are the same as those of section 5 of the Act of February 25, 1862, on page 165, and section 6 of the Act of July 14, 1870, on page 207.]

1877-78, Chap. CXLVI. — *An Act to forbid the further retirement of United States legal-tender notes.*

Be it enacted, . . . That from and after the passage of this act it shall not be lawful for the Secretary of the Treasury or other officer under him to cancel or retire any more of the United States legal-tender notes. And when any of said notes may be redeemed or be received into the Treasury under any law from any source whatever and shall belong to the United States, they shall not be retired cancelled or destroyed but they shall be reissued and paid out again and kept in circulation : *Provided,* That nothing herein shall prohibit the cancellation and destruction of mutilated notes and the issue of other notes of like denomination in their stead, as now provided by law.

All acts and parts of acts in conflict herewith are hereby repealed.

[Approved, May 31, 1878. 20 Statutes at Large, 87.]

1878-79, Chap. XXIV. — *An Act to facilitate the refunding the national debt.*

Be it enacted, . . . That the Secretary of the Treasury is hereby authorized in the process of refunding the national debt under existing laws to exchange directly at par the bonds of the United States bearing interest at four per centum per annum authorized by law for the bonds of the United States commonly known as five-twenties outstanding and uncalled, and, whenever all such five-twenty bonds shall have been redeemed, the provisions of this section and all existing provisions of law authorizing the refunding of the national debt shall apply to any bonds of the United States bearing interest at five per centum per annum or a higher rate, which may be redeemable. In any exchange made under the provisions of this section interest may be allowed, on the bonds redeemed, for a period of three months.

[Approved, January 25, 1879. 20 Statutes at Large, 265.]

1878–79, Chap. CII. — *An Act to authorize the issue of certificates of deposit in aid of the refunding of the public debt.*

Be it enacted, . . . **That the Secretary of the Treasury is** hereby authorized and directed to issue, in exchange for lawful money of the United States that may be presented for such exchange, certificates of deposit, of the denomination of ten dollars, bearing interest at the rate of four per centum per annum, and convertible at any time, with accrued interest into the four per centum bonds described in the refunding act ; and the money so received shall be applied only to the payment of the bonds bearing interest at a rate of not less than five per centum in the mode prescribed by said act, and he is authorized to prescribe suitable rules and regulations in conformity with this act.

[Approved, February 26, 1879.   20 Statutes at Large, 321.]

1879–80, Chap. XXV. — *An Act authorizing the conversion of national gold banks.*

Be it enacted, . . . That any national gold bank organized under the provisions of the laws of the United States, may, in the manner and subject to the provisions prescribed by section fifty-one hundred and fifty-four of the Revised Statutes of the United States, for the conversion of banks incorporated under the laws of any State, cease to be a gold bank, and become such an association as is authorized, by section fifty-one hundred and thirty-three, for carrying on the business of banking, and shall have the same powers and privileges, and shall be subject to the same duties, responsibilities, and rules, in all respects, as are by law prescribed for such associations : *Provided,* That all certificates of organization which shall be issued under this act shall bear the date of the original organization of each bank respectively as a gold bank.

[Approved, February 14, 1880.   21 Statutes at Large, 66.]

[The provisions of sections 5133 and 5154 of the Revised Statutes are in substance those of section 5 of the Act of June 3, 1864, on page 179, and section 44 of the same Act, on page 188.]

1880-81, Chap. CXXXIII. — *An Act making appropriations for sundry civil expenses of the Government for the fiscal year ending June thirtieth, eighteen hundred and eighty-two, and for other purposes.*

SEC. 2. That the Secretary of the Treasury may at any time apply the surplus money in the Treasury not otherwise appropriated, or so much thereof as he may consider proper, to the purchase or redemption of United States bonds : *Provided,* That the bonds so purchased or redeemed shall constitute no part of the sinking-fund, but shall be cancelled.

[Approved, March 3, 1881. 21 Statutes at Large, 457.]

1881-82, Chap. CCXC. — *An Act to enable national-banking associations to extend their corporate existence, and for other purposes.*

Be it enacted, . . . That any national banking association organized under the acts of February twenty-fifth, eighteen hundred and sixty-three, June third, eighteen hundred and sixty-four, and February fourteenth, eighteen hundred and eighty, or under sections fifty-one hundred and thirty-three, fifty-one hundred and thirty-four, fifty-one hundred and thirty-five, fifty-one hundred and thirty-six, and fifty-one hundred and fifty-four of the Revised Statutes of the United States, may, at any time within the two years next previous to the date of the expiration of its corporate existence under present law, and with the approval of the Comptroller of the Currency, to be granted as hereinafter provided, extend its period of succession by amending its articles of association for a term of not more than twenty years from the expiration of the period of succession named in said articles of association, and shall have succession for such extended period, unless sooner dissolved by the act of shareholders owning two thirds of its stock, or unless its franchise becomes forfeited by some violation of law, or unless hereafter modified or repealed.

[The sections 5133 5136 and 5154 of the Revised Statutes contain in substance the provisions of sections 5, 6, 8, and 44 of the Act of June 3, 1864; see pages 179 and 188.]

[Sections 2, 3, and 4 provide that the amended articles of association must receive the written consent of shareholders owning not less than two thirds of the capital stock, and shall not be valid until the Comptroller shall have certified his approval, after making a special examination of the association to determine its condition; and that any association so extending the period of its succession "shall continue to be in all respects the identical association it was before the extension of its period of succession."

Section 5 provides that any shareholder not assenting to the amended articles shall be entitled to receive the appraised value of his shares, and that his shares shall then be sold at public sale.]

SEC. 6. That the circulating notes of any association so extending the period of its succession which shall have been issued to it prior to such extension shall be redeemed at the Treasury of the United States, as provided in section three of the act of June twentieth, eighteen hundred and seventy-four, entitled "An act fixing the amount of United States notes, providing for redistribution of national-bank currency, and for other purposes," and such notes when redeemed shall be forwarded to the Comptroller of the Currency, and destroyed as now provided by law; and at the end of three years from the date of the extension of the corporate existence of each bank the association so extended shall deposit lawful money with the Treasurer of the United States sufficient to redeem the remainder of the circulation which was outstanding at the date of its extension, as provided in sections fifty-two hundred and twenty-two, fifty-two hundred and twenty-four, and fifty-two hundred and twenty-five of the Revised Statutes; and any gain that may arise from the failure to present such circulating notes for redemption shall inure to the benefit of the United States; and from time to time, as such notes are redeemed or lawful money deposited therefor as provided herein, new circulating notes shall be issued as provided by this act, bearing such devices, to be approved by the Secretary of the Treasury, as shall make them readily distinguishable from the circulating notes heretofore issued: *Provided however*, That each banking association which shall obtain the benefit of this act shall reimburse to the Treasury the cost of preparing the plate or plates for such new circulating notes as shall be issued to it.

[Sections 5222, 5224, and 5225 of the Revised Statutes contain in substance the provisions of sections 42 and 43 of the Act of June 3, 1864, on page 188.]

[Section 7 provides that any bank which does not avail itself of the provisions of this act shall be wound up as if the shareholders had voted to go into liquidation, that it shall within six months deposit with the Treasurer of the United States lawful money sufficient to redeem all its outstanding circulating notes, and shall thereupon be discharged from all liability therefor, and that the bonds deposited to secure the same shall then be re-assigned to it.]

SEC. 8. That national banks now organized or hereafter organized, having a capital of one hundred and fifty thousand dollars, or less, shall not be required to keep on deposit, or deposit with the Treasurer of the United States, United States bonds in excess of one fourth of their capital stock as security for their circulating notes; but such banks shall keep on deposit, or deposit with the Treasurer of the United States, the amount of bonds as herein required. And such of those banks having on deposit bonds in excess of that amount are authorized to reduce their circulation by the deposit of lawful money as provided by law; *provided,* That the amount of such circulating notes shall not in any case exceed ninety per centum of the par value of the bonds deposited as herein provided. . . .

SEC. 9. That any national banking association now organized, or hereafter organized, desiring to withdraw its circulating notes, upon a deposit of lawful money with the Treasurer of the United States, as provided in section four of the act of June twentieth, eighteen hundred and seventy-four, entitled "An act fixing the amount of United States notes, providing for a redistribution of national-bank currency, and for other purposes," or as provided in this act, is authorized to deposit lawful money and withdraw a proportionate amount of the bonds held as security for its circulating notes in the order of such deposits; and no national bank which makes any deposit of lawful money in order to withdraw its circulating notes shall be entitled to receive any increase of its circulation for the period of six months from the time it made such deposit of lawful money for the purpose aforesaid : *Provided,* That not more than three millions of dollars of lawful money shall be deposited during any calendar month for this purpose : *And provided further,* That the provisions of this section shall not apply to bonds called for redemption by the Secretary of the Treasury, nor to the withdrawal of circulating notes in consequence thereof.

Sec. 10. That upon a deposit of bonds as described by sections fifty-one hundred and fifty-nine and fifty-one hundred and sixty, except as modified by section four of an act entitled "An act fixing the amount of United States notes, providing for a redistribution of the national-bank currency, and for other purposes," approved June twentieth, eighteen hundred and seventy-four, and as modified by section eight, of this act, the association making the same shall be entitled to receive from the Comptroller of the Currency circulating notes of different denominations, in blank, registered and countersigned as provided by law, equal in amount to ninety per centum of the current market value, not exceeding par, of the United States bonds so transferred and delivered, and at no time shall the total amount of such notes issued to any such association exceed ninety per centum of the amount at such time actually paid in of its capital stock; and the provisions of sections fifty-one hundred and seventy-one and fifty-one hundred and seventy-six of the Revised Statutes are hereby repealed.

[Sections 5159 and 5160 of the Revised Statutes correspond to section 16 of the Bank Act of 1864, on page 180, and sections 5171 and 5176 state the limit of circulating notes to be allowed to each bank, as given on pages 199 and 203.]

Sec. 11. That the Secretary of the Treasury is hereby authorized to receive at the Treasury any bonds of the United States bearing three and a half per centum interest, and to issue in exchange therefor an equal amount of registered bonds of the United States of the denominations of fifty, one hundred, five hundred, one thousand, and ten thousand dollars, of such form as he may prescribe, bearing interest at the rate of three per centum per annum, payable quarterly at the Treasury of the United States. Such bonds shall be exempt from all taxation by or under State authority, and be payable at the pleasure of the United States: *Provided*, That the bonds herein authorized shall not be called in and paid so long as any bonds of the United States heretofore issued bearing a higher rate of interest than three per centum, and which shall be redeemable at the pleasure of the United States, shall be outstanding and uncalled. The last of the said bonds originally issued under this act, and their substitutes, shall be first called in, and this order of payment shall be followed until all shall have been paid.

Sec. 12. That the Secretary of the Treasury is authorized and directed to receive deposits of gold coin with the Treasurer or assistant treasurers of the United States, in sums not less than twenty dollars, and to issue certificates therefor in denominations of not less than twenty dollars each, corresponding with the denominations of United States notes. The coin deposited for or representing, the certificates of deposits shall be retained in the Treasury for the payment of the same on demand. Said certificates shall be receivable for customs, taxes, and all public dues, and when so received may be reissued; and such certificates, as also silver certificates, when held by any national banking association, shall be counted as part of its lawful reserve; and no national banking association shall be a member of any clearing-house in which such certificates shall not be receivable in the settlement of clearing-house balances: *Provided*, That the Secretary of the Treasury shall suspend the issue of such gold certificates whenever the amount of gold coin and gold bullion in the Treasury, reserved for the redemption of United States notes falls below one hundred millions of dollars; and the provisions of section fifty-two hundred and seven of the Revised Statutes shall be applicable to the certificates herein authorized and directed to be issued.

Sec. 14. That Congress may at any time amend, alter, or repeal this act and the acts of which this is amendatory.

[Approved, July 12, 1882. 22 Statutes at Large, 162.]

[Section 5207 of the Revised Statutes is the Act of February 19, 1869, on page 201.]

1882-83, Chap. CXXI. — *An act to reduce internal-revenue taxation, and for other purposes.*

Be it enacted, . . . That the taxes herein specified imposed by the laws now in force be, and the same are hereby, repealed, as hereinafter provided, namely: On capital and deposits of banks, bankers, and national banking associations, except such taxes as are now due and payable; and on and after the first day of July, eighteen hundred and eighty-three, the stamp tax on bank checks, drafts, orders, and vouchers, . . .

[Approved, March 3, 1883.   22 Statutes at Large, 488.]

1885-86, Chap. LXXIII. — *An Act to enable national banking associations to increase their capital stock and to change their names or locations.*

[This act authorizes any national bank, with the approval of the Comptroller of the Currency and by the vote of shareholders owning two thirds of its stock, to increase its capital to any sum approved by the Comptroller, to change its name, or to change its place of business to any other within the same State and not more than thirty miles distant. All liabilities, rights, and powers of the bank under its old name devolve upon and inure to it under the new name, and it is not released from any liability, nor shall any proceeding at law to which it is a party be affected, by change of location under this act.]

[Approved, May 1, 1886.   24 Statutes at Large, 18.]

1885-86, Chap. DCCCXVIII. — *An act to prohibit the passage of local or special laws in the Territories of the United States, to limit Territorial indebtedness, and for other purposes.*

[Section 5 amends section 1889 of the Revised Statutes, so as to allow any Territory by general act to incorporate "banks of discount and deposit (but not of issue)."]

[Approved, July 30, 1886.   24 Statutes at Large, 170.]

1886-87, Chap. CCCLXXVIII. — *An act to amend sections five thousand one hundred and ninety-one and five thousand one hundred and ninety-two of the Revised Statutes of the United States, and for other purposes.*

Be it enacted . . . That whenever three-fourths in number of the national banks located in any city of the United States having a population of fifty thousand people shall make application to the Comptroller of the Currency, in writing, asking that the name of the city in which such banks are located shall be added to the cities named in sections, fifty-one hundred and ninety-one and fifty-one hundred and ninety-two of the Revised Statutes, the Comptroller shall have authority to grant such request, and every bank located in such city shall at all times thereafter have on hand, in lawful money of the United States, an amount equal to at least twenty-five per centum of its deposits, as provided in sections fifty-one hundred and ninety-one and fifty-one hundred and ninety-five of the Revised Statutes.

SEC. 2. That whenever three-fourths in number of the national banks located in any city of the United States having a population of two hundred thousand people shall make application to the Comptroller of the Currency, in writing, asking that such city may be a central reserve city, like the city of New York, in which one-half of the lawful-money reserve of the national banks located in other reserve cities may be deposited, as provided in section fifty-one hundred and ninety-five of the Revised Statutes, the Comptroller shall have authority, with the approval of the Secretary of the Treasury, to grant such request, and every bank located in such city shall at all times thereafter have on hand, in lawful money of the United States, twenty-five per centum of its deposits, as provided in section fifty-one hundred and ninety-one of the Revised Statutes.

SEC. 3. That section three of the act of January fourteenth, eighteen hundred and seventy-five, entitled "An act to provide for the resumption of specie payments, be, and the same is, hereby amended by adding after the words "New York" the words "and the city of San Francisco, California."

[Approved, March 3, 1887. 24 Statutes at Large, 559.]

[Sections 5191 and 5192 of the Revised Statutes correspond to section 31 of the Bank Act of June 3, 1864, on page 184, and section 5195 corresponds to section 32 of the same Act.]

15

1889-90, Chap. DCCVIII. — *An act directing the purchase of silver bullion and the issue of Treasury notes thereon, and for other purposes.*

[Sections 1 and 2 of this act authorize the issue of Treasury notes in payment for silver bullion, the notes to be redeemable in coin, to be a legal tender for all debts, receivable for customs and public dues, and to be counted by banks as a part of their lawful reserve; and section 6 provides for covering into the Treasury all moneys held for the redemption of bank notes, except the five per cent. redemption fund required by the act of June 20, 1874, on page 210. The act is given in full *below*, on page 250.]

[Approved, July 14, 1880.   26 Statutes at Large, 289.]

PART III.

COINS AND COINAGE.
1789–1890.

1789, Chap. V. — *An Act to regulate the Collection of the Duties imposed by law on the tonnage of ships or vessels, and on goods, wares, and merchandises imported into the United States.*

[Section 30 of this act, fixing the rates at which foreign coins shall be received in payment of duties and fees under this act, is printed *above*, on page 7.

The same rates are repeated in section 56 of the revised collection act of August 4, 1790, 1 Statutes at Large, 173.]

[Approved, July 31, 1789. 1 Statutes at Large, 45.]

1791–92, Chap. XVI. — *An Act establishing a Mint, and regulating the Coins of the United States.*

Sec. 9. *And be it further enacted*, That there shall be from time to time struck and coined at the said mint, coins of gold, silver, and copper, of the following denominations, values and descriptions, viz. Eagles — each to be of the value of ten dollars or units, and to contain two hundred and forty-seven grains and four-eighths of a grain of pure, or two hundred and seventy grains of standard gold.

[Half-eagles and quarter-eagles of corresponding weights and fineness.]

Dollars or Units — Each to be of the value of a Spanish milled dollar as the same is now current, and to contain three hundred and seventy-one grains and four-sixteenth parts of a grain of pure, or four hundred and sixteen grains of standard silver.

[Half-dollars, quarter-dollars, dimes, and half-dimes of corresponding weights and fineness, and cents and half-cents of copper.]

SEC. 11. *And be it further enacted,* That the proportional value of gold to silver in all coins which shall by law be current as money within the United States, shall be as fifteen to one, according to quantity in weight, of pure gold or pure silver; that is to say, every fifteen pounds weight of pure silver shall be of equal value in all payments, with one pound weight of pure gold, and so in proportion as to any greater or less quantities of the respective metals.

SEC. 12. *And be it further enacted,* . . . That the standard for all gold coins of the United States shall be eleven parts fine to one part alloy; and accordingly that eleven parts in twelve of the entire weight of each of the said coins shall consist of pure gold, and the remaining one twelfth part of alloy; and the said alloy shall be composed of silver and copper, in such proportions not exceeding one half silver as shall be found convenient; to be regulated by the director of the mint, for the time being, with the approbation of the President of the United States, until further provision shall be made by law. . . .

SEC. 13. *And be it further enacted,* That the standard for all silver coins of the United States, shall be one thousand four hundred and eighty-five parts fine to one hundred and seventy-nine parts alloy; and accordingly that one thousand four hundred and eighty-five parts in one thousand six hundred and sixty-four parts of the entire weight of each of the said coins shall consist of pure silver, and the remaining one hundred and seventy-nine parts of alloy; which alloy shall be wholly of copper.

SEC. 14. *And be it further enacted,* That it shall be lawful for any person or persons to bring to the said mint gold and silver bullion, in order to their being coined; and that the bullion so brought shall be there assayed and coined as speedily as may be after the receipt thereof, and that free of expense to the person or persons by whom the same shall have been brought. And as soon as the said bullion shall have been coined, the person or persons by whom the same shall have been delivered, shall upon demand receive in lieu thereof coins of the same species of bullion which shall have been so delivered, weight for weight, of the pure gold or pure silver therein contained : *Provided nevertheless*, That it shall be at the mutual option of the party or parties bringing such bullion, and of the director of the said mint, to make an immediate exchange of coins for standard bullion, with a deduction of one-half per cent. from the weight of the pure gold, or pure silver contained in the said bullion, as an indemnification to the mint for the time which will necessarily be required for coining the said bullion, and for the advance which shall have been so made in coins. . . .

SEC. 16. *And be it further enacted*, That all the gold and silver coins which shall have been struck at, and issued from the said mint, shall be a lawful tender in all payments whatsoever, those of full weight according to the respective values herein before declared, and those of less than full weight at values proportional to their respective weights.

SEC. 20. *And be it further enacted*, That the money of account of the United States shall be expressed in dollars or units, dismes or tenths, cents or hundredths, and milles or thousandths, a disme being the tenth part of a dollar, a cent the hundredth part of a dollar, a mille the thousandth part a dollar, and that all accounts in the public offices and all proceedings in the courts of the United States shall be kept and had in conformity to this regulation.

[Approved, April 2, 1792.   1 Statutes at Large, 246.]

1792–93, Chap. V. — *An Act regulating foreign Coins, and for other purposes.*

SECTION 1. *Be it enacted*, . . . That from and after the first day of July next, foreign gold and silver coins shall pass current as money within the United States, and be a legal tender for the payment of all debts and demands, at the several and respective rates following, and not otherwise, viz :

[The gold coins of Great Britain and Portugal at 100 cents for every 27 grains of weight; gold coins of France, Spain, and the dominions of Spain at 100 cents for every 27⅘ grains ; Spanish milled dollars at 100 cents each, the weight being not less than 17 pennyweights and 7 grains, and so for the parts of a dollar ; crowns of France at 110 cents each, the weight being not less than 18 pennyweights and 17 grains, and so for the parts of a crown. But no foreign coin issued after January 1, 1792, shall be a tender until proclamation by the President that it has been found by assay at the Mint to be of the required standard.]

SEC. 2. *Provided always, and be it further enacted,* That at the expiration of three years next ensuing the time when the coinage of gold and silver, agreeably to the act, entitled "An act establishing a mint, and regulating the coins of the United States," shall commence at the mint of the United States, (which time shall be announced by the proclamation of the President of the United States,) all foreign gold coins, and all foreign silver coins, except Spanish milled dollars and parts of such dollars, shall cease to be a legal tender, as aforesaid.

[Section 3 provides that, from the time when coining shall begin at the Mint, all foreign gold and silver coins, except Spanish milled dollars and parts thereof, received by the United States, shall be recoined at the Mint.

Section 4 repeals from July 1, 1793, section 56 of the collection act of 1790, fixing the rates at which foreign coins shall be received for duties. See *above,* page 227.]

[Approved, February 9, 1793. 1 Statutes at Large, 300.]

NOTE. — The proclamation required by section 2 of the above act was issued July 22, 1797. See 11 Statutes at Large, 755.

The collection act of March 2, 1799, provides for the collection of all duties and fees in money of the United States or in foreign coins at the rates prescribed by section 1 *above;* and also provides that no foreign coins which are not by law a tender for debts shall be received, except under a proclamation of the President authorizing the same. 1 Statutes at Large, 680.

1797-98, Chap. XI. — *An Act supplementary to the act intituled "An Act regulating Foreign Coins, and for other purposes."*

Be it enacted, . . . That the second section of an act, intituled "An act regulating foreign coins, and for other purposes," be, and the same is hereby suspended, for and during the space of three years from and after the first day of January, one thousand seven hundred and ninety-eight, and until the end of the next session of Congress thereafter, during which time the said gold and silver coins shall be and continue a legal tender, as is provided in and by the first section of the act aforesaid ; and that the same coins shall thereafter cease to be such tender.

[Approved, February 1, 1798. 1 Statutes at Large, 539.]

NOTE. — By the Act of April 30, 1802, this suspension is continued for three years from the end of the present session of Congress. 2 Statutes at Large, 173.

1805–06, Chap. XXII. — *An Act regulating the currency of foreign coins in the United States.*

[Section 1 provides that foreign gold and silver coin shall pass current as money and be a legal tender for debt, specifying the same coins as are named in section 1 of the Act of February 9, 1793, and fixing the same rates. It is also required that assays shall be made, at least annually, of the coins thus made current and of similar coins subsequently issued, in order that Congress may determine the real value at which such coins should be current.

Section 2 repeals section 1 of the act of February 9, 1793, and suspends the operation of section 2 of the same act for three years.]

[Approved, April 10, 1806. 2 Statutes at Large, 374.]

1815–16, Chap. CXXXIX. — *An Act regulating the currency within the United States, of the gold coins of Great Britain, France, Portugal and Spain, and the crowns of France, and five-franc pieces.*

Be it enacted, . . . That from the passage of this act and for three years thereafter, and no longer, the following gold and silver coins shall pass current as money within the United States, and be a legal tender for the payment of all debts and demands, at the several and respective rates following, and not otherwise, videlicet : the gold coins of Great Britain and Portugal, of their present standard, at the rate of one hundred cents for every seventy [twenty]-seven grains, or eighty-eight cents and eight-ninths per pennyweight ; the gold coins of France, of their present standard, at the rate of one hundred cents for every twenty-seven and a half grains, or eighty-seven and a quarter cents per pennyweight ; the gold coins of Spain, at the rate of one hundred cents for every twenty-eight and a half grains, or eighty-four cents per pennyweight ; the crowns of France, at the rate of one hundred and seventeen cents and six-tenths per ounce, or one hundred and ten cents for each crown weighing eighteen pennyweights and seventeen grains ; the five-franc pieces at the rate of one hundred and sixteen cents per ounce, or ninety-three cents and three mills for each five-franc piece, weighing sixteen pennyweights and two grains.

SEC. 2. *And be it further enacted*, That it shall be the duty of the Secretary of the Treasury to cause assays of the foregoing gold and silver coins, made current by this act, to be had at the mint of the United States, at least once in every year : and to make report of the result thereof to Congress.   •

[Approved, April 29, 1816.   3 Statutes at Large, 322.]

NOTE.—By the Act approved March 3, 1819, so much of the above Act as relates to foreign gold coins was continued in force until November 1, 1819, and so much as relates to foreign silver coins until April 29, 1821. See 3 Statutes at Large, 525.   And by acts approved March 3, 1821, and March 3, 1823, the provisions relating to foreign silver coins were further continued in force until March 4, 1827.   See *ibid.*, 645, 777.

1822-23, Chap. LIII. — *An Act making the gold coins of Great Britain, France, Portugal and Spain, receivable in payments on account of public lands.*

[Section 1 makes the gold coins of Great Britain, France, Portugal and Spain, of their present standard, receivable in all payments on account of public lands, at rates identical with those specified in the Act of April 29, 1816 ; and section 2 makes it the duty of the Secretary of the Treasury to cause assays of the said coins to be made at least once in every year, and to report the results to Congress.]

[Approved, March 3, 1823.   3 Statutes at Large, 779.]

1827-28, Chap. LXVII. — *An Act to continue the mint at the city of Philadelphia, and for other purposes.*

SEC. 2. *And be it further enacted*, That, for the purpose of securing a due conformity in weight of the coins of the

United States, to the provisions of the ninth section of the act, passed the second of April, one thousand seven hundred and ninety-two, entitled "An act establishing a mint, and regulating the coins of the United States," the brass troy pound weight procured by the minister of the United States at London, in the year one thousand eight hundred and twenty-seven, for the use of the mint, and now in the custody of the director thereof, shall be the standard troy pound of the mint of the United States, conformably to which the coinage thereof shall be regulated.

[Approved, May 19, 1828.   4 Statutes at Large, 277.]

1833–34, Chap. LXXI. — *An Act regulating the value of certain foreign silver coins within the United States.*

. *Be it enacted*, . . . That from and after the passage of this act, the following silver coins shall be of the legal value, and shall pass current as money within the United States, by tale, for the payment of all debts and demands, at the rate of one hundred cents the dollar, that is to say, the dollars of Mexico, Peru, Chili, and Central America, of not less weight than four hundred and fifteen grains each, and those re-stamped in Brazil of the like weight, of not less fineness than ten ounces fifteen pennyweights of pure silver, in the troy pound of twelve ounces of standard silver : and the five franc pieces of France, when of not less fineness than ten ounces and sixteen pennyweights in twelve ounces troy weight of standard silver, and weighing not less than three hundred and eighty-four grains each at the rate of ninety-three cents each.

SEC. 2. *And be it further enacted*, That it shall be [the] duty of the Secretary of the Treasury to cause assays of the aforesaid silver coins, made current by this act, to be had at the mint of the United States at least once in every year, and to make report of the result thereof to Congress.

[Approved, June 25, 1834.   4 Statutes at Large, 681.]

1833–34, Chap. XCV. — *An Act concerning the gold coins of the United States, and for other purposes.*

Be it enacted, . . . That the gold coins of the United States shall contain the following quantities of metal, that is to say : each eagle shall contain two hundred and thirty-two grains of pure gold, and two hundred and fifty-eight grains of standard gold ; each half eagle one hundred and sixteen grains of pure gold, and one hundred and twenty-nine grains of standard gold ; each quarter eagle shall contain fifty-eight grains of pure gold, and sixty-four and a half grains of standard gold ; every such eagle shall be of the value of ten dollars ; every such half eagle shall be of the value of five dollars ; and every such quarter eagle shall be of the value of two dollars and fifty cents ; and the said gold coins shall be receivable in all payments, when of full weight, according to their respective values ; and when of less than full weight, at less values, proportioned to their respective actual weights.

SEC. 2. *And be it further enacted*, That all standard gold or silver deposited for coinage after the thirty-first of July next, shall be paid for in coin under the direction of the Secretary of the Treasury, within five days from the making of such deposit, deducting from the amount of said deposit of gold and silver one-half of one per centum : *Provided*, That no deduction shall be made unless said advance be required by such depositor within forty days.

SEC. 3. *And be it further enacted*, That all gold coins of the United States, minted anterior to the thirty-first day of July next, shall be receivable in all payments at the rate of ninety-four and eight-tenths of a cent per pennyweight.

[Approved, June 28, 1834. 4 Statutes at Large, 699.]

1833–34, Chap. XCVI. — *An Act regulating the value of certain foreign gold coins within the United States.*

Be it enacted, . . . That, from and after the thirty-first day of July next, the following gold coins shall pass as current as money within the United States, and be receivable in all payments, by weight, for the payment of all debts

and demands, at the rates following, that is to say : the gold
coins of Great Britain, Portugal, and Brazil, of not less than
twenty-two carats fine, at the rate of ninety-four cents and
eight-tenths of a cent per pennyweight; the gold coins of
France nine-tenths fine, at the rate of ninety-three cents and
one-tenth of a cent per pennyweight; and the gold coins of
Spain, Mexico, and Colombia, of the fineness of twenty
carats three grains and seven-sixteenths of a grain, at the
rate of eighty-nine cents and nine-tenths of a cent per
pennyweight.

Sec. 2. *And be it further enacted*, That it shall be the
duty of the Secretary of the Treasury to cause assays of
the aforesaid gold coins, made current by this act, to be
had at the mint of the United States, at least once in
every year, and to make a report of the result thereof to
Congress.

[Approved, June 28, 1834.   4 Statutes at Large, 700.]

1836–37, Chap. III. — *An Act supplementary to the act entitled "An act establishing a mint, and regulating the
coins of the United States."*

Sec. 8. *And be it further enacted*, That the standard for
both gold and silver coins of the United States shall hereafter
be such, that of one thousand parts by weight, nine hundred
shall be of pure metal, and one hundred of alloy; and the
alloy of the silver coins shall be of copper; and the alloy of
the gold coins shall be of copper and silver, provided that the
silver do not exceed one-half of the whole alloy.

Sec. 9. *And be it further enacted*, That of the silver coins,
the dollar shall be of the weight of four hundred and twelve
and one-half grains ; the half dollar of the weight of two hundred and six and one-fourth grains ; the quarter dollar of the
weight of one hundred and three and one-eighth grains ; the
dime, or tenth part of a dollar, of the weight of forty-one and
a quarter grains ; and the half dime, or twentieth part of a
dollar, of the weight of twenty grains, and five-eighths of a
grain.   And that dollars, half dollars, and quarter dollars,

dimes, and half dimes, shall be legal tenders of payment, according to their nominal value, for any sums whatever.

SEC. 10. *And be it further enacted*, That of the gold coins, the weight of the eagle shall be two hundred and fifty-eight grains; that of the half eagle one hundred and twenty-nine grains; and that of the quarter eagle sixty-four and one-half grains. And that for all sums whatever, the eagle shall be a legal tender of payment for ten dollars; the half eagle for five dollars; and the quarter eagle for two and a half dollars.

SEC. 11. *And be it further enacted*, That the silver coins heretofore issued at the mint of the United States, and the gold coins issued since the thirty-first day of July, one thousand eight hundred and thirty-four, shall continue to be legal tenders of payment for their nominal values, on the same terms as if they were of the coinage provided for by this act.

[Sections 14-19 provide that gold and silver bullion brought to the Mint shall be received and coined for the benefit of the depositor, and that the only subjects of charge to him shall be for refining, toughening, and separating, and for metal used for alloy, the rate of charge being fixed from time to time so as not to exceed the actual expense incurred. For the net amount of the deposit a certificate shall be given, payable in coins of the same metal as the deposit. Sections 30 and 31 require that when the coins which are the equivalent to any deposit of bullion are ready for delivery they shall be paid over, payment being made to depositors in the order of priority of deposit. And to enable the Mint to make returns to depositors with as little delay as possible, it is made the duty of the Secretary of the Treasury to keep in the Mint, when practicable, a deposit not exceeding one million dollars, out of which the value of bullion brought to the Mint may be paid as soon as ascertained; but no discount or interest is to be charged on moneys so advanced.]

[Approved, January 18, 1837. 5 Statutes at Large, 136.]

1842-43, Chap. LXIX. — *An Act regulating the currency of foreign gold and silver coins in the United States.*

Be it enacted, . . . That from and after the passage of this act, the following foreign gold coins shall pass current as money within the United States, and be receivable, by weight, for the payment of all debts and demands, at the rates following, that is to say: the gold coins of Great Britain, of not less than nine hundred and fifteen and a half thousandths in fineness, at ninety-four cents and six-tenths of a cent per pennyweight; and the gold coins of France, of not less than eight hundred and ninety-nine thousandths in fineness, at ninety-two cents and nine-tenths of a cent per pennyweight.

Sec. 2. *And be it further enacted,* That from and after the passage of this act, the following foreign silver coins shall pass current as money within the United States, and be receivable by tale, for the payment of all debts and demands, at the rates following, that is to say: the Spanish pillar dollars, and the dollars of Mexico, Peru, and Bolivia, of not less than eight hundred and ninety-seven thousandths in fineness, and four hundred and fifteen grains in weight, at one hundred cents each; and the five franc pieces of France, of not less than nine hundred thousandths in fineness, and three hundred and eighty-four grains in weight, at ninety-three cents each.

Sec. 3. *And be it further enacted,* That it shall be the duty of the Secretary of the Treasury to cause assays of the coins made current by this act to be had at the mint of the United States, at least once in every year, and to make report of the result thereof to Congress.

[Approved, March 3, 1843.   5 Statutes at Large, 607.]

1848–49, Chap. CIX. — *An Act to authorize the Coinage of Gold Dollars and Double Eagles.*

[This act authorizes the coinage of gold dollars and double eagles "conformably in all respects to the standard for gold coins now established by law," and to be a legal tender in payment for all sums.]

[Approved, March 3, 1849.   9 Statutes at Large, 397.]

1849–50, Chap. XII. — *An Act supplementary to the Act entitled "An Act supplementary to the Act entitled 'An Act establishing a Mint, and regulating the Coins of the United States.'"*

Be it enacted, . . . That, for the purpose of enabling the mint and branch mints of the United States to make returns to depositors with as little delay as possible, it shall be lawful

for the President of the United States, when the state of the
treasury shall admit thereof, to direct transfers to be made
from time to time to the mint and branch mints for such sums
of public money as he shall judge convenient and necessary,
out of which those who bring bullion to the mint may be paid
the value thereof, as soon as practicable after this value has
been ascertained; that the bullion so deposited shall become
the property of the United States; that no discount or interest shall be charged on money so advanced; and that the
Secretary of the Treasury may at any time withdraw the said
deposite, or any part thereof, or may, at his discretion, allow
the coins formed at the mint to be given for their equivalent
in other money. . . .

[Approved, May 23, 1850.   9 Statutes at Large, 436.]

1852–3, Chap. LXXIX. — *An Act amendatory of Existing
Laws relative to the Half Dollar, Quarter Dollar,
Dime, and Half Dime.*

Be it enacted, . . . That from and after the first day of
June, eighteen hundred and fifty-two [three], the weight of
the half dollar or piece of fifty cents shall be one hundred and
ninety-two grains, and the quarter dollar, dime, and half dime,
shall be, respectively, one half, one fifth, and one tenth of the
weight of said half dollar.

SEC. 2. *And be it further enacted,* That the silver coins
issued in conformity with the above section, shall be legal
tenders in payment of debts for all sums not exceeding five
dollars.

SEC. 3. *And be it further enacted,* That in order to procure bullion for the requisite coinage of the subdivisions of
the dollar authorized by this act, the Treasurer of the Mint
shall, with the approval of the Director, purchase such bullion
with the bullion fund of the mint. He shall charge himself
with the gain arising from the coinage of such bullion into
coins of a nominal value exceeding the intrinsic value thereof,
and shall be credited with the difference between such intrinsic value and the price paid for said bullion, and with the

expense of distributing said coins as hereinafter provided. The balances to his credit, or the profit of said coinage, shall be, from time to time, on a warrant of the Director of the mint, transferred to the account of the Treasury of the United States.

Sec. 4. *And be it further enacted,* That such coins shall be paid out at the mint, in exchange for gold coins at par, in sums not less than one hundred dollars ; and it shall be lawful, also, to transmit parcels of the same from time to time to the assistant treasurers, depositaries, and other officers of the United States, under general regulations, proposed by the Director of the Mint, and approved ·by the Secretary of the Treasury : *Provided, however,* That the amount coined into quarter dollars, dimes, and half dimes, shall be regulated by the Secretary of the Treasury.

Sec. 5. *And be it further enacted,* That no deposits for coinage into the half dollar, quarter dollar, dime, and half dime, shall hereafter be received, other than those made by the Treasurer of the Mint, as herein authorized, and upon account of the United States.

[Section 6 provides that when gold or silver is deposited for coinage, there shall be a charge to the depositor, in addition to the charge for refining or parting the metals, of one half of one per centum, this provision not applying to silver coined into the subdivisions of the dollar.]

Sec. 7. *And be it further enacted,* That from time to time there shall be struck and coined at the Mint of the United States, and the branches thereof, conformably in all respects to law, and conformably in all respects to the standard of gold coins now established by law, a coin of gold of the value of three dollars, or units. . . . .

[Approved, February 21, 1853. 10 Statutes at Large, 160

1852-53, Chap. XCVII. — *An Act making Appropriations for the Civil and Diplomatic Expenses of Government for the year ending the thirtieth of June, eighteen hundred and fifty-four.*

[Section 10 provides for the establishment of an Assay Office in the city of New York.]

SEC. 11. *And be it further enacted*, That the owner or owners of any gold or silver bullion, in dust or otherwise, or of any foreign coin, shall be entitled to deposite the same in the said office, and the Treasurer thereof shall give a receipt, stating the weight and description thereof, in the manner and under the regulations that are or may be provided in like cases or deposits at the Mint of the United States with the Treasurer thereof. And such bullion shall, without delay, be melted, parted, refined, and assayed, and the net value thereof, and of all foreign coins deposited in said office, shall be ascertained ; and the Treasurer shall thereupon forthwith issue his certificate of the net value thereof, payable in coins of the same metal as that deposited, either at the office of the Assistant Treasurer of the United States, in New York, or at the Mint of the United States, at the option of the depositor, to be expressed in the certificate, which certificates shall be receivable at any time within sixty days from the date thereof in payment of all debts due to the United States at the port of New York for the full sum therein certified. . . .

[Approved, March 3, 1853.   10 Statutes at Large, 212.]

1856–57, Chap. LVI. — *An Act relating to Foreign Coins and to the Coinage of Cents at the Mint of the United States.*

Be it enacted, . . . That the pieces commonly known as the quarter, eighth, and sixteenth of the Spanish pillar dollar, and of the Mexican dollar, shall be receivable at the treasury of the United States, and its several offices, and at the several post-offices and land-offices, at the rates of valuation following, — that is to say, the fourth of a dollar, or piece of two reals, at twenty cents ; the eighth of a dollar, or piece of one real, at ten cents ; and the sixteenth of a dollar, or half real, at five cents.

[Section 2 provides that the said coins, when so received, shall not be paid out again, but shall be recoined at the Mint, and that the expenses of transmission and recoinage "shall be charged against the account of silver profit and loss."]

SEC. 3. *And be it further enacted,* That all former acts authorizing the currency of foreign gold or silver coins, and declaring the same a legal tender in payment for debts, are hereby repealed; but it shall be the duty of the director of the mint to cause assays to be made, from time to time, of such foreign coins as may be known to our commerce, to determine their average weight, fineness, and value, and to embrace in his annual report a statement of the results thereof.

[Approved, February 21, 1857. 11 Statutes at Large, 163]

NOTE. — Section 3566 of the Revised Statutes of 1874 provides that "all foreign gold and silver coins received in payment for moneys due to the United States shall, before being issued in circulation, be coined anew."

1872–73, Chap. CXXXI. — *An Act revising and amending the Laws relative to the Mints, Assay-offices, and Coinage of the United States.*

SEC. 13. That the standard for both gold and silver coins of the United States shall be such that of one thousand parts by weight nine hundred shall be of pure metal and one hundred of alloy; and the alloy of the silver coins shall be of copper, and the alloy of the gold coins shall be of copper, or of copper and silver; but the silver shall in no case exceed one tenth of the whole alloy.

SEC. 14. That the gold coins of the United States shall be a one-dollar piece, which, at the standard weight of twenty-five and eight-tenths grains, shall be the unit of value; a quarter-eagle, or two-and-a-half dollar piece; a three-dollar piece; a half-eagle, or five-dollar piece; an eagle or ten-dollar piece; and a double eagle, or twenty-dollar piece. And the standard weight of the gold dollar shall be twenty-five and eight-tenths grains; of the quarter-eagle, or two-and-a-half dollar piece, sixty-four and a half grains; of the three-dollar piece, seventy-seven and four-tenths grains; of the half-eagle, or five-dollar piece, one hundred and twenty-nine grains; of the eagle, or ten-dollar piece, two hundred and fifty-eight grains; of the double-eagle, or twenty-dollar piece, five hun-

16

dred and sixteen grains; which coins shall be a legal tender in all payments at their nominal value when not below the standard weight and limit of tolerance provided in this act for the single piece, and, when reduced in weight, below said standard and tolerance, shall be a legal tender at valuation in proportion to their actual weight; and any gold coin of the United States, if reduced in weight by natural abrasion not more than one-half of one per centum below the standard weight prescribed by law, after a circulation of twenty years, as shown by its date of coinage, and at a ratable proportion for any period less than twenty years, shall be received at their nominal value by the United States treasury and its offices, under such regulations as the Secretary of the Treasury may prescribe for the protection of the government against fraudulent abrasion or other practices; and any gold coins in the treasury of the United States reduced in weight below this limit of abrasion shall be recoined.

SEC. 15. That the silver coins of the United States shall be a trade-dollar, a half-dollar, or fifty cent piece, a quarter-dollar, or twenty-five cent piece, a dime, or ten-cent piece; and the weight of the trade-dollar shall be four hundred and twenty grains troy; the weight of the half-dollar shall be twelve grams (grammes) and one-half of a gram, (gramme); the quarter-dollar and the dime shall be respectively, one-half and one-fifth of the weight of said half-dollar; and said coins shall be a legal tender at their nominal value for any amount not exceeding five dollars in any one payment.

SEC. 16. That the minor coins of the United States shall be a five-cent piece, a three-cent piece, and a one-cent piece, and the alloy for the five and three-cent pieces shall be of copper and nickel, to be composed of three-fourths copper and one-fourth nickel, and the alloy of the one-cent piece shall be ninety-five per centum of copper and five per centum of tin and zinc, in such proportions as shall be determined by the director of the mint. The weight of the piece of five cents shall be seventy-seven and sixteen hundredths grains, troy; of the three-cent piece, thirty grains; and of the one-cent piece, forty-eight grains; which coins shall be a legal tender, at their nominal value, for any amount not exceeding twenty-five cents in any one payment.

SEC. 17. That no coins, either of gold, silver, or minor coinage, shall hereafter be issued from the mint other than those of the denominations, standards, and weights herein set forth.

SEC. 21. That any owner of silver bullion may deposit the same at any mint, to be formed into bars, or into dollars of the weight of four hundred and twenty grains, troy, designated in this act as trade-dollars, and no deposit of silver for other coinage shall be received; but silver bullion contained in gold deposits, and separated therefrom, may be paid for in silver coin, at such valuation as may be, from time to time, established by the director of the mint.

SEC. 25. That the charge for converting standard gold bullion into coin shall be one-fifth of one per centum; and the charges for converting standard silver into trade-dollars, for melting and refining when bullion is below standard, for toughening when metals are contained in it which render it unfit for coinage, for copper used for alloy when the bullion is above standard, for separating the gold and silver when these metals exist together in the bullion, and for the preparation of bars, shall be fixed, from time to time, by the director, with the concurrence of the Secretary of the Treasury, so as to equal but not exceed, in their judgment, the actual average cost to each mint and assay-office of the material, labor, wastage, and use of machinery employed in each of the cases aforementioned.

[Approved, February 12, 1873.   17 Statutes at Large, 424.]

NOTE. — By an Act approved March 3, 1875, the coinage of a twenty-cent piece, in conformity with the provisions made as to other subsidiary silver coins, was authorized. See 18 Statutes at Large, part 3, 478.

This act was repealed May 2, 1878.   20 *ibid.*, 47.

1872–73, Chap. CCLXVIII. — *An Act to establish the Custom-house Value of the Sovereign or Pound sterling of Great Britain, and to fix the Par of Exchange.*

Be it enacted, . . . That the value of foreign coin as expressed in the money of account of the United States shall be that of the pure metal of such coin of standard value; and the values of the standard coins in circulation of the various nations of the world shall be estimated annually by the director of the mint, and be proclaimed on the first day of January by the Secretary of the Treasury.

SEC. 2. That in all payments by or to the treasury, whether made here or in foreign countries, where it becomes necessary to compute the value of the sovereign or pound sterling, it shall be deemed equal to four dollars eighty-six cents and six and one-half mills, and the same rule shall be applied in appraising merchandise imported where the value is, by the invoice, in sovereigns or pounds sterling, and in the construction of contracts payable in sovereigns or pounds sterling; and this valuation shall be the par of exchange between Great Britain and the United States; and all contracts made after the first day of January, eighteen hundred and seventy-four, based on an assumed par of exchange with Great Britain of fifty-four pence to the dollar, or four dollars forty-four and four-ninth cents to the sovereign or pound sterling, shall be null and void.

SEC. 3. That all acts and parts of acts inconsistent with these provisions be, and the same are hereby, repealed.

[Approved, March 3, 1873. 17 Statutes at Large, 602.]

NOTE. — For previous determinations of the value of the pound sterling see the acts of July 14, 1832, 4 Statutes at Large, 593, and July 27, 1842, 5 *ibid.*, 496.

1873-74. — *Revised Statutes of the United States: Title* XXXIX., *Legal Tender.*

SEC. 3584. No foreign gold or silver coins shall be a legal tender in payment of debts.

SEC. 3585. The gold coins of the United States shall be a legal tender in all payments at their nominal value when not below the standard weight and limit of tolerance provided by law for the single piece, and, when reduced in weight below such standard and tolerance, shall be a legal tender at valuation in proportion to their actual weight.

SEC. 3586. The silver coins of the United States shall be a

legal tender at their nominal value for any amount not exceed-ing five dollars in any one payment.

[By section 2 of the joint resolution of July 22, 1876, the trade dollar ceased to be a legal tender, and by section 1 of the Act of February 28, 1878, the standard silver dollar became a legal tender without limit of amount. See *below*, page 246.]

SEC. 3587. The minor coins of the United States shall be a legal tender, at their nominal value for any amount not exceed-ing twenty-five cents in any one payment.

[Approved, June 22, 1874. Revised Statutes, 712.]

NOTE.— An Act of June 22, 1874, authorizes the Secretary of the Treasury to exchange gold mint bars for coin certificates or gold coins, at not less than par nor less than market value. 18 Statutes at Large, part 3, 202.

1874–75, Chap. XV. — *An Act to provide for the resumption of specie payments.*

[For sections 1 and 2 of this act, providing for the coinage of small silver coins and their issue in redemption of fractional currency, and for the discontinuance of the charge made for coining gold bullion, see *ante*, page 214.]

[Approved, January 14, 1875. 18 Statutes at Large, part 3, 296.]

1875–76, Resolution No. XVII. — *Joint Resolution for the Issue of silver coin.*

Resolved, . . . That the Secretary of the Treasury, under such limits and regulations as will best secure a just and fair distribution of the same through the country, may issue the silver coin at any time in the Treasury to an amount not ex-ceeding ten million dollars, in exchange for an equal amount of legal-tender notes ; and the notes so received in exchange shall be kept as a special fund separate and apart from all other money in the Treasury, and be reissued only upon the retirement and destruction of a like sum of fractional currency received at the Treasury in payment of dues to the United States ; and said fractional currency, when so substituted, shall be destroyed and held as part of the sinking fund, as provided in the act approved April seventeen, eighteen hun-dred and seventy-six.

[Under section 3 of the Act of June 21, 1879, making appropriations for legislative, executive, and judicial expenses, in order to provide for the speedy payment of arrearages of pensions, the Secretary of the Treasury is directed to issue immediately in payment thereof, the legal-tender notes held as a special fund under the authority given above, and it is further provided that "fractional currency presented for redemption shall be redeemed in any moneys in the Treasury not otherwise appropriated." See 21 Statutes at Large, 30.]

SEC. 2. That the trade dollar shall not hereafter be a legal tender, and the Secretary of the Treasury is hereby authorized to limit from time to time, the coinage thereof to such an amount as he may deem sufficient to meet the export demand for the same.

SEC. 3. That in addition to the amount of subsidiary silver coin authorized by law to be issued in redemption of the fractional currency it shall be lawful to manufacture at the several mints, and issue through the Treasury and its several offices, such coin, to an amount, that, including the amount of subsidiary silver coin and of fractional currency outstanding, shall, in the aggregate, not exceed, at any time, fifty million dollars.

[Section 4 authorizes the Secretary of the Treasury to purchase bullion for the purposes of this resolution, and requires any gain arising from the coinage thereof to be paid into the Treasury.]

[Approved, July 22, 1876.   19 Statutes at Large, 215.]

1877–78, Chap. XX. — *An Act to authorize the coinage of the standard silver dollar, and to restore its legal-tender character.*

Be it enacted, . . . That there shall be coined, at the several mints of the United States, silver dollars of the weight of four hundred and twelve and a half grains Troy of standard silver, as provided in the act of January eighteenth, eighteen hundred thirty-seven, on which shall be the devices and superscriptions provided by said act; which coins together with all silver dollars heretofore coined by the United States, of like weight and fineness, shall be a legal tender, at their nominal value, for all debts and dues public and private, except where otherwise expressly stipulated in the contract.   And the Secretary of the Treasury is authorized and directed to purchase, from time to time, silver bullion, at the market price thereof, not less than two million dollars worth per month, nor more than four million dollars worth per month, and cause the same to be coined monthly, as fast as so purchased, into such dollars ; and a sum sufficient to carry out the foregoing provision of this act is hereby appropriated out of any money in the Treasury not otherwise appropriated. And any gain or seigniorage arising from this coinage shall be accounted for and paid into the Treasury, as provided under existing laws relative to the subsidiary coinage : *Provided,* That the amount of money at any one time invested in such silver bullion, exclusive of such resulting coin, shall not exceed five million dollars : *And provided further,* That nothing in this act shall be construed to authorize the payment in silver of certificates of deposit issued under the provisions of section two hundred and fifty-four of the Revised Statutes.

[The provisions of section 254 of the Revised Statutes are contained in section 5 of the act of March 3, 1863, on page 170.]

SEC. 2. That immediately after the passage of this act, the President shall invite the governments of the countries composing the Latin Union, so called, and of such other European nations as he may deem advisable, to join the United States in a conference to adopt a common ratio between gold and silver, for the purpose of establishing, internationally, the use of bi-metallic money, and securing fixity of relative value between those metals ; such conference to be held at such place, in Europe or in the United States, at such time within six months, as may be mutually agreed upon by the executives of the governments joining in the same, whenever the governments so invited, or any three of them, shall have signified their willingness to unite in the same.

The President shall, by and with the advice and consent of the Senate, appoint three commissioners, who shall attend such conference on behalf of the United States, and shall report the doings thereof to the President, who shall transmit the same to Congress.

Said commissioners shall each receive the sum of twenty-five hundred dollars and their reasonable expenses, to be approved by the Secretary of State ; and the amount necessary to pay such compensation and expenses is hereby appropriated out of any money in the Treasury not otherwise appropriated.

Sec. 3. That any holder of the coin authorized by this act may deposit the same with the Treasurer or any assistant treasurer of the United States, in sums not less than ten dollars, and receive therefor certificates of not less than ten dollars each, corresponding with the denominations of the United States notes. The coin deposited for or representing the certificates shall be retained in the Treasury for the payment of the same on demand. Such certificates shall be receivable for customs, taxes, and all public dues, and, when so received, may be reissued.

[By the Act of August 4, 1886, making appropriations for sundry civil expenses for the fiscal year 1887, the issue of silver certificates·in denominations of one, two, and five dollars is required, the certificates to be receivable, redeemable, and payable as is provided in the above section, and, upon the presentation of those of larger denominations, to be issued in lieu thereof. 24 Statutes at Large, 227.]

Sec. 4. All acts and parts of acts inconsistent with the provisions of this act are hereby repealed.

Note. — The above act having been returned by the President of the United States, with his objections, to the House of Representatives, February 28, 1878, was passed by both Houses, and became a law on the same day.

[20 Statutes at Large, 25.]

1879, Chap. XII. — *An Act to provide for the exchange of subsidiary coins for lawful money of the United States under certain circumstances, and to make such coins a legal tender in all sums not exceeding ten dollars, and for other purposes.*

Be it enacted, . . . That the holder of any of the silver coins of the United States of smaller denominations than one dollar, may, on presentation of the same in sums of twenty dollars, or any multiple thereof, at the office of the Treasurer or any assistant treasurer of the United States, receive therefor lawful money of the United States.

SEC. 2. The Treasurer or any assistant treasurer of the United States who may receive any coins under the provision of this act shall exchange the same in sums of twenty dollars, or any multiple thereof, for lawful money of the United States, on demand of any holder thereof.

SEC. 3. That the present silver coins of the United States of smaller denominations than one dollar shall hereafter be a legal tender in all sums not exceeding ten dollars in full payment of all dues public and private.

SEC. 4. That all laws or parts of laws in conflict with this act be, and the same are hereby, repealed.

[Approved, June 9,.1879.   21 Statutes at Large, 7.]

1881–82, Chap. CXC. — *An Act to authorize the receipt of United States gold coin in exchange for gold bars.*

Be it enacted, . . . That the superintendents of the coinage mints, and of the United States assay-office at New York, are hereby authorized to receive United States gold coin from any holder thereof in sums not less than five thousand dollars, and to pay and deliver in exchange therefor gold bars in value equalling such coin so received.

[Approved, May 26, 1882.   22 Statutes at Large, 97.]

1886–87, Chap. CCCXCVI. — *An Act for the retirement and recoinage of the trade-dollar.*

Be it enacted, . . . That for a period of six months after the passage of this act, United States trade-dollars, if not defaced, mutilated, or stamped, shall be received at the office of the Treasurer, or any assistant-treasurer of the United States in exchange for a like amount, dollar for dollar, of standard silver dollars, or of subsidiary coins of the United States.

SEC. 2. That the trade-dollars received by, paid to, or deposited with the Treasurer or any assistant treasurer or national depositary of the United States shall not be paid out or in any other manner issued, but, at the expense of the United States, shall be transmitted to the coinage mints and recoined into standard silver dollars or subsidiary coin, at the discretion of the Secretary of the Treasury : *Provided;* That the trade-dollars recoined under this act shall not be counted as part of the silver bullion required to be purchased and coined into standard dollars as required by the act of February twenty-eighth, eighteen hundred and seventy-eight.

SEC. 3. That all laws and parts of laws authorizing the coinage and issuance of United States trade-dollars are hereby repealed.

Received by the President, February 19, 1887.

[NOTE BY THE DEPARTMENT OF STATE. — The foregoing act having been presented to the President of the United States for his approval, and not having been returned by him to the house of Congress in which it originated within the time prescribed by the Constitution of the United States, has become a law without his approval.]

[24 Statutes at Large, 634.]

1889–90, Chap. DCCVIII. — *An Act directing the purchase of silver bullion and the issue of Treasury notes thereon, and for other purposes.*

Be it enacted, . . . That the Secretary of the Treasury is hereby directed to purchase, from time to time, silver bullion to the aggregate amount of four million five hundred thousand ounces, or so much thereof as may be offered in each month, at the market price thereof, not exceeding one dollar for three hundred and seventy-one and twenty-five hundredths grains of pure silver, and to issue in payment for such purchases of silver bullion Treasury notes of the United States to be prepared by the Secretary of the Treasury, in such form and of such denominations, not less than one dollar nor more than one thousand dollars, as he may prescribe, and a sum sufficient to carry into effect the provisions of this act is hereby appropriated out of any money in the Treasury not otherwise appropriated.

SEC. 2. That the Treasury notes issued in accordance with

the provisions of this act shall be redeemable on demand, in coin, at the Treasury of the United States, or at the office of any assistant treasurer of the United States, and when so redeemed may be reissued; but no greater or less amount of such notes shall be outstanding at any time than the cost of the silver bullion and the standard silver dollars coined therefrom, then held in the Treasury purchased by such notes; and such Treasury notes shall be a legal tender in payment of all debts, public and private, except where otherwise expressly stipulated in the contract, and shall be receivable for customs, taxes, and all public dues, and when so received may be reissued; and such notes, when held by any national banking association, may be counted as a part of its lawful reserve. That upon demand of the holder of any of the Treasury notes herein provided for the Secretary of the Treasury shall, under such regulations as he may prescribe, redeem such notes in gold or silver coin, at his discretion, it being the established policy of the United States to maintain the two metals on a parity with each other upon the present legal ratio, or such ratio as may be provided by law.

Sec. 3. That the Secretary of the Treasury shall each month coin two million ounces of the silver bullion purchased under the provisions of this act into standard silver dollars until the first day of July eighteen hundred and ninety-one, and after that time he shall coin of the silver bullion purchased under the provisions of this act as much as may be necessary to provide for the redemption of the Treasury notes herein provided for, and any gain or seigniorage arising from such coinage shall be accounted for and paid into the Treasury.

Sec. 4. That the silver bullion purchased under the provisions of this act shall be subject to the requirements of existing law and the regulations of the mint service governing the methods of determining the amount of pure silver contained, and the amount of charges or deductions, if any, to be made.

Sec. 5. That so much of the act of February twenty-eighth, eighteen hundred and seventy-eight, entitled "An act to authorize the coinage of the standard silver dollar and to restore its legal-tender character," as requires the monthly purchase and coinage of the same into silver dollars of not less than two million dollars, nor more than four million dollars worth of silver bullion, is hereby repealed.

Sec. 6. That upon the passage of this act the balances standing with the Treasurer of the United States to the respective credits of national banks for deposits made to redeem the circulating notes of such banks, and all deposits thereafter received for like purpose, shall be covered into the Treasury as a miscellaneous receipt, and the Treasury of the United States shall redeem from the general cash in the Treasury the circulating notes of said banks which may come into his possession subject to redemption; and upon the certificate of the Comptroller of the Currency that such notes have been received by him and that they have been destroyed and that no new notes will be issued in their place, reimbursement of their amount shall be made to the Treasurer, under such regulations as the Secretary of the Treasury may prescribe, from an appropriation hereby created, to be known as National bank notes: Redemption account, but the provisions of this act shall not apply to the deposits received under section three of the act of June twentieth, eighteen hundred and seventy-four, requiring every National bank to keep in lawful money with the Treasurer of the United States a sum equal to five per centum of its circulation, to be held and used for the redemption of its circulating notes; and the balance remaining of the deposits so covered shall, at the close of each month, be reported on the monthly public debt statement as debt of the United States bearing no interest.

See. 7. That this act shall take effect thirty days from and after its passage.

[Approved, July 14, 1890. 26 Statutes at Large, 289.]

1889-90, Chap. DCCCCXLV. — *An Act to discontinue the coinage of the three-dollar and one-dollar gold pieces and three-cent nickel piece.*

[Approved, September 26, 1890. 26 Statutes at Large, 485.]

1890-91, Chap.   . — *An Act making appropriations for the legislative, executive, and judicial expenses of the Government for the fiscal year ending June thirtieth, eighteen hundred and ninety-two, and for other purposes.*

SEC. 3. That an act to authorize the receipt of United States gold coin in exchange for gold bars, approved May twenty-sixth, eighteen hundred and eighty-two, be amended to read as follows:

That the superintendents of the coinage mints and of the United States assay office at New York may, with the approval of the Secretary of the Treasury, but not otherwise, receive United States gold coin from any holder thereof in sums of not less than five thousand dollars, and pay and deliver in exchange therefor gold bars in value equaling such coin so received: *Provided,* That the Secretary of the Treasury may impose for such exchange a charge which in his judgment shall equal the cost of manufacturing the bars.

[Approved, March 3, 1891. Printed for Congress.]

PART IV.

VETOED BILLS AND OTHER DOCUMENTS.

Resolves of the Confederation respecting Coinage.

July 6, 1785.

Resolved, That the money unit of the United States of America be one dollar.

Resolved, That the smallest coin be of copper, of which 200 shall pass for one dollar.

Resolved, That the several pieces shall increase in a decimal ratio.

[Journal of Congress, 1785, p. 225.]

August 8, 1786.

Resolved, That the standard of the United States of America, for gold and silver, shall be eleven parts fine and one part alloy.

That the money unit of the United States, being by the resolve of Congress of the 6th July, 1785, a dollar, shall contain of fine silver, three hundred and seventy-five grains, and sixty-four hundredths of a grain.

That the money of account, to correspond with the division of coins, agreeably to the above resolve, proceed in a decimal ratio, agreeably to the forms and manner following, viz.

> Mills, — The lowest money of accompt, of which one thousand shall be equal to the federal dollar, or money unit, ... 0.001
>
> Cents, — The highest copper piece, of which one hundred shall be equal to the dollar, ... 0.010
>
> Dimes, — The lowest silver coin, ten of which shall be equal to the dollar, ... 0.100
>
> Dollar, — The highest silver coin, ... 1.000

That betwixt the dollar and the lowest copper coin, as fixed by the resolve of Congress of the 6th July, 1785, there shall be three silver coins, and one copper coin.

That the silver coins shall be as follows : One coin containing one hundred and eighty-seven grains, and eighty-two hundredths of a grain of fine silver, to be called *A Half Dollar :* One coin containing seventy-five grains, and one hundred and twenty-eight thousandths of a grain of fine silver, to be called *A Double Dime :* And one coin containing thirty-seven grains and five hundred and sixty-four thousandths of a grain of fine silver, to be called *A Dime.*

That the two copper coins shall be as follows ; one equal to the one hundredth part of the federal dollar, to be called *A Cent :* And one equal to the two hundredth part of the federal dollar, to be called *A Half Cent.*

That two pounds and a quarter avoirdupois weight of copper, shall constitute one hundred cents.

That there shall be two gold coins : One containing two hundred and forty-six grains, and two hundred and sixty-eight thousandths of a grain of fine gold, equal to ten dollars, to be stamped with the impression of the American eagle, and to be called *An Eagle :* One containing one hundred and twenty-three grains, and one hundred and thirty-four thousandths of a grain of fine gold, equal to five dollars, to be stamped in like manner, and to be called *A Half-Eagle.*

That the mint price of a pound troy weight of uncoined silver, eleven parts fine and one part alloy, shall be nine dollars, nine dimes and two cents.

That the mint price of a pound troy weight of uncoined gold, eleven parts fine and one part alloy, shall be two hundred and nine dollars, seven dimes and seven cents.

Ordered, That the board of treasury report the draft of an ordinance for the establishment of a mint.

[Journal of Congress, 1786, p. 179.]

Ordinance for Settling Accounts with the States.

May 7, 1787.

An ordinance for settling the accounts between the United States and individual States.

Be it ordained by the United States in Congress assembled, that five commissioners be appointed by the board of treasury, whose duty it shall be to go to the several states in the districts hereinafter mentioned, for which they may be respectively appointed, for the purpose of stating the accounts of the states within those districts, against the United States. . . .

That it shall be the duty of the said commissioners respectively to receive of the states for which they are appointed, all their accounts and vouchers for payments made on account of bounties, pay and depreciation of pay, to the late army of the United States : and for advances to the militia, called out under the authority of the United States, and actually in their service, and to give descriptive acknowledgments thereof to the states from which they may be received, which accounts and vouchers shall be immediately forwarded to the commissioner of army accounts, whose duty it shall be to examine and pass such as are authorized by the resolves of Congress, and supported by proper vouchers ; and to state such as may not fall under the above description, together with such remarks as may tend to elucidate the nature of these claims.

That it shall further be the duty of the said commissioners, to receive in like manner, the accounts and vouchers for monies paid, and supplies furnished on the requisitions of Congress, made previously to Oct. 1781, and to forward the same to the office of the comptroller of the treasury.

That it shall also be the duty of the said commissioners to receive and examine all the claims of the states to which they are appointed, against the United States for advances or disbursements by them made for the use of the late commissary, quarter master, cloathing, marine and hospital depart-

ments, or under any other description whatsoever, to pass
upon all such as are authorized by the resolves of Congress,
and supported by proper vouchers, so far as it respects the
evidence offered in support of the said claims, and to state
such as are not thus warranted or supported, together with
such remarks as may explain the nature of these accounts,
and the reasons offered for the deficiency of vouchers.

And be it further ordained by the authority aforesaid, that
on all the accounts aforesaid interest shall be allowed at the
rate of six per cent. per annum, agreeably to the resolves of
Congress.

[The space of six months is allowed to the several States for exhibit-
ing their claims against the United States, and within twelve months the
commissioners are to deliver all accounts and vouchers to the comptroller
of the Treasury. A board of three commissioners is to be appointed by
Congress, to receive all the accounts and claims of the several States,
and to examine such accounts as have been passed by the district commissioners, in order that the same may be finally adjusted on uniform
and equitable principles, but such revision is not to affect the validity of
vouchers admitted by the district commissioners.]

And be it further ordained, That wherever it shall appear
to the said board of commissioners, that advances or disbursements, payments or supplies, of the description aforesaid, have been made by any of the states, subsequent to
the 18th of April, 1775, for articles or services for the use
of the United States, That the said commissioners be, and
they are hereby vested with full power and authority to make
such allowance for the same as they shall think consistent
with the principles of general equity, although such advances
or disbursements may not be sanctioned by the resolves of
Congress, or supported by regular vouchers, so as to enable
the said commissioners to make a final adjustment of all the
accounts subsisting between the United States and the several
members thereof, agreeably to such quota as Congress shall
hereafter determine.

[The decision of a majority of the commissioners on the claims submitted is to be final, and the commission is to continue in force for one
year and a half from the time of entering upon their office, unless sooner
revoked by Congress.

The ordinance of October 13, 1786, establishing a board to settle all accounts with the individual States, is then repealed.]

[Journal of Congress, 1787, p. 65.]

The United States Bank bill of 1815.

[Printed in the Journal of the Senate, January 31, 1815, p. 315.]

An Act to incorporate the subscribers to the Bank of the United States of America.

Be it enacted, ... That a bank of the United States of America shall be established, the capital stock of which shall be thirty millions of dollars, divided into three hundred thousand shares, of one hundred dollars each share; and that subscriptions for thirty millions of dollars, towards constituting the said capital stock, shall be opened on the last Monday of February next, . . .

[The places for receiving subscriptions and the commissioners who are to receive the same are then named, and provision is made for the allotment of shares if the subscriptions exceed the proposed capital, and for an extension of time for receiving subscriptions if they fall short.]

SEC. 2. *And be it further enacted,* That it shall be lawful for any person, copartnership, or body politic, to subscribe for so many shares of the said capital stock of the said bank, as he, she, or they, shall think fit, not exceeding three thousand shares, except as is hereinafter provided for the subscription on behalf of the United States, and the sums respectively subscribed, except on behalf of the United States, as is hereinafter provided, shall be payable in the manner following, that is to say: five millions of dollars thereof in gold or silver coin of the United States, or of foreign coin at the value heretofore established by the act of congress, entitled " An act regulating the currency of foreign coins," passed the tenth of April, one thousand eight hundred and six; ten millions of dollars thereof in gold or silver coin as aforesaid, or in the public debt of the United States, contracted by virtue of the act of congress, entitled

17

"An act authorizing a loan for a sum not exceeding eleven millions of dollars," passed the fourteenth day of March, one thousand eight hundred and twelve, or contracted, or to be contracted by virtue of any subsequent act and acts of congress heretofore passed, authorizing a loan or loans; and fifteen millions of dollars thereof in gold or silver coin, or in treasury notes issued under the act of congress, entitled "An act to authorize the issuing of treasury notes," passed the thirtieth day of June, one thousand eight hundred and twelve, or issued or to be issued under the authority of any subsequent act or acts of congress, authorizing or which shall authorize treasury notes to be issued, previously to the final closing of the subscriptions to the said bank. . . .

SEC. 3. *And be it further enacted,* That the United States may, at any time before the expiration of this act, in pursuance of any law which may be passed by congress for that purpose, cause to be subscribed, for the use of the United States, to said bank, fifty thousand additional shares, to be paid in public stock, bearing an interest of four per cent. per annum, redeemable in any sums, and at any periods, which the government may deem fit.

SEC. 4. *And be it further enacted,* That whenever and as often as any of the treasury notes, subscribed as aforesaid, to the said capital stock of the said bank, shall be due and payable, it shall be lawful for the secretary of the treasury (and he is hereby authorized and required) to pay and redeem the same, principal and interest, by causing certificates of public stock for an equal amount, bearing an interest of six per cent. per annum, and redeemable in any sums, and at any periods, which the government may deem fit, to be prepared and made in the usual form, and the same to be delivered to the president and directors of the said bank, in satisfaction and discharge of such treasury notes.

[Section 5, making the subscribers a corporation under the name of "The President, Directors, and Company, of the Bank of the United States," to continue until March 3, 1835, follows the phraseology of the act of February 25, 1791, establishing the first Bank of the United States, on page 23, but limits the property to be held to not exceeding thirty-five millions of dollars, including the amount of the capital stock.]

SEC. 6. *And be it further enacted*, That, for the management of the affairs of the said corporation, there shall be twenty-five directors, who shall be elected at the banking house in Philadelphia, on the first Monday of January, in each year, by the stockholders or proprietors of the capital stock of the said corporation, and by a plurality of votes then and there actually given, according to the scale of voting hereinafter prescribed. And the directors, so duly chosen, shall be capable of serving by virtue of such choice, ' until the end or expiration of the first Monday in January next ensuing the time of such election, and no longer: Provided always, That the first election and appointment of directors shall be at the time, and for the period, hereinafter declared.

[Section 7 requires that, as soon as twelve millions of dollars, in gold and silver coin and in public debt and treasury notes, shall have been received on account of the subscription to stock, exclusive of the subscription by the United States, a time shall be fixed for the election of directors, the directors then elected to elect one of their number as president, and the operations of the bank then to begin at the city of Philadelphia.

Section 8 empowers the directors to appoint and pay the necessary officers, clerks, and servants, and to govern the affairs of the corporation.]

SEC. 9. *And be it further enacted,* That the following rules, restrictions, limitations, and provisions, shall form and be fundamental articles of the constitution of the said corporation, to wit:

[Article 1, prescribing the method of voting by stockholders and forbidding any but stockholders actually resident in the United States to vote by proxy, is identical with article I. of section 7 of the act of February 25, 1791, on page 24.]

2. Not more than three fourths of the directors in office, at the time of an annual election, shall be elected for the next succeeding year, and no person shall be a director more than three out of four years; but the director who shall be the president at the time of an election, may always be re-elected.

3. None but a resident citizen of the United States, and holding at the time of his election not less than ten shares, bona fide in his own right, shall be a director; and if any director shall cease to be a stockholder to that amount, he shall cease to be a director.

4. No director shall be entitled to any emolument. The stockholders may make such compensation to the president, for his extraordinary attendance at the bank, as shall appear to them reasonable.

5. Not less than seven directors shall constitute a board for the transaction of business, of whom the president shall always be one, except in case of sickness or necessary absence, in which case his place may be supplied by any other director whom he, by writing under his hand, shall depute for the purpose. And the director so deputed, may do and transact all the necessary business belonging to the office of the president of the said corporation, during the continuance of the sickness or necessary absence of the president.

6. A number of stockholders, not less than sixty, who, together, shall be proprietors of one thousand shares or upwards, shall have power at any time to call a general meeting of the stockholders, for purposes relative to the institution, giving at least ten weeks' notice in two public newspapers of the place where the bank is seated, and specifying in such notice the object or objects of such meeting.

[Articles 7, 8, and 9, requiring bonds from every cashier, limiting the lands to be held by the corporation, prescribing a limit for the total amount of its debts, and fixing the liability of the directors in case of excess beyond that limit, are the same as articles VII., VIII., and IX. of section 7 of the act of 1791, on page 25, except that the limit of debts is fixed at thirty millions of dollars.]

10. The said corporation shall not directly or indirectly deal or trade in anything except bills of exchange, gold or silver bullion, or in the sale of goods really and truly pledged for money lent, and not redeemed in due time, or goods which shall be the proceeds of its lands. It shall not be at liberty to purchase any public debt whatsoever; nor shall it take more than at the rate of six per cent. per annum, for or upon its loans or discounts.

11. The said corporation shall not, in any one year, sell any portion of the public debt constituting a part of its capital stock aforesaid, to an amount exceeding five millions of dollars, without the consent of Congress.

12. No loan shall be made by the said corporation, for the use, or on account, of the government of the United States, to an amount exceeding five hundred thousand dollars; or of any particular state, to an amount exceeding fifty thousand dollars; or to any foreign prince or state, unless previously authorized by a law of the United States.

[Articles 13 and 14, providing for the transfer of shares in the corporation and for the assignment and negotiation of its bills and notes, follow closely the phraseology of articles XII. and XIII. of section 7 of the act of 1791, on page 26.]

15. Half yearly dividends shall be made of so much of the profits of the bank as shall appear to the directors advisable; and once in every three years, the directors shall lay before the stockholders, at a general meeting, for their information, an exact and particular statement of the debts which shall have remained unpaid after the expiration of the original credit, for a period of treble the term of that credit, and of the surplus of profits, if any, after deducting losses and dividends. If there shall be a failure in the payment of any part of any sum subscribed by any person, copartnership, or body politic, the party failing shall lose the benefit of any dividend which may have accrued prior to the time for making such payment, and during the delay of the same.

16. The directors of said corporation shall be bound to establish a competent office of discount and deposite in the District of Columbia, whenever any law of the United States shall require such establishment; and it shall be lawful for the said directors to establish offices wheresoever they shall think fit, within the United States, or the territories thereof, for the purposes of discount, deposite, and distribution, or for the purposes of deposite and distribution only; and upon the same terms, and in the same manner, as shall be practised at the bank; and to commit the management of the said offices, and the business thereof respectively, to such persons, and

under such regulations, as they shall deem proper, not being contrary to law or to the constitution of the bank. Or, instead of establishing such offices, it shall be lawful for the directors of the said corporation, from time to time, to employ any other bank or banks, at any place or places, that they may deem safe and proper, to manage and transact the business proposed as aforesaid, to be managed and transacted by such offices, under such agreements, and subject to such regulations, as they shall deem just and proper. But the managers or directors of every office of discount, deposite, and distribution, established as aforesaid, shall be annually appointed by the directors of the bank, to serve one year; each of them shall be a citizen of the United States; and shall hold, at the time of his appointment, not less than five shares in the said bank, bona fide in his own right; and, if he shall cease to be a stockholder to that amount, he shall cease to be a manager or director of such office of discount, deposite, and distribution; and not more than three-fourths of the said managers or directors in office at the time of an annual appointment, shall be reappointed for the next succeeding year; nor shall any person be a manager or director for more than three out of four years; but the president may be always reappointed.

17. The said corporation, all offices of discount, deposite, and distribution, and of deposite and distribution only, which shall be established by the said directors as aforesaid, and all banks by the said directors employed in lieu of such offices as aforesaid, shall be bound to receive upon deposite, the treasury notes of the United States which have been, or may be hereafter issued by virtue of any law or laws of the United States; but it shall be optional with the said corporation to pay and discharge the checks or drafts of the persons making such deposite, in treasury notes, for the amount thereof, either in gold or silver coin, or in the notes of the bank, or in treasury notes. And all banks by the said directors employed as aforesaid, in lieu of the offices aforesaid, shall be further bound to receive on deposite, and to circulate the notes of the said corporation, on the same terms, and in the same manner, as the notes of the said banks respectively

are received and circulated, and from time to time issue and exchange for the said notes of the said corporation, other notes of the said corporation, or the notes of the said banks respectively, or treasury notes, at the option of the persons applying for such issue or exchange. The said corporation shall, at all times, distribute among the offices of discount, deposite, and distribution, and of deposite and distribution only, and at all the banks employed in lieu of such offices as aforesaid, a sufficient sum, in the various denominations of the notes of the said corporation, and in the treasury notes which it may receive upon deposite from the government, to answer the demand therefor, and to establish a sufficient circulating medium throughout the United States and the territories thereof.

[Article 18, providing for statements of the condition of the bank to be made to the Treasury Department, is identical with article XVI. of section 7 of the act of 1791, on page 27.

Sections 10 and 11, providing for the punishment of unlawful dealings in merchandise and unlawful loans, contrary to articles 10 and 12 of section 9, follow the language of sections 8 and 9 of the act of 1791, on page 28.]

SEC. 12. *And be it further enacted,* That the bills or notes of the said corporation, originally made payable, or which shall have become payable, on demand, shall be receivable in all payments to the United States, until otherwise directed by act of congress.

SEC. 13. *And be it further enacted,* That, if the subscriptions and payments to the said bank shall not be made and completed, so as to enable the same to commence its operations, or if the said bank shall not commence its operations on or before the first day of March, one thousand eight hundred and sixteen, then, and in that case, this act shall be null and void.

[Section 14 providing for the examination of the proceedings of the corporation at any time by a committee of either House of Congress, and for a scire facias and forfeiture of the charter in case of any violation of the same, is identical with section 23 of the act of April 10, 1816, establishing the second Bank of the United States, on page 93.]

SEC. 15. *And be it further enacted,* That, during the continuance of this act, and whenever required by the secretary of the treasury, the said corporation shall do and perform the several and respective duties of the commissioners of loans for the several states, or of any one or more of them, at the times, in the manner, and upon the terms, to be prescribed by the secretary of the treasury.

SEC. 16. *And be it further enacted,* That no other bank shall be established by any future law of the United States, during the continuance of the corporation hereby created; for which the faith of the United States is hereby pledged: Provided, Congress may renew existing charters for banks in the District of Columbia, not increasing the capital thereof; and may grant charters, if they deem it expedient, to any banking associations now in operation, in the said district, and renew the same, not increasing the capital thereof. And notwithstanding the expiration of the term for which the said corporation is created, it shall be lawful to use the corporate name, style, and capacity, for the purposes of suits, for the final settlement and liquidation of the affairs and accounts of the corporation, and for the sale and disposition of their estate, real, personal, and mixed, but not for any other purpose, or in any other manner whatsoever; nor for a period exceeding two years, after the expiration of the said term of incorporation.

NOTE. — The above bill was returned to the Senate, where it originated, by the President of the United States with his objections, January 30, 1815, and then failing to receive the votes of two thirds of that house, did not become a law.

———

The Agreement for Resumption of Specie Payments, 1817.

[Printed in State Papers on Finance, iv. 709.]

Propositions respectfully submitted to the convention of State banks by the committee on the part of the Bank of the United States:

1. That the incorporated banks of New York, Philadelphia, Baltimore, and Richmond, engage, on the 20th instant,

to commence, and thenceforth to continue, specie payments for all demands upon them.

2. That in the liquidation of the balances which may be due by the receiving banks, the Bank of the United States will credit those banks, respectively, with the amount of their checks upon banks which may be parties to this agreement.

3. That the whole of the public balances in the receiving banks in New York, Philadelphia, Baltimore, and Virginia, be transferred to the Bank of the United States on the 20th of this month, and retained by the said bank until the 1st of July next, when the same shall be paid off, together with the interest thereon.

4. The payment of the balances which may accumulate against the aforesaid banks subsequently to the transfer of the balances first mentioned shall not be demanded by the Bank of the United States until the said bank and its branches shall have discounted for individuals (other than those having duties to pay) subsequently to the 19th instant the following sums, to wit: For those in New York, two millions; for those in Philadelphia, two millions; for those in Baltimore, one and a half million; for those in Virginia, five hundred thousand dollars; provided, that if the said bank shall be willing to discount, and shall not have the required amount of good paper offered within the term of sixty days from the 20th instant at New York, Philadelphia, and Baltimore, and within the same term after the operation of the offices of the said bank in Virginia shall have commenced, the aforesaid banks shall, at the expiration of that time, at the aforesaid places, respectively, pay to the Bank of the United States the balance due by them respectively.

5. That the Bank of the United States will engage to discount the required amount at the respective places, and within the time mentioned in the preceding articles, provided good paper to that amount shall be offered.

6. That in the event of the Bank of the United States and its branches not having a sufficient amount of good paper offered at the respective places mentioned in the fourth article within the period therein stipulated, then the Bank of the

United States will engage to discount for the said banks the amount of the deficiency at the respective places, according to the amount of the capitals of the said banks respectively.

7. That the aforesaid banks shall exchange with the Bank of the United States and its branches, from day to day, all such notes of either as the said banks may receive; and an interest account from the 20th instant to the 1st of July shall be liquidated and settled in the usual manner.

8. That the Bank of the United States, and the incorporated banks of New York, Philadelphia, Baltimore, and Virginia, will interchange pledges of good faith and friendly offices, and upon any emergency which may menace the credit of any of the aforesaid banks or the branches of the United States Bank, will cheerfully contribute their resources to any reasonable extent in support thereof — the Bank of the United States confiding in the justice and discretion of the State banks, respectively, to circumscribe their affairs within the just limits indicated by their respective capitals as soon as the interest and convenience of the community will admit.

9. That upon the mutual agreement of the parties to these stipulations, the same shall be submitted to the Secretary of the Treasury for his decision upon those points which involve the public balances, and when approved by him shall be obligatory upon all the contracting parties.

Bank of the United States, February 1, 1817.

The United States Bank Bill of 1832.

[Printed in the Journal of the Senate, July 11, 1832, page 451.]

An act to modify and continue the act entitled "An act to incorporate the subscribers to the Bank of the United States."

Be it enacted, . . . That the act entitled "An act to incorporate the subscribers to the Bank of the United States," approved on the tenth day of April, in the year one thousand eight hundred and sixteen, shall continue in full force and effect for the term of fifteen years from and after the period therein limited for its expiration, to wit, the third day of March, in the year one thousand eight hundred and thirty-six; and that all the rights, interests, properties, powers and privileges, secured by the said act, with all the rules, conditions, restrictions, and duties, therein prescribed and imposed, be and remain after the said third day of March, in the year one thousand eight hundred and thirty-six, during the said fifteen years, as if the said limitation in the said act had not been made; subject, nevertheless, to the modifications and changes hereinafter expressed.

SEC. 2. *And be it further enacted,* That the directors of the said corporation shall have power to appoint two or more officers, with authority to sign and countersign any or all the notes thereof, the denomination of each of which shall be less than one hundred dollars; which notes, when signed and countersigned by the said officers, respectively, shall, to all intents and purposes, be binding and obligatory upon the said corporation as if the same had been signed by the President, and countersigned by the principal Cashier or Treasurer thereof; and it shall be the duty of the directors of the said corporation to make known, in writing, and as soon as may be, to the Secretary of the Treasury, the names of the officers who shall be appointed by virtue of this provision: *Provided,* That from and after the third day of March, one thousand eight hundred and thirty-six, no branch bank draft, or other bank paper not payable at the place where issued, shall be put in circulation, as currency, by the bank, or any of its offices, except notes of the denomination of fifty dollars, or of some greater sum.

SEC. 3. *And be it further enacted,* That it shall not be lawful for the said corporation to issue, pay out, or put in circulation, any note or notes of a denomination less than fifty dollars, which shall not, upon the faces thereof, respectively, be payable at the bank or office of discount and deposite, whence they shall be issued, paid out, or put in circulation.

SEC. 4. *And be it further enacted,* That the notes or bills of the said corporation, although the same be, upon the faces thereof, respectively, made payable at one place only, shall, nevertheless, be received by the said corporation at the bank, or at any of the offices of discount and deposite thereof, if tendered in liquidation or payment of any balance or balances due to said corporation, or to such office of discount and deposite, from any other incorporated bank.

SEC. 5. *And be it further enacted*, That it shall not be lawful, after the said third day of March, in the year one thousand eight hundred and thirty-six, for the said corporation to hold, keep, and retain, for a period exceeding five years after the date of acquiring the same, any right, title, or interest, except by way of mortgage or judgment lien in security of debts, to any lands, tenements, and hereditaments, other than those requisite for its accommodation in relation to the convenient transacting of its business; and it shall be the duty of said corporation, within the aforesaid period of five years, to sell, dispose of, or otherwise bona fide divest itself of all right, title, and interest to any lands, tenements, and hereditaments, conveyed to it in satisfaction of debts previously contracted in the course of its dealings, or purchased at sales upon judgments which shall have been obtained for such debts; and for any and every violation of this provision, the said corporation shall be subject to a penalty of ten thousand dollars, to be recovered in the name of the United States of America by a qui-tam action of debt instituted in any court of the United States having jurisdiction of the same; one half of which shall enure to the benefit of the informer, and the other half to the use of the United States.

SEC. 6. *And be it further enacted*, That from and after the said tenth day of April, in the year one thousand eight hundred and thirty-six, it shall not be lawful for the directors of the said corporation to have, establish, or retain, more than two offices of discount and deposite in any State. *Provided*, That nothing herein contained shall prevent the said corporation from retaining any of the branches which are now established.

SEC. 7. *And be it further enacted*, That, in consideration of the exclusive benefits and privileges continued by this act to the said corporation for fifteen years as aforesaid, the said corporation shall pay to the United States the annuity, or yearly sum of two hundred thousand dollars ; which said sum shall be paid on the fourth day of March in each and every year during the said term of fifteen years.

SEC. 8. *And be it further enacted*, That it shall be lawful for Congress to provide, by law, that the said bank shall be restrained, at any time after the third day of March, in the year one thousand eight hundred and thirty-six, from making, issuing, or keeping in circulation, any notes or bills of said bank, or any of its offices, of a less sum or denomination than twenty dollars.

SEC. 9. *And be it further enacted*, That the Cashier of the bank shall, annually, report to the Secretary of the Treasury the names of all stockholders who are not resident citizens of the United States ; and, on application of the Treasurer of any State, shall make out and transmit to such Treasurer a list of stockholders residing in, or citizens of, such State, with the amount of stock owned by each.

SEC. 10. *And be it further enacted*, That so much of any act or acts of Congress heretofore passed, and now in force, supplementary to, or in any wise connected with, the said original act of incorporation, approved on the tenth day of April, in the year one thousand eight hundred and sixteen, as is not inconsistent with this act, shall be continued in full force and effect during the said fifteen years after the said third day of March, in the year one thousand eight hundred and thirty-six.

SEC. 11. *And be it further enacted*, That it shall be the duty of the President and directors of the said Bank, on or before the first day of the next session of Congress, to signify to the President of the United States their acceptance, on behalf of the Bank of the United States, of the terms and conditions in this act contained ; and if they shall fail to do so on or before the day above mentioned, that then this act shall cease to be in force.

NOTE.— Senate bill No. 147 of 1831-32 was returned to the Senate by the President of the United States with his objections, July 10, 1832, and failing to obtain the votes of two thirds of that house, did not become a law.

The Specie Circular of 1836.

[Printed in Senate Documents, 1836–37, No. 2, p. 96.]

Circular to Receivers of Public Money, and to the Deposite Banks.

TREASURY DEPARTMENT, July 11, 1836.

In consequence of complaints which have been made of frauds, speculations, and monopolies, in the purchase of the public lands, and the aid which is said to be given to effect these objects by excessive bank credits, and dangerous if not partial facilities through bank drafts and bank deposites, and the general evil influence likely to result to the public interests, and especially the safety of the great amount of money in the Treasury, and the sound condition of the currency of the country, from the further exchange of the national domain in this manner, and chiefly for bank credits and paper money, the President of the United States has given directions, and you are hereby instructed, after the 15th day of August next, to receive in payment of the public lands nothing except what is directed by the existing laws, viz: gold and silver, and in the proper cases, Virginia land scrip; provided that till the 15th of December next, the same indulgences heretofore extended as to the kind of money received, may be continued for any quantity of land not exceeding 320 acres to each purchaser who is an actual settler or bona fide resident in the State where the sales are made.

In order to ensure the faithful execution of these instructions, all receivers are strictly prohibited from accepting for land sold, any draft, certificate, or other evidence of money, or deposite, though for specie, unless signed by the Treasurer of the United States, in conformity to the act of April 24, 1820. And each of those officers is required to annex to his monthly returns to this Department, the amount of gold, and of silver, respectively, as well as the bills received under the foregoing exception; and each deposite bank is required to annex to every certificate given upon a deposite of money, the proportions of it actually paid in gold, in silver, and in bank notes. All former instructions on these subjects, except as now modified, will be considered as remaining in full force.

The principal objects of the President in adopting this measure being to repress alleged frauds, and to withhold any countenance or facilities in the power of the Government from the monopoly of the public lands in the hands of speculators and capitalists, to the injury of the actual settlers in the new States, and of emigrants in search of new homes, as well as to discourage the ruinous extension of bank issues, and bank credits, by which those results are generally supposed to be promoted, your utmost vigilance is required, and relied on, to carry this order into complete execution.

LEVI WOODBURY,
Secretary of the Treasury.

The bill to rescind the Specie Circular.

[Printed in Senate Miscellaneous Documents, 1886-87, No. 53, page 157.]

An act designating and limiting the funds receivable for the revenues of the United States.

Be it enacted, . . . That the Secretary of the Treasury be, and hereby is, required to adopt such measures as he may deem necessary to effect a collection of the public revenue of the United States, whether arising from duties, taxes, debts, or sales of lands, in the manner and on the principles herein provided ; that is, that no such duties, taxes, debts, or sums of money, payable for lands, shall be collected or received otherwise than in the legal currency of the United States, or in notes of banks which are payable and paid on demand in the said legal currency of the United States, under the following restrictions and conditions in regard to such notes, to wit : from and after the passage of this act, the notes of no bank which shall issue or circulate bills or notes of a less denomination than five dollars shall be received on account of the public dues ; and, from and after the thirtieth day of December, eighteen hundred and thirty-nine, the notes of no bank which shall issue or circulate bills or notes of a less denomination than ten dollars shall be so receivable ; and, from and after the thirtieth day of December, one thousand eight hundred and forty-one, the like prohibition shall be extended to the notes of all banks issuing bills or notes of a less denomination than twenty dollars.

Sec. 2. *And be it further enacted,* That no notes shall be received by the collectors or receivers of the public money which the banks in which they are to be deposited, shall not, under the supervision and control of the Secretary of the Treasury, agree to pass to the credit of the United States as cash : *Provided,* That, if any deposite bank shall refuse to receive and pass to the credit of the United States, as cash, any notes receivable under the provisions of this act, which said bank, in the ordinary course of business, receives on general deposite, the Secretary of the Treasury is hereby authorized to withdraw the public deposites from said bank.

Sec. 3. *And be it further enacted,* That this act shall not be so construed as to prohibit receivers or collectors of the dues of the Government from receiving for the public lands any kind of land scrip or Treasury certificates now authorized by law, but the same shall hereafter be received for the public lands, in the same way and manner as has heretofore been practised ; and it shall not be lawful for the Secretary of the Treasury to make any discrimination in the funds receivable between the different branches of the public revenue, except as is provided in this section.

Note. — Senate bill No. 144 of 1836–37, having been passed by both houses of Congress, was presented to the President of the United States for his approval, March 2, 1837, but, not having been acted upon by him when the session ended, March 3, did not become a law.

The Fiscal Bank bill of August, 1841.

[Printed in the Journal of the Senate, August 19, 1841, page 178.]

An Act to incorporate the subscribers to the Fiscal Bank of the United States.

Be it enacted, . . . That a Fiscal Bank of the United States shall be established in the District of Columbia, with a capital of thirty millions of dollars, divided into three hundred thousand shares, of one hundred dollars each share. One hundred thousand shares shall be subscribed for by the United States, and the residue of the said capital may be subscribed and paid for by individuals, companies, corporations, or States, the said individuals being citizens of the United States, and the said companies and corporations being of the several States, or of these United States, or Territories thereof, in the manner hereinafter specified. But Congress reserves to itself the power of augmenting the capital of the said bank, at any time after the 1st of January, 1851, by authorizing the addition thereto of a sum not exceeding twenty millions of dollars, divided into shares as aforesaid, which may be subscribed for, at not less than their par value, by the United States, or by any State, corporation, company, or individuals, in the manner directed by law: *Provided*, That the United States shall not subscribe for more than one third of the said additional capital.

[Section 2 provides for the appointment of commissioners to receive subscriptions, and for the time, place, and manner of receiving, and gives directions as to the course of proceeding in case the amount subscribed exceeds or falls short of the twenty millions to be raised.]

SEC. 3. *And be it further enacted*, That it shall be lawful for any individual, company, corporation, or State, when the subscriptions shall be opened as heretofore directed, to subscribe for any number of shares of the capital of the said bank, not exceeding two thousand five hundred shares; and that the sums so subscribed shall be payable and paid in bullion, in gold or silver coin of the United States, or in foreign coins, made and declared current in the United States by the act of Congress of the 25th of June, 1834, entitled, "An act regulating the value of certain foreign silver coins in the United States," and by the act of the 28th of June, 1834, entitled, "An act regulating the value of certain gold coins within the United States," at the following rates, to wit:

[The section then prescribes the rates for a large number of foreign coins respectively, and continues]

... and in foreign silver coins at the value fixed upon them severally in the act first above named, or in Treasury notes of the United States, or in certificates of stock issued under the act entitled, "An act authorizing a loan not exceeding the sum of twelve millions of dollars," approved July 21st, 1841. And the payments made in Treasury notes or in the said certificates of stock shall be paid and received at the par value thereof, including all interest which shall have accrued thereon on the day of such payment. And the payments of the said subscriptions shall be made and completed by the subscribers, respectively, at the time and in the manner following, that is to say: at the time of subscribing there shall be paid ten dollars on each share in bullion, in gold or silver coin, in the Treasury notes of the United States, or in the said certificates of stock, and twenty-five dollars more in bullion, in coin, Treasury notes, or certificates of stock, as aforesaid, at the expiration of three calendar months from the first Monday in September, 1841 ; and there shall be paid the further sum of twenty-five dollars on each share in bullion, in gold or silver coin, Treasury notes, or certificates of stock, as aforesaid, in eight calendar months from the first Monday in September, 1841 ; and forty dollars more in bullion, in coin, Treasury notes, or certificates of stock, as aforesaid, at the expiration of twelve calendar months from the said first Monday.

[Section 4 provides that if, in consequence of an excess of subscriptions and the allotment of shares among the subscribers, any subscriber shall have made a larger payment than was necessary at the time of subscribing, the surplus shall be returned to him ; and provision is made for the delivery to the Fiscal Bank of money and certificates of stock, received from the subscribers by the commissioners, as soon as shall be required after the organization of the Bank.]

SEC. 5. *And be it further enacted*, That no certificate of stock, or any subscription, or any right thereto, shall be transferred except by operation of law, until after the whole amount of the second instalment shall have been fully paid, and every contract or agreement made or entered into for the transfer of such stock, or for the holding of the same in trust for the use of any other person, except the person in

whose name it is subscribed in the books, or for whose use it
is therein expressed, shall be wholly and absolutely null and
void in law. That it shall be lawful for the president, directors, and company of the said bank, to sell and transfer for
gold and silver coin, or [the] bullion, Treasury notes and certificates of stock subscribed to the capital of the said bank,
as aforesaid.

SEC. 6. *And be it further enacted,* That at the opening of
the subscription to the capital stock of the said bank, the
Secretary of the Treasury shall subscribe, or cause to be subscribed, on behalf of the United States, the said number of
one hundred thousand shares, amounting to ten millions of
dollars, as aforesaid; which said subscriptions, so made by
the Secretary of the Treasury, as aforesaid, shall be paid in
bullion, in gold or silver coin, or in stock of the United States,
bearing interest at the rate of five per centum per annum;
and if payment thereof, or of any part thereof, be made in
public stock, bearing interest as aforesaid, the said interest
shall be payable half yearly, to commence from the time of
making such payments on account of the said subscription;
and the principal of the said stock shall be redeemable in any
sums, and at any periods, which the Government shall deem
fit, after the expiration of fifteen years. And the Secretary
of the Treasury shall cause certificates of public stock, to the
amount of ten millions of dollars, to be prepared and made in
the usual form, and shall, at his discretion, and whensoever he
shall think fit, sell the same for gold or silver coin, or bullion,
at not less than the par value thereof, or he shall pay over
and deliver three millions five hundred thousand dollars of the
same to the said bank, on the first day of January, eighteen
hundred and forty-two, and two millions five hundred thousand
dollars on the first day of May, and four millions of dollars of
the same on the first day of September, in the same year;
which said stock it shall be lawful for the said bank to sell
and transfer for gold and silver coin, or bullion, at their discretion. And if the Secretary of the Treasury shall sell the
whole, or any part of the said stock, he shall pay to the said
bank gold and silver coin, or bullion, to the nominal amount

of stock so sold in like instalments: *Provided, nevertheless,* That if the amount of stock which may be offered for the subscription of individuals, States, or corporations, shall not be fully taken prior to the twentieth of December next, and the deficiency do not exceed one third, the residue shall be subscribed for by the Secretary of the Treasury, on behalf of the United States, and shall be sold by him as soon thereafter as he can obtain its par value; and for which the Secretary of the Treasury is hereby authorized to issue stocks of the United States, in manner as before provided.

[Section 7 incorporates the subscribers by the name of "The Fiscal Bank of the United States," until the first day of June, 1862; and authorizes them to hold property without specified limit, and to dispose of the same, to have a common seal, to establish necessary regulations, and generally to do all needful acts, subject to the restrictions otherwise prescribed in this law.]

SEC. 8. *And be it further enacted,* That, for the management of the affairs of the said corporation, there shall be nine directors, three of whom shall be annually appointed by the President of the United States, by and with the advice and consent of the Senate, and six of whom shall be annually elected at the banking-house in the city of Washington, on the first Monday of January in each year, by the qualified stockholders of the capital of said bank, other than the United States, and by a plurality of votes then and there actually given, according to the scale of voting hereinafter prescribed.

[The section then makes certain public offices incompatible with the position of director, forbids any director to act as a director of any other bank, and provides that the board shall annually elect one of their number to be president of the corporation, and that in case of his death, resignation, or removal, they shall elect another. Any vacancy occurring among the directors is to be supplied by the President of the United States, or by the remaining directors, as the case may be; "but the President of the United States alone shall have power to remove either of the directors appointed by him as aforesaid."]

SEC. 9. *And be it further enacted,* That as soon as the sum of ten dollars on each share, in bullion, gold or silver coin, Treasury notes, or certificates of stock, shall have been actually received on account of the subscriptions to the capital of the said bank, (exclusively of the subscription aforesaid on the part of the United States,) notice thereof shall be given, . . .

[And the subscribers shall then proceed to elect six directors, and the President of the United States to appoint three on behalf of the government "whether they be stockholders or not," and the directors thus elected and appointed shall elect one of their number president of the bank and shall serve until the first Monday of January next ensuing; and,]

. . . as soon as the sum of six millions five hundred thousand dollars, in bullion, gold or silver coin, or in Treasury notes, or certificates of stock, shall have been actually received on account of the subscriptions to the capital of the said bank, (exclusively of the subscription of ten millions aforesaid on the part of the United States,) the operations of the same shall thenceforth commence and continue at the city of Washington.

[Section 10 authorizes the directors to employ such officers, clerks, and servants as may be necessary, and to exercise such other powers for ordering their affairs as shall be prescribed by their by-laws.]

SEC. 11. *And be it further enacted,* That the following rules, restrictions, limitations, and provisions, shall form and be fundamental articles of the constitution of said corporation, to wit:

[Article 1 provides for the number of votes to which any stockholder may be entitled in voting for directors, in the same manner as article 1 of section 11 of the act of 1816 establishing the second United States Bank on page 85.]

. . . but no person, copartnership, or body politic, shall be entitled to a greater number than sixty votes; and, after the first election, no share or shares shall confer a right of voting, which shall not have been holden three calendar months previous to the day of election; no proxy to any officer of the bank, or of more than ninety days standing, shall be valid; no proxy shall have a right to give more than three hundred votes; and stockholders actually resident citizens of the United States, and none others, may vote in elections, by proxy or otherwise; and any person holding a proxy may be required by any stockholder, at the time of voting, to make oath that he believes his principal, in whose behalf he votes, to be the bona fide holder of the share or shares, and that no sale or transfer has been made for the purpose of evading the scale of voting established by this act.

2d. Not more than five-sixths of the directors elected by the stockholders, who shall be in office at the time of an annual election, shall be elected for the succeeding year; and no director shall hold his office for more than five years out of six in succession; but the director who shall be president at the time of an election, may always be reappointed, or [s]elected, as the case may be.

3d. None but a stockholder, resident citizen, shall be a director. Not more than two directors shall be elected, and not more than one appointed, out of any one State; and they shall be paid by said bank such reasonable compensation for their services as the stockholders, at their annual meeting, shall direct; but the salary of the president shall be fixed by the directors.

4th. Not less than five directors shall constitute a board for the transaction of business, of whom the President shall always be one; and at least three of the five shall be of the directors elected by the stockholders; and in case of sickness or necessary absence of the president, his place shall be supplied by any other director whom he, by writing, under his hand, shall depute for that purpose; and the director so deputed may do and transact all the necessary business belonging to the office of the president of the said corporation, during the continuance of the sickness or necessary absence of the president.

[Articles 5 and 6, providing for the calling of a general meeting of stockholders and for the bonds to be given by any cashier or treasurer, follow the corresponding articles of the act of 1816 on page 86, except that only four weeks' notice is required for the general meeting.]

7th. The lands, tenements, and hereditaments, which it shall be lawful for the said corporation to hold, shall be only such as shall be requisite for its immediate accommodation, in relation to the convenient transaction of its business, and such as shall have been purchased at sales upon judgments or decrees, or shall have been assigned or set off to said bank in satisfaction of said judgment or decrees, which shall have been obtained for debts due, or as have been bona fide mortgaged to it by way of security ; *Provided*, That no loan shall be made on the security of real estate ; nor shall the said corporation hold any one parcel of such lands or tenements, not necessary for the convenient transaction of its business, for a longer period than five years.

[Article 8, limiting the total amount of debts which the corporation shall at any time owe, is identical with article 8 in the act of 1816, on page 87, except that the limit of debts is now fixed at twenty-five millions of dollars.]

9th. The said corporation shall not directly or indirectly deal or trade in anything except bills of exchange, gold or silver coin, or bullion, or goods, or lands purchased on execution, sued out on judgments, or decrees obtained for the benefit of said bank, or taken bona fide in the payment of debts due to it, or goods which shall be the proceeds of its lands. It shall not be at liberty to purchase any public debt whatever, nor make any loan upon the pledge thereof, nor shall it take more than at the rate of six per centum per annum, for or upon its loans or discounts ; nor shall the board of directors of the said corporation make donations or presents of its funds to any officer or director for any purpose whatever.

10th. No loan shall be made by the said corporation, for the use or on account of the Government of the United States, to an amount exceeding one million of dollars, nor for any period exceeding one hundred and eighty days, or on account of any particular State, to an amount exceeding one hundred thousand dollars, or for any period exceeding one hundred and eighty days, unless previously authorized by a law of the United States.

11th. The stock of the said corporation shall be assignable and transferrable, according to such rules as shall be instituted in that behalf, by the by-laws and ordinances of the same. *Provided*, No assignment or transfer of stock shall at any time be made to others than citizens of the

United States, or corporations and companies of the several
States, or of the United States, or Territories thereof; and
if otherwise made, the same shall be void, and the stock so
unlawfully transferred shall be forfeited and accrue to the
surplus fund of the bank.

[Articles 12 and 13, providing for bills obligatory under seal and for
bills and notes payable on demand, follow closely the language of article
12 in the act of 1816, on page 88, except that no bill under seal shall be
made for a longer period than one year, and that all bills and notes are
to be made payable on demand.]

14th. Half-yearly dividends may be made of so much of
the profits of the bank as shall appear to the directors advisable, not exceeding three and a half per cent. for any one half
year. When a surplus beyond that limit shall have accumu-
lated in the said bank to an amount exceeding two millions
of dollars, the excess beyond that sum and beyond the annual
dividends, as such excess accrues, shall be annually transferred and paid over to the Treasurer of the United States;
and, upon the expiration of this charter, any surplus which
may be in the said bank, after the payment of dividends as
aforesaid, and after reimbursing the capital of the stockholders, shall in like manner be paid into the Treasury of the
United States. If the dividends shall in any half year fall
below the above limitation of three and a half per cent., the
Secretary of the Treasury shall, out of the surpluses which
shall have been previously paid over to the Treasurer, but
out of no other funds or money in the Treasury of the United
States, pay a sum sufficient to make up the deficiency. The
directors shall make no dividends except from the nett profits
arising from the business of the corporation, and shall not at
any time, or in any manner, pay to the stockholders, or any
of them, any part of the capital stock of the said corporation;
nor shall they at any time, or in any way or manner, reduce
the capital stock of the said corporation without the consent
of Congress; nor shall the said directors, either of the said
principal bank or of any branch or office of discount and deposit, or any agency, discount or suffer to be discounted, or
received in payment, or suffer to be received in payment,

any note or other evidence of debt as a payment of or upon
any instalment of the said capital stock actually called for
and required to be paid, or with the intent of providing the
means of making such payment; nor shall any of the said directors receive or discount, or suffer to be received or discounted, any note or other evidence of debt, with intent of
enabling any stockholder to withdraw any part of the money
paid in by him on his stock; nor shall the said directors apply, or suffer to be applied, any portion of the funds of the
said corporation, directly or indirectly, to the purchase of
shares of its own stock; nor shall the said directors, or any
of them, receive as a security for any loan or discount, or in
payment or satisfaction of any debt due to the said corporation, except in the necessary course of collection of debts previously contracted in a bona fide manner in the ordinary
course of its banking operations, and actually due and unpaid, any shares of the capital stock of the said corporation;
and any shares of the said capital stock so received in payment of any such debts shall be, in good faith, sold and transferred from the hands and ownership of the said corporation
within ten months from the time of its transfer to and recep-
tion by the same, in the manner and for the purposes aforesaid; nor shall the said directors, or any of them, receive
from any other banking or other stock corporation shares of
the stock of any such banking or other stock corporation, or
any notes, bonds, or other evidences of debt issued by or upon
the credit of such corporation, in exchange for the shares of
stock, notes, bonds, or other evidences of debt of the corporation created by this act.

And the said directors, in determining what are "nett
profits" of the said corporation, from which the dividends
allowed by this article may be made, shall first deduct from
the profits of the business of the said corporation all expenses
paid or incurred, both ordinary and extraordinary, attending
the management of the affairs, and the transaction of the business of the said corporation; all interest paid, or then accrued,
due and unpaid, on debts owed by the said corporation; and
all losses sustained by the said corporation; and in the com-

putation of such losses, all debts owing to the corporation shall be included which shall have remained due, without prosecution, and no interest shall have been paid thereon for more than one year, or on which judgments shall have been recovered that shall have remained for more than two years unsatisfied, and on which no interest shall have been paid during that period. If there shall be a failure in the payment of any part of any sum subscribed to the capital of the said bank, the stockholder so delinquent shall lose the benefit of any dividend which may have accrued prior to the time for making such payment, and during the delay of the same.

15th. Once in every year the directors shall lay before the stockholders, at a general meeting, or publish for their information, an exact and particular statement of the debts which shall remain unpaid after the expiration of the original credit, and of the surplus of the profits, if any, after deducting losses and dividends.

16th. The directors of the said corporation shall establish one competent office of discount and deposit in any State in which two thousand shares shall have been subscribed, or may be held, whenever, upon application of the Legislature of such State, Congress may by law require the same. And the said directors may also establish one or more competent offices of discount and deposit in any Territory or District of the United States, and in any State, with the assent of such State; and when established, the said office or offices shall be only withdrawn or removed by the said directors prior to the expiration of this charter, with the previous assent of Congress: *Provided*, in respect to any State that shall not, at the first session of the Legislature thereof held after the passage of this act, by resolution or other usual legislative proceeding, unconditionally assent or dissent to the establishment of such office or offices within it, such assent of the said State shall be thereafter presumed: *And provided, nevertheless*, That whenever it shall become necessary and proper for carrying into execution any of the powers granted by the Constitution, to establish an office or offices in any of the States whatever, and the establishment thereof shall be directed by law, it shall be the duty of the said directors to establish such office or offices accordingly. And the said directors shall have power to commit the management of the said offices, and the business thereof, respectively, to such persons, and under such regulations as they may deem proper, not being contrary to law or to this charter. Or, instead of establishing such offices, it shall be lawful for the directors of the said corporation, from time to time, to employ any agent or agents, or any other bank or banks, to be approved by the Secretary of the Treasury, at any place or places that the said directors may deem safe and proper, to manage and transact the business proposed as aforesaid, other than for the purposes of discount, and to perform the duties hereinafter required of the said corporation, to be managed and transacted by such officers, under such agreements, and subject to such regulations as they shall deem just and proper. Not more than nine, nor less than five managers or directors of every office, established as aforesaid, shall be annually appointed by the directors of the said corporation, to serve one year. The said managers or directors shall choose a president from their own number ; they shall be citizens of the United States, and residents of the State, Territory, or District wherein such office is established ; and at least one of the said managers or directors shall be ineligible to reappointment at the end of every first and each succeeding year ; but the president may be always reappointed.

17th. The officer at the head of the Treasury Department of the United States shall be furnished, from time to time, as often as he may require, not exceeding once a week, with such statements of the condition and business of said corporation as he may specially direct ; and he shall also have a right to inspect, or cause to be inspected by some one by him duly authorized, all the books, papers, and accounts of the said corporation, of every kind, including the accounts of individuals, and to make, or cause to be made, an examination into the affairs, transactions, and condition of the corporation ; and the condition of the bank shall be published monthly, in such manner, and with such particularity as the Secretary of the Treasury shall direct. And the said bank, and its offices of discount and deposit, shall be open at all times to the full and unrestricted inspection and examination of a committee of either House of Congress, a committee of the stockholders, and to each and all of the directors of the bank. And, for the purpose of securing a full and unrestricted inspection and examination as aforesaid, the Secretary of the Treasury, or any one by him duly authorized, or a committee of either House of Congress, may respectively summon and examine, under oath, all the directors, officers, or agents of the said corporation, and of any branch or agency thereof, and such other witnesses as they may think proper, in relation to the affairs, transactions, and condition of the corporation ; and any such director, officer, agent, or other person, who shall refuse, without justifiable cause, to appear and testify when thereto required, as aforesaid, shall, on conviction, be subject to a fine not exceeding one thousand dollars, and imprisonment for a term not exceeding one year. And upon the question of any loan or discount exceeding one thousand dollars, where the same is granted, if any member shall dissent, the vote shall be taken by ayes and noes, and shall be entered on the books of the bank, and be subject to the same inspection as the other proceedings of said bank ; and no part of the proceedings of the bank, nor any loans, discounts, or payments made by it, nor any order given by it, shall be concealed or kept secret from the Government directors, nor shall said directors be excluded from the free and full participation in all the transactions and business of the institution.

18th. No note shall be issued of a less denomination than five dollars ; but Congress may hereafter, if it shall think fit, restrain the lowest denomination of notes to ten dollars ; nor shall the said bank knowingly increase the amount of the debts due to it, when the notes in circulation exceed three times the amount of specie in its vaults ; and whenever such excess takes place, it shall be the duty of the said corporation to return to such proportion as soon as shall be safe and practicable.

19th. The debts due and becoming due to said bank shall

never, at any one time, exceed the amount of the capital stock actually paid in, and seventy-five per cent. advance thereon.

20th. No paper shall be discounted, or any loan made by said bank for a longer period than one hundred and eighty days; nor shall any note, or bill, or other debt, or evidence of debt, be renewed or extended by any engagement or contract of said bank, after the time for which it was negótiated shall have expired.

21st. The said bank shall not hold any public debt or stocks, or the stocks of any incorporated institution, unless taken for the security, or in satisfaction of debts previously contracted.

22d. The said bank shall not pay out the notes of any other bank, or anything except legal coin, or its own notes.

23d. The directors of the said bank shall not, within the District of Columbia, discount any promissory note or bill of exchange, nor make any loan whatever, except it be a loan to the Government of the United States, according to the provisions of law.

24th. All notes or bills, adapted and intended to circulate as money, shall be prepared under the direction of the parent institution at Washington, shall be signed as hereinbefore provided for, and shall be made payable at the banking-house in Washington, or at some one of the offices of discount and deposit, to be specified on the face of the note or bill, except notes of a denomination not exceeding twenty dollars, which may be signed by the president and cashier of any office of discount and deposit at which they may be issued and made payable, but shall, nevertheless, be prepared at and authorized by the parent institution at Washington. And no notes or bills but such as are prepared and signed, as aforesaid, shall be issued by any of the said offices of discount and deposit: *Provided*, That nothing herein contained shall be so construed as to prohibit the said offices from selling drafts for fifty dollars and upwards, each, drawn and intended for the purpose of remittance.

The notes or bills of the said corporation, although the

same be upon their face, respectively, made payable at
a particular place only, shall, nevertheless, be received by
the said corporation, or at any of its offices of discount and
deposit, when tendered in liquidation or payment of any debt
or balance due to said corporation.

25th. The officers of the corporation shall not be permitted
to borrow money from the said corporation, or contract any
debt therewith in any manner whatever; and no note or bill,
of which such officer is maker, drawer, endorser, acceptor, or
otherwise a party, shall be discounted: *Provided*, That the
entire liability of any one director of any of said offices to
said corporation may exist to an amount not exceeding ten
thousand dollars: *And provided*, *also*, That no note or bill
shall be discounted for any member of either House of Congress of the United States.

[Sections 12 and 13 prescribe the penalties to be imposed in case the
corporation, or any person to its use, shall deal in goods, wares, or merchandise, contrary to the provisions of this act, or shall lend any sum of
money for the use of the Government of the United States, to an amount
exceeding one million of dollars, or of any particular State, to an amount
exceeding one hundred thousand dollars, unless specially authorized
by law.]

Sec. 14. *And be it further enacted*, That the bills or
notes of the said corporation originally made payable, or
which shall have become payable on demand, shall be receivable in all payments to the United States, unless otherwise directed by act of Congress: *Provided, however,* That
if the said bank, or any of its branches, shall at any time
suspend specie payments, or shall neglect or refuse to discharge, on demand, any and all of its liabilities in specie,
then its bills or notes shall not, during such suspension, be
received in payment of any debt or demand of the United
States; and such suspension of specie payments shall be held
and adjudged a cause of forfeiture of the charter hereby
granted.

Sec. 15. *And be it further enacted*, That during the continuance of this act, and whenever required by the Secretary
of the Treasury, the said corporation shall give the necessary

facilities for transferring the public funds from place to place within the United States, or the Territories thereof, and for distributing the same in payment of the public creditors, and shall also do and perform the several respective duties formerly required of the pension agents and commissioners of loans for the several States, or of any one or more of them, without charging commissions, or claiming allowances on account of difference of exchange.

SEC. 16. *And be it further enacted*, That the deposits of the money of the United States in places in which the said bank and branches thereof may be established, shall be made in said bank or branches thereof, unless Congress shall otherwise direct by law ; and that all public moneys in deposit in said bank, or standing on its books to the credit of the Treasurer, shall be taken and deemed to be in the Treasury of the United States, and all payments made by the Treasurer shall be in checks drawn on said bank : *Provided*, That if the said bank shall suspend specie payments during the recess of Congress, it shall be the duty of the Secretary of the Treasury to provide for the safe keeping of the public moneys until the action of Congress can be had thereon, and he shall report the same to Congress on the first day of the session next after such suspension.

[Section 17, forbidding the suspension of specie payment upon any of the obligations of the bank, and providing the remedy therefor, follows the language of section 17 of the act of 1816, on page 92, except that under the final clause no jurisdiction in the courts of the several States is provided for.

Sections 18 and 19 prescribe the penalties for forging, counterfeiting, or altering bills or notes of the bank or checks drawn upon it, and for the like offences. Section 20 provides for punishing embezzlement, or false entries upon the books of the bank, by any of its officers.

Section 21 engages that no other bank shall be established by Congress during the continuance of this corporation, except that in the District of Columbia banks may be established until there is an aggregate capital not exceeding five millions of dollars, and follows closely the language of section 21 of the act of 1816, on page 93.]

SEC. 22. *And be it further enacted*, That if the subscriptions and payments to said bank shall not be made and completed, so as to enable the same to commence its operations ; or, if the said bank shall not commence its operations on or before the first Monday in April next, then, and in that case, Congress may, at any time within twelve months thereafter, declare, by law, this act null and void.

[Section 23 provides for summoning the corporation by *scire facias* to answer charges of violating its charter and for the forfeiture of the charter upon proof of the alleged violation. Section 24 provides for restraining the bank by injunction from exercising any franchise or carrying on any business not allowed by this act. Both sections provide that every issue of fact joined between the United States and the corporation shall be tried by a jury, and that any final judgment or decree under these sections shall be examinable in the Supreme Court of the United States.]

NOTE. — Senate bill No. 5 of 1841 was returned to the Senate by the President of the United States with his objections, August 16, 1841, and then failing to receive the vote of two thirds of that house, did not become a law.

The Fiscal Corporation bill of September, 1841.

[Printed in the Journal of the House of Representatives, September 10, 1841, page 497.]

An Act to provide for the better collection, safe-keeping, and disbursement of the public revenue, by means of a corporation to be styled the Fiscal Corporation of the United States.

Be it enacted, . . . That a Fiscal Corporation of the United States shall be established in the District of Columbia, with a capital of twenty-one millions of dollars, divided into two hundred and ten thousand shares, of one hundred dollars each share. Seventy thousand shares shall be subscribed for by the United States, and the residue of the said capital may be subscribed and paid for by individuals, companies, corporations, or States, the said individuals being citizens of the United States, and the said companies and corporations being of the several States, or of these United States, or Territories, thereof, in the manner hereinafter specified. But Congress reserves to itself the power of augmenting the capital of the said corporation, at any time after the 1st of January, 1851, by authorizing the addition thereto of a sum not exceeding fourteen millions of dollars, divided into shares as aforesaid, which may be subscribed for, at not less than their par value, by the United States, or by any State, corporation, company, or individuals, in the manner directed by law: *Provided*, That the United States shall not subscribe for more than one-third of the said additional capital.

[Section 2 provides for the appointment of commissioners to receive subscriptions, and for the time, place, and manner of receiving them, and gives directions as to the course of proceeding in case the amount subscribed exceeds or falls short of the fourteen millions thus to be raised.

Section 3 provides that it shall be lawful for any individual, company, corporation, or State to subscribe for not exceeding two thousand shares of the capital ; and then makes the same provisions as those in the Fiscal Bank bill for the medium of payment and for the rates at which foreign coins shall be received ; and also the same provisions as to the time and manner of payment, except however that the time is in all cases to be calculated from the first Monday in October, 1841.

Sections 4 and 5 are identical with sections 4 and 5 of the Fiscal Bank bill, with the exception of the change of name.

Section 6 provides for the subscription of seven millions of dollars on behalf of the United States, to be made in the same manner as in section 6 of the Fiscal Bank bill, and the instalments to be payable, $2,450,000 on the first day of January, 1842, $1,750,000 on the first day of May, and $2,800,000 on the first day of September. Stock not subscribed for by individual States or corporations before the first day of January, and not exceeding one third of the amount offered, may be subscribed for on behalf of the United States, to be sold as soon as its par value can be obtained.

Section 7 incorporates the subscribers by the name of "The Fiscal Corporation of the United States," until the first day of June, 1862 ; and authorizes them to hold property without specified limit, and to dispose of the same, to have a common, seal, to establish all necessary regulations, and generally to do all needful acts, subject to the restrictions otherwise prescribed in this law.

Section 8 makes the same provisions as to the number and choice or appointment of directors and president as are made in section 8 of the Fiscal Bank bill.

Sections 9 and 10 are also identical with the corresponding sections of the Fiscal Bank bill, except that it is provided that the corporation may begin its operations at the city of Washington, as soon as four millions of dollars shall have been received on account of the subscriptions to capital, exclusive of the subscription made on behalf of the United States.]

SEC. 11. *And be it further enacted,* That the following rules, restrictions, limitations, and provisions shall form and be fundamental articles of the constitution of said corporation, to wit:

[Articles 1, 2, 3, 4, 5, and 6 are identical with the corresponding articles of section 11 of the Fiscal Bank bill.

Article 7 is identical with the corresponding article of the Fiscal Bank bill, omitting the provision "that no loan shall be made on the security of real estate."

Article 8 provides that the total amount of debts owed by the corporation, over and above its deposits, shall not exceed seventeen million five hundred thousand dollars, unless previously authorized by law; and is otherwise identical with the corresponding article of section 11 of the Fiscal Bank bill.]

9th. The said corporation shall not, directly or indirectly, deal or trade in anything except foreign bills of exchange, including bills or drafts drawn in one State or Territory, the District of Columbia included, and payable in another, or gold or silver coin, or bullion, or goods, or lands purchased on execution, sued out on judgments, or decrees obtained for the benefit of said corporation, or taken bona fide in the payment of debts due to it, or goods which shall be the proceeds of its lands. It shall not be at liberty to purchase any public debt whatever; nor shall the board of directors of the said corporation make donations or presents of its funds to any officer or director for any purpose whatever.

10th. It shall be lawful for the said corporation to loan to the Government of the United States to an amount not exceeding one million of dollars, and for a period not exceeding one hundred and eighty days, or to any particular State to an amount not exceeding one hundred thousand dollars, or for any period not exceeding one hundred and eighty days; but such loans may be for a larger amount and for a longer period if previously authorized by a law of the United States.

11th. The stock of the said corporation shall be assignable and transferable, according to such rules as shall be instituted in that behalf, by the by-laws and ordinances of the same.

[Articles 12, 13, 14, and 15, are nearly the same as the corresponding articles of section 11 of the Fiscal Bank bill, except that in article 14 the

[clauses forbidding the directors to discount or receive any note as a payment upon the capital stock, beginning " nor shall the said directors," and ending " on his stock " are omitted.]

16th. That, for the purpose of carrying on and transacting the business of the said corporation herein and hereby authorized, and fulfilling the duties herein and hereby required, it shall be lawful for the directors of the said corporation, from time to time, to establish agencies in any State or Territory of the United States, at any place or places they may deem safe and proper, and to employ any agent or agents, or, with the approbation of the Secretary of the Treasury, any bank or banks, under such agreements, and subject to such regulations, as they may deem just and proper, not being contrary to law or to this charter ; and the same agencies, at their pleasure, to relinquish or discontinue, and the same agent or agents to remove, and to commit to such agents, agencies, or banks, such portions of the business and concerns of the said corporation as they may think fit : *Provided, always,* That neither the said corporation, nor any agent or agents thereof, nor any bank or banks employed by the same, shall be authorized to discount promissory notes with the moneys or means of the said corporation, but shall employ the same in the business and dealing in foreign bills of exchange, including bills and drafts drawn in one State or Territory and payable in another.

[Article 17 is the same as the corresponding article of section 11 of the Fiscal Bank bill, except that the clause to enable any director to call for the ayes and noes upon any loan exceeding one thousand dollars is omitted.

Articles 18 and 19 are identical with the corresponding articles of section 11 of the Fiscal Bank bill; articles 20 and 21 with articles 21 and 22 of the Fiscal Bank bill; and article 20 of that bill is omitted.]

22d. The directors of the said corporation shall not, within the District of Columbia, buy or discount any bill of exchange, nor make any loan whatever, except it be a loan to the Government of the United States, according to the provisions of law.

23d. All notes or bills, adapted and intended to circulate as money, shall be prepared under the direction of the parent institution at Washington, shall be signed as hereinbefore provided for, and shall be made payable at the house of said corporation in Washington, or at some one of its agen ;ies, to be specified on the face of the note or bill, except notes of a denomination not exceeding ten dollars, which may be signed by an authorized person at the agency at which they may be issued and made payable, but shall, nevertheless, be prepared at, and authorized by, the parent institution at Washington. And no notes or bills but such as are prepared and signed, as aforesaid, shall be issued by any of the said agencies: *Provided,* That nothing herein contained shall be so construed as to prohibit the said agencies from selling drafts for fifty dollars and upwards, each, drawn and intended for the purpose of remittance.

24th. The notes or bills of the said corporation, although the same be upon their face, respectively, made payable at a particular place only, shall, nevertheless, be received by the said corporation, or at any of its agencies, when tendered in liquidation or payment of any debt or balance due to said corporation.

25th. The officers of the corporation, and the agents thereof, shall not be permitted to borrow money from the said corporation, or contract any debt therewith, in any manner whatever; and no bill or other evidence of debt, of which such officer or agent is maker, drawer, endorser, accepter, or otherwise a party, shall be discounted.

[Sections 12 and 13 prescribe the penalties to be imposed if the corporation, or any person to its use, shall deal in goods, wares, or merchandise, contrary to the provisions of this act, or if it shall lend any sum of money for the use of the Government of the United States to an amount exceeding one million of dollars, or of any particular State to an amount exceeding one hundred thousand dollars, unless specially authorized by law.]

Sec. 14. *And be it further enacted,* That the bills or notes of the said corporation originally made payable, or which shall have become payable on demand, shall be receivable in all payments to the United States, unless otherwise directed by act of Congress: *Provided, however,* That if the said corporation, or any of its agencies, shall at any time suspend specie payments, or shall neglect or refuse to discharge, on demand, any and all of its liabilities in specie, then its bills or notes shall not, during such suspension, be received in payment of any debt or demand of the United States; and such suspension of specie payments for thirty days in any one year shall be held and adjudged a cause of forfeiture of the charter hereby granted.

[Sections 15, 16, 17, 18, 19, and 20 provide for the facilities to be given by the corporation to the Treasury of the United States, and for the deposit of the money of the United States in the corporation or its agencies; forbid the suspension of specie payment by the corporation; prescribe the penalties for forging, counterfeiting, or altering notes of the corporation or checks drawn upon it, and for embezzlement of its funds, or false entries upon its books; and are substantially identical with sections 15-20 of the Fiscal Bank act.

Section 21 provides "that no bank or other corporation, with powers similar to those herein and hereby conferred," shall be established by Congress during the continuance of this corporation, except that in the District of Columbia banks may be established until there is an aggregate capital not exceeding five millions of dollars, and follows closely the language of the corresponding section of the act of 1816, on page 93, and of the Fiscal Bank bill.]

SEC. 22. *And be it further enacted,* That if the subscriptions and payments to said corporation shall not be made and completed, so as to enable the same to commence its operations, or if the said corporation shall not commence its operations on or before the first Monday in May next, then, and in that case, Congress may, at any time within twelve months thereafter, declare, by law, this act null and void.

[Section 23 provides for summoning the corporation by *scire facias* to answer charges of violating its charter and for the forfeiture of the charter upon proof of the alleged violation. Section 24 provides for restraining the corporation by injunction from exercising any franchise or carrying on any business not allowed by this act. Both sections provide that every issue of fact joined between the United States and the corporation shall be tried by a jury, and that any final judgment or decree under these sections shall be examinable in the Supreme Court of the United States.]

NOTE. — House bill No. 14 of 1841 was returned to the House of Representatives by the President of the United States with his objections, September 9, 1841, and, then failing to receive the votes of two thirds of the House, did not become a law.

The Refunding Bill of 1868.

[Printed in the Congressional Globe, 1867–68, p. 4406, and now corrected
by reference to the original in the department of State.]

*An Act providing for the payment of the national debt, and
for the reduction of the rate of interest thereon.*

Be it enacted, . . . That the Secretary of the Treasury is
hereby authorized to issue coupon or registered bonds of the
United States in such form as he may prescribe, and of denominations of one hundred dollars, or any multiple of that
sum, redeemable in coin at the pleasure of the United States
after thirty, and forty years, respectively, and bearing the
following rates of yearly interest, payable semi-annually in
coin, that is to say : The issue of bonds falling due in thirty
years shall bear interest at four and a half per centum ; and
bonds falling due in forty years shall bear interest at four per
centum, which said bonds and the interest thereon shall be
exempt from the payment of all taxes or duties to the United
States other than such income tax as may be assessed upon
other incomes, as well as from taxation in any form by or
under State, municipal, or local authority, and the said bonds
shall be exclusively used, par for par for the redemption of or
in exchange for an equal amount of any of the present outstanding bonds of the United States, known as the five twenty
bonds, and may be issued to an amount, in the aggregate,
sufficient to cover the principal of all such five twenty bonds
and no more.

SEC. 2. *And be it further enacted,* That there is hereby
appropriated out of the duties derived from imported goods
the sum of one hundred and thirty-five millions of dollars annually, which sum, during each fiscal year, shall be applied to
the payment of the interest and to the reduction of the principal of the public debt in such a manner as may be determined
by the Secretary of the Treasury, or as Congress may hereafter direct ; and such reduction shall be in lieu of the sinking fund contemplated by the fifth section of the act entitled
" An act to authorize the issue of United States notes, and

for the redemption or funding thereof, and for funding the floating debt of the United States," approved February twenty-fifth, eighteen hundred and sixty-two.

SEC. 3. *And be it further enacted*, That from and after the passage of this act no percentage, deduction, commission or compensation of any amount or kind shall be allowed to any person for the sale, negotiation, redemption or exchange of any bonds or securities of the United States, or of any coin or bullion disposed of at the Treasury Department or elsewhere on account of the United States; and all acts and parts of acts authorizing or permitting, by construction or otherwise, the Secretary of the Treasury to appoint any agent, other than some proper officer of his department, to make such sale, negotiation, redemption or exchange of bonds and securities, are hereby repealed.

NOTE. — Senate bill No. 207 of 1867–68, having passed the Senate and the House of Representatives, was sent to the President of the United States, July 27, 1868, and was deposited by him in the State Department endorsed as follows : —

> Received 11⁵⁹ A. M. July 27th, 1868, on which day, at 12 o'clock M., the two Houses of Congress adjourned until the third Monday in September, 1868.
>
> ANDREW JOHNSON.

The Currency Bill of 1874.

[Printed in Senate Executive Documents of 1873–74, No. 44.]

An act to fix the amount of United States notes and the circulation of national banks, and for other purposes.

Be it enacted, . . . That the maximum amount of United States notes is hereby fixed at four hundred million dollars.

SEC. 2. That forty-six millions in notes for circulation, in addition to such circulation now allowed by law, shall be issued to national banking associations now organized and which may be organized hereafter ; and such increased circulation shall be distributed among the several States as provided in section one of the act entitled " An act to provide for the redemption of the three-per-centum temporary-loan certificates, and for an increase of national bank notes," approved July twelfth, eighteen hundred and seventy; and each national banking association, now organized or hereafter to be organized, shall keep and maintain, as a part of its reserve required by law, one-fourth part of the coin received by it as interest on bonds of the United States deposited as security for circulating notes or Government deposits ; and that hereafter only one-fourth of the reserve now prescribed by law for national banking associations shall consist of balances due to an association available for the redemption of its circulating notes from associations in cities of redemption, and upon which balances no interest shall be paid.

NOTE. — Senate bill No. 617 of 1873–74 was returned to the Senate by the President of the United States with his objections, April 22, 1874, and then failing to receive the votes of two-thirds of that house, did not become a law.

The Funding Bill of March, 1881.

[Printed in the Congressional Record, 1880–81, p. 2433, and now corrected by reference to the bill as ordered to be printed for the Senate, February 17, 1881.]

An act to facilitate the refunding of the national debt.

Be it enacted, . . . That all existing provisions of law authorizing the refunding of the national debt shall apply to any bonds of the United States bearing a higher rate of interest than four and one-half per centum per annum which may hereafter become redeemable : *Provided,* That in lieu of the bonds authorized to be issued by the act of July fourteenth, eighteen hundred and seventy, entitled "An act to authorize the refunding of the national debt," and the acts amendatory thereto, and the certificates authorized by the act of February twenty-sixth, eighteen hundred and seventy-nine, entitled "An act to authorize the issue of certificates of deposit in aid of the refunding of the public debt," the Secretary of the Treasury is hereby authorized to issue bonds to an amount not exceeding four hundred million dollars, of denominations of

fifty dollars, or some multiple of that sum, which shall bear
interest at the rate of three per centum per annum, payable semi-annually, redeemable, at the pleasure of the United
States, after five years, and payable twenty years from the
date of issue; and also Treasury notes to an amount not
exceeding three hundred million dollars, in denominations
of ten dollars, or some multiple of that sum not exceeding
one thousand dollars, either registered or coupon, bearing
interest at a rate not exceeding three per centum per annum,
payable semi-annually, redeemable at the pleasure of the
United States, after one year, and payable in ten years from
the date of issue; and no Treasury note of a less denomination than one hundred dollars shall be registered. The
bonds and Treasury notes shall be, in all other respects, of
like character and subject to the same provisions as the
bonds authorized to be issued by the act of July fourteenth,
eighteen hundred and seventy, entitled "An act to authorize the refunding of the national debt," and acts amendatory
thereto: *Provided*, That nothing in this act shall be so construed as to authorize an increase of the public debt: *Provided further*, That interest upon the six per cent. bonds
hereby authorized to be refunded shall cease at the expiration
of thirty days after publication of notice that the same have
been designated by the Secretary of the Treasury for redemption. It shall be the duty of the Secretary of the Treasury,
under such rules and regulations as he may prescribe, to
authorize public subscriptions, at not less than par, to be
received at all depositories of the United States, and at all
national banks, and such other banks as he may designate,
for the bonds and for the Treasury notes herein provided for,
for thirty days before he shall contract for or award any
portion of said bonds or Treasury notes to any syndicate of
individuals or bankers, or otherwise than under such public
subscriptions; and if it shall happen that more than the entire amount of said bonds and Treasury notes, or of either of
them, has been subscribed within said thirty days, he shall
award the full amount subscribed to all persons who shall
have made bona-fide subscriptions for the sum of two thou-

sand dollars or less, at rates most advantageous to the United States, and the residue ratably among the subscribers in proportion to the amount by them respectively subscribed, at rates most advantageous to the United States.

SEC. 2. The Secretary of the Treasury is hereby authorized, in the process of refunding the national debt, to exchange, at not less than par, any of the bonds or Treasury notes herein authorized for any of the bonds of the United States outstanding and uncalled bearing a higher rate of interest than four and one-half per centum per annum; and on the bonds so redeemed the Secretary of the Treasury may allow to the holders the difference between the interest on such bonds from the date of exchange to the time of their maturity, and the interest for a like period on the bonds or Treasury notes issued; and the bonds so received and exchanged in pursuance of the provisions of this act shall be cancelled and destroyed; but none of the provisions of this act shall apply to the redemption or exchange of any of the bonds issued to the Pacific Railway Companies.

SEC. 3. The Secretary of the Treasury is hereby authorized and directed to make suitable rules and regulations to carry this act into effect; and the expense of preparing, issuing, advertising, and disposing of the bonds and Treasury notes authorized to be issued shall not exceed one half of one per centum.

SEC. 4. That the Secretary of the Treasury is hereby authorized, if in his opinion it shall become necessary, to use temporarily not exceeding fifty million dollars of the standard gold and silver coin in the Treasury in the redemption of the five and six per cent. bonds of the United States authorized to be refunded by the provisions of this act, which shall from time to time be repaid and replaced out of the proceeds of the sale of the bonds or Treasury notes authorized by this act; and he may at any time apply the surplus money in the Treasury not otherwise appropriated, or so much thereof as he may consider proper, to the purchase or redemption of United States bonds or Treasury notes authorized by this act: *Provided*, That the bonds and Treasury notes so purchased or redeemed shall constitute no part of the sinking fund, but shall be cancelled.

SEC. 5. From and after the first day of July, eighteen hundred and eighty-one, the three per centum bonds authorized by the first section of this act shall be the only bonds receivable as security for national-bank circulation, or as security for the safe-keeping and prompt payment of the public money deposited with such banks ; but when any such bonds deposited for the purposes aforesaid shall be designated for purchase or redemption by the Secretary of the Treasury, the banking association depositing the same shall have the right to substitute other issues of the bonds of the United States in lieu thereof: *Provided,* That no bond upon which interest has ceased shall be accepted or shall be continued on deposit as security for circulation or for the safe-keeping of the public money ; and in case bonds so deposited shall not be withdrawn, as provided by law, within thirty days after interest has ceased thereon, the banking association depositing the same shall be subject to the liabilities and proceedings on the part of the Comptroller provided for in section fifty-two hundred and thirty-four of the Revised Statutes of the United States : *And provided further,* That section four of the act of June twentieth, eighteen hundred and seventy-four, entitled "An act fixing the amount of the United States notes, providing for a redistribution of the national-bank currency, and for other purposes," be, and the same is hereby, repealed ; and sections fifty-one hundred and fifty-nine and fifty-one hundred and sixty of the Revised Statutes of the United States be, and the same are hereby, re-enacted.

SEC. 6. That the payment of any of the bonds hereby authorized, after the expiration of five years, shall be made in amounts to be determined from time to time by the Secretary of the Treasury, at his discretion, the bonds so to be paid to be distinguished and described by the dates and numbers, beginning for each successive payment with the bonds of each class last dated and numbered ; of the time of which intended payment or redemption the Secretary of the Treasury shall give public notice, and the interest on the particular bonds so selected at any time to be paid shall cease at the expiration of thirty days from the publication of such notice.

Sec. 7. That this act shall be known as "The funding act of eighteen hundred and eighty-one;" and all acts and parts of acts inconsistent with this act are hereby repealed.

Note. — House bill No. 4592 of 1880–81, having been presented to the President of the United States, was returned by him, with his objections, to the House of Representatives, March 3, 1881, and did not become a law.

TABLE

OF ACTS, RESOLUTIONS, AND DOCUMENTS, PRINTED, ABRIDGED, OR DESCRIBED, IN THIS VOLUME.

For convenience, most of the following titles are much abridged, and in case of complete variance from the original they are bracketed.

PART I.

PART II.

PART III.

PART IV.

www.ingramcontent.com/pod-product-compliance
Lightning Source LLC
Chambersburg PA
CBHW031400270326
41929CB00010BA/1264